MW01601825

WAKING TO THE INFINITE UNIVERSE

Disclosure of Extraterrestrials, UFOs, Spirituality, and the Divine Conscious Universe

Aaron Kuhn

ISBN-13: 9798323716180

Cover design by: Tyler Kiwala
Edited by: Amanda Kuhn
Library of Congress Control Number: 2018675309
Printed in the United States of America

This book is dedicated to my amazing, beautiful, divine love, Amanda. You are my greatest blessing and I love you more than I could ever put into words.

"Do not feel lonely, the entire universe is inside you.
Stop acting so small. You are the universe in ecstatic motion.
Set your life on fire. Seek those who fan your flames."

RUMI

CONTENTS

ACKNOWLEDGEMENTS

So many people have helped and blessed me on my journey, in writing this book, and with Journey to Truth. I give my deepest gratitude and appreciation to the following people:

My love Amanda, for being the love of my life, my greatest blessing, editing this book, and for encouraging me even when it meant many super late nights and one incident that involved a smoke alarm in the wee hours of the morning.

Jackie Kenner for helping me accomplish this book through her amazing leadership and guidance in her book writing course. Thank you so much Jackie!!
Everyone go buy Jackie's book "Parked by the Exit"!

My soul brother and podcast partner Tyler Kiwala, thank you for your amazing friendship, your leadership, and your continual support and encouragement. It's been a blessing and an honor doing our life missions together.

My parents for their constant love and support. My brother Andy and my sister Heather.

From the bottom of my heart, thank you to everyone who has supported me and/or Journey to Truth. None of this would've happened without you:

Aage Nost, Aaron Moriarity, Abby Lynn, Adam AstroYogi Sánchez, Adrienne Youngblood, Aida Farhat, Alara Sirius, Alberto Sanchez, Alex Bloom, Alex Kiwala, Alex Murphy, Alex Patout, Alexis Buck, Alisha Braché, Alisha Haugland, Allison and Will Brown, Allison Coe, Allison Gee, Amanda Bahr, Amanda Joan Quimper, Amária Sweet, Amber Francois, Amber Jean Wheeler, Amber Light, Amy Nicole Akers, Angel Varela, Anita Napier, Ann Marie Morales-Ear, Anna Multanen, Annora Mournian, Anthony DeStefano, Anthony Zender, Antonio Arilo, Apolla Asteria, Arkheim Ra, Arlyn Ruddy, Aurora Diamondheart, Aurora Quezada, Axel Verstraeten, Barry Everson, Barry Littleton, Beata Partynska, Becky Lou, Ben Chasteen, Ben Cehic, Ben Gordon, Ben Talford, Beth Noyes, Beth Rachel, Bethany Mannina, Bex Marie, Billy Carson, Brad GetZ, Brad Olsen, Braden Missall, Brandon Michael Keys, Bret Lueder, Brian Larson, Brian Tseng, Brooke Van Horn (Brookie Smallz), Brooks Agnew, Candace Craw-Goldman, Caressa Ayres, Cassandra Cohen, Cathleena Hailley, Catherine Gentle, Chad Potratz, Chad Wagner, Chastity Campbell, Chasity Munoz, Chief Golden Light Eagle, Chiraya Dharma, Chris Lopidollisathanasthaisiopolous, Chris Pyne, Christina Lee Dobbs, Christina Love, Christine Sanders, Christi Catlett, Christopher Musgrave, Christy Campbell, Ciel Walko, CJ Haessley, Claudette Karma Lewis, Clifford Mahooty (RIP), Cody Press, Colin Joe Byrne, Constance Victoria Briggs, Corinne Roman, Craig Martin Walker, Cynthia Clark, Cyrus A. Parsa, Dale Triplett (RIP), Damian Gutierrez, Dan Cooper, Dan Hecmanczuk, Dan Willis, Dana Sauvan, Daniel Sala, Darius Barazandeh, Dave Trilles, David Benson, David Icke, David Nino Rodriguez, David Pace, David Sherjan, Dawn Holliday, Dean Pratt-DeRøsa, Deanne Adamson, Deb Fox, Debbi Dachinger, Debbie Ziegelmeyer, Debra Dosch, Debra Harvey, Derek and Daniel of Shred the Veil, Deserie Foley, Devara ThunderBeat, Diana Adair, Diana Dunbar, Diana Indigo, Dillon Louis Monroe, Dillon Macy, Donald Scoggins, Donna Hill, Dr. Courtney Brown, Dr. Michael Salla, Dr. Sharnael Wolverton

Sehon, Drago Reid, Dylan Louis Monroe, Ed Spina, Elee Lew, Elisabeth Carson, Elise Brown, Ellen Carnahan, Erika Simmons, Eric Dadmehr (Eric the Healer), Eric Raines, Eric and Nancy of Hopewell Farm, Erica Amoreena, Erica Gallo, Erica Lynn, Erin Lynn, Eve Howard, Eve Lorgen, Floyd Wills, Forest Crawford, Gene Decode, Geraldine Orozco, Glenn Bert, Glen Roos, Gordon Chase Sorensen, Graham Simms, Gregg Braden, Gregg Prescott, Greta Reid, Harry Gale, Harry Hubbard, Heidi Popp, Holly Marie, Irene Ingalls, Ivan Teller, Ileana the Star Traveler, Isaac Mars, Ismael Perez, Jack Ryan, Jaime Gomez Baquero, James Bartley, James Gilliland, James Rink, Jami Lee Mayfield, Jason Ballay, Jason Depatie, Jason Quitt, Jayse Kulesa, Jean Broida, Jean-Charles Moyen, Jean Letellier (SunBow TrueBrother), Jeff Demmers, Jeff Lake, Jena Frey, Jennifer Jarvis, Jennifer Nunez, Jennifer Santella, Jennie Byers, Jenny Constantine, Jerome Headley, Jermaine Chavis, Jessica Jones, Jessica Arael Marrocco of AndronETalks, Jewel Yi, Jillian Willow, Jim Eppelin, Jim Kiwala, Jimi Wilson, Joanna Partynska-Vogel, Joaquin Escobar, Jodi Reynosa, Joe Anderton, Joe Joyce, John Jordan, John Vivanco, John DeSouza, John Popeck, John W. Warner IV, Jonathon Shalomar, Jordan Dreste, Jordan Sather, Josh Sorenson, Julie Porter, Julia Gordon-Bramer, Julia Kamman, Julia Marie, Kara Mooney Henkel, Karen Ann Macdonald, Karen Swain, Kate Buckley (The Kate Awakening), Kate Catinella, Kathryn Faulkner, Katie Mabrey, Katie Weiss (Katie and the Chorus), Kb Werx, Ken Rohla, Kendra Strand, Keira Ingalls, Kerry Cassidy, Kevin Mcgirt, Kimberly Gafter, Kirk Sig, Kitty McFeisty, Kristen Boyesen, Kristin Bredimus, Laura Borgatta, Laura Eisenhower, Laura Loncaric Kays, Laura Matsue, Laura Van Tyne, LaLa Deaton, Lance Schuttler, Lelie Carroll, Leon Isaac Kennedy, Lily Hayes, Lily Nova, Lisa DeMartino, Lorie Ladd, Louis Maschi, Loyal2ThaFoil, Lozza Lou, Lyci Jane, Maggie Federhart, Maighread Birdsong, Marc Wallin, Maria Cabeza, Marina Seren, Mark Alexander, Mark Domizio, Mark Sabbas, Mary Beaver, Mason Feary, Mary Bledsoe, Mary Rodwell, Matthew Starseed,

Matthew Ryan, Matthew T. Goss, Maureen Richmond, Megan Rose, Melissa Kinion, Melody Ash, Melody Clark, Michael Newkopf, Michael Scott, Michael Tellinger, Michele Hartz Aiello, Michelle Anderson, Mickey Megistus, Miesha Johnston, Mike Collins of Wandering Wolf Productions, Mike Huhman, Mike Paterson, Mikki Willis, Monica Hethcote, Natly Denise, Natalie Anne, Natalie Anne Chavez, Natalie Rustichelli, Nancy Thames, Neil Gaur of Portal to Ascension, Nereeda McInnes, Nicole Garwood, Nikkiana Jones, Noah Morin, Nyla Nguyen, Orville Murphy of Board Camp Crystal Mine, Patricia of The Keystone Channel, Paul Peter Straat, Penny Bradley, Peter Maxwell Slattery, Phoenix H Lux, Piper Paprika, Preston Dennett, Ra Cloud, Rachel Celler, Rachel Farris, Randi Ubl, Rebecca Rose, Rebecca Willis, Regina Cornelio, Rene Armenta, Rhonda Elliott, Rick Maki, Ricky Roehr, River Speak, Rob Grand, Rob Gauthier, Rob Potter, Rob Sullivan, Rob Vannoy, Robert Bergquist, Robert D. Morningstar, Robert Earl White, Robert Gartner, Robert Kalil of Typical Skeptic Podcast, Robert RJ Johnston (RIP), Robert Sepehr, Robin Martin, Roger Richards, Ron Dale Jr., Ron Starr, Ross Feinstein, Rozy Alize, Ryan DeLarme, Ryushin Malone, Sami Ingalls, Sammie Nicole, Sarah Breskman Cosme, Sarah Borgatta, Scoobs Aims, Scott Deans, Scott Savoy, Scott Wolter, Sean Bond, Sean Cannon, Sean David Morton, Sean Hessman, Sev Tok, Sharnael Wolverton Sehon, Shavon Ayala, Sheryl Arbogast, Shevann Hill, Shem El-Jamal, Sherri Divband, Sibyl Haynes, Simon Esler, Soo McClure, Sophia Forbes, Sorsha Shannon, Stephanie Farlow, Stephanie Kraft, Stephanie Sheets, Stephanie Williams, Steve Cefalo, Steve Malloch, Susan Long, Susan Manewich, Susan Walter, Suzanne Spooner, Su Walker, Tamara Stier, Tammy Blythe, Tarek Bliss Bibi, Tarot by Janine, Taylor Jane Green, Taylor O'Steen, Teresa Warren, Teri Wade, Tiffany Sunburst, Tim McClure, Tim Sandars of Omnia, Tim Williams, Tobi Lew, Todd Cunningham, Tom Nieman, Tom Paladino, Tom Zamara, Tone Mellard, Tony Oomen, Tony Rodrigues, Tracy Kroeker, Tricia Margis of Ninety Degree Turns, Tyler

Dwight, UFO Johnny, Velentaya Reece, Victoria Gabrielson, Victoria Jean, Vivian Chauvet, Von Galt of Merkaba Chakras, Will Nutter (Johan Fritz), Yeme Jeaneè, Yuvonda Wells, Zach Vorhies, Zachary Fisher, Zaphiera Nicole, Zen God

And thank you to all our Patreon subscribers!

My sincere apologies if I missed anyone!

FOREWORD

by Tyler Kiwla

"Do you want to start a podcast?" Little did I know that saying yes to this question would quite literally change my life forever. Without Aaron asking me this simple question shortly after we met in 2018, there would be no Journey To Truth Podcast as you know it today and I would most likely not be writing this. As a matter of fact, many of the stories you are about to read in this book are a direct result of what it looks like to take that leap of faith and journey into the uncharted territories just outside of your comfort zone.

When Aaron and I met I knew very little of him aside from the brotherly soul connection that was immediately apparent. We started the podcast solely on this bond and a common goal to somehow be a part of this truth movement that was rapidly changing our lives and sparking a Great Awakening within both of us. It was throughout the past 5 years when I truly got to know who Aaron was and realize the significant role he is playing in not only my life, but in the world. A mutual friend nicknamed Aaron 'The walking heart chakra' and I'm here to tell you there could be no better name for him as he radiates love and positivity. Aaron is a wealth of information and a wisdom keeper of esoteric knowledge. His journey tells a story of an innocent loving soul born into a religious family and walking that path for the better part of his life until one day breaking free from the dogmatic chains that kept him tethered to beliefs that were not his own and to the church, the unnecessary middle man standing in the way of our true spiritual path and our true connection to the God within.

When Aaron speaks it's beautiful to watch him tap into the stream of consciousness and bring forward information from the higher planes. This ability has allowed him to plant seeds and enlighten thousands of souls all around the world. His story is a true inspiration for anyone who finds themselves questioning their purpose, their reality or even their existence. External information is a necessary stepping stone for breaking free from our programming and exiting the matrix. Aaron's story is a reminder that it's only meant to be a stepping stone and nothing more. And more importantly, a reminder to not give your power away to anything outside of yourself. To question everything and go within to find the real truth that's already there just waiting to be rediscovered.

Each and every one of us holds the keys to unlocking the secrets of the infinite universe. We all carry a piece of the puzzle and every voice deserves to be heard. This book will help you find those keys, lock in the missing puzzle piece, and inspire you to find your voice and speak your truth during this crucial time on our planet when we are all direly needed. It's time to stand up! We can stay divided no longer. We are the true creators, we have the numbers and we carry the light that will outshine the dark and transform this planet into the paradise it was always meant to be.

PREFACE

This goal of this book is to explore the truths of life and the Universe. It is an attempt to answer the questions:

Who are we?
What is the true nature of reality?
Is there more to reality than we're told by our society and institutions?
Are we alone in the Universe?
Are Extraterrestrials and UFOs real?
Do other dimensions exist?
Are there beings in other dimensions?
Are we more than just a physical body?
What happens after we die?
Is there a Divine Intelligence behind our reality?
Is the Universe Conscious?
Are we all One and connected to everything?
Is our Inner World and Outer World connected?
Is a Great Shift happening on the planet?
Is there a Control System attempting to keep humanity and these truths suppressed?

The answers to these questions have long been hidden from humanity. Truth will not be handed to you by the systems or institutions of this world. You must seek it out. I do not claim to know everything or have all the answers. I'm still learning and growing each and every day. However, this book is somewhat of an encapsulation of the information, knowledge, and wisdom I've gained so far on my journey to Truth. It is an invitation to open your mind and heart to the wonders of the

Universe, and it's a call to awaken to the truth of who you are.

You will find that there are many quotes and excerpts throughout this book. They serve to corroborate, enhance, and drive home the information and concepts that are presented. I do not expect nor even want you to believe anything in this book at face value. My only wish is that you keep an open mind and heart, and that you consider the information and investigate what is presented here on your own. As they say, "Take what resonates and leave the rest."

Note:

Much of the beggining part of the book details my story and the experiences that led me to where I am today. Don't worry, I eventually get to the meat of the information on the topics covered in this book. If you picked up this book only wanting that information, then after chapter 3, feel free to skip ahead to Chapter 11 on.

INTRODUCTION

"To develop a complete mind: Study the science of art; Study the art of science. Learn how to see. Realize that everything connects to everything else."
— Leonardo da Vinci

"When I despair, I remember that all through history the way of truth and love have always won. There have been tyrants and murderers, and for a time, they can seem invincible, but in the end, they always fall. Think of it—always."
— Mahatma Gandhi

"Truth lies within ourselves; it takes no rise from outward things, whatever you may believe. There is an inmost center in us all, where truth abides in fullness."
— Robert Browning, Paracelsus

I genuinely believe we'll all eventually end up where we're meant to be on our journeys, and that ultimately, there are no mistakes in the universe. There are only experiences. And what you get out of them is ultimately and entirely up to you. The universe is constantly growing and expanding through our own personal growth, expansion, and evolution. We are players in the great cosmic game, and the universe is playing that game through you. I've been saying a lot in recent years: "You are the universe experiencing Itself" or "We are all God experiencing Itself through different points of awareness."

Through years of spiritual growth, seeking, downloads of information, research, reading and hearing about others' testimonies, information on Near Death Experiences (NDEs), and through my own experiences and intuition, this is what I truly believe is going on. What I know is going on. It's a deep inner knowing, well beyond just "belief."

I do not claim to have all the answers, to know the entire truth of everything, or to be fully enlightened. But I am on my own personal journey toward truth, love, and enlightenment. I've realized that it's not about trying to be perfect or complete. It's about realizing you are already perfect and complete. We've just forgotten this eternal truth.

CHAPTER 1

Seeking Truth

"Truth is by nature self-evident. As soon as you remove the cobwebs of ignorance that surround it, it shines clear."
— Mahatma Gandhi

"An error does not become truth by reason of multiplied propagation, nor does truth become error because nobody sees it. Truth stands, even if there be no public support. It is self sustained."
— Mahatma Gandhi

"As the least drop of wine tinges the whole goblet, so the least particle of truth colors our whole life. It is never isolated, or simply added as treasure to our stock. When any real progress is made, we unlearn and learn anew what we thought we knew before."
— Henry David Thoreau

"The unexamined life is not worth living."
— Socrates

The concept of Truth has been at the center of philosophical discussion for thousands of years. Every person throughout history, to some degree or another (usually to a high degree), has been taught and told what is true and what to believe by their parents, teachers, friends, religions, churches, governments, media...go down the list.

Most people are programmed from a very young age with beliefs and identities. But how many people have truly embarked on their own journey to truth? How many people have dedicated their lives to seeking and finding truth, and finding out who they really are? I would say not very many. But I can see that rapidly changing now as humanity is waking up.

So what is Truth? You could say Truth is simply what exists. Truth is what IS.

What is reality? Is it only what we can experience with the five senses? Is it only what we are taught in schools, or by various institutions and "authorities"? Or is there a reality beyond the five senses that isn't readily apparent to us, but that we're all connected to? What if there is a reality beyond what we are taught and told?

The next question is, how do we find Truth? Are we to blindly believe and trust that what we are taught is Truth just because it is told to us by various perceived "authorities"? We love our parents and family, but loving someone does not equate to giving your power away to them or blindly accepting information and ideas. How can we be sure what they've handed to us is true unless we find out those things for ourselves?

This process takes introspection, self-examination, and getting extremely honest with yourself. These things can be much easier said than done, and the stronger and more entrenched a belief is, the more complex and painful it can be to go through this process, let alone break free from old beliefs and programs. When you reach the point that you desire truth, love, and self-authenticity above all else, the Universe will synchronistically start bringing to you the people, things, and situations that will help you on that journey. When you start waking up from the deep sleep you've been in your whole life, you are then forced to make a choice. You can either live a lie and continue trying to "fit in" with society and the current people in your life, or you can be brave enough to start living authentically and true to yourself without caring what anyone else may say, think, or do. The former will lead to a life of misery and suffering. The latter will lead to joy, peace, and fulfillment beyond words. I highly recommend the latter.

My search for truth brought me to information regarding UFOs, Extraterrestrials, and Spiritual and Metaphysical concepts. I came from a place of purely wanting truth, no matter how, where, or in what form it showed up. When I expanded out of the extremely limiting and dogmatic "reality box" I was in, my search for truth began for the first time. I was finally free to discover the truth and everything it encapsulated for myself, instead of just continuing to accept a prepackaged "truth" that someone else handed to me.

My internal guidance system was the engine and compass leading the way on my "Journey to Truth." What do I mean by "internal guidance system?" This would be the guidance of my intuition, gut, heart, and soul or higher self. The heart's intelligence (which is the intelligence of your higher self) is *infinitely* greater than the 3D mind and intellect. It's your connection to God/Source/Divine Spirit. Using your intellect is a crucial and wonderful tool. It absolutely needs to be honed and utilized. But it's only meant to be a tool for us to navigate this 3D realm. It's not meant to be the ultimate and only guidance system that we use. This is where many people have gone off track and are stuck. They're completely disconnected from their heart (higher self) and are purely operating from their mind. The ego lives and operates in the mind. It forms beliefs and judgements about self, the universe, and "outside" reality. When someone is disconnected from their heart and their higher self, essentially what happens is they become completely overtaken by their unconscious ego. Basically that means they think they *are* their ego's thoughts, beliefs, and judgements.

When I went through my awakening I started to connect to my heart and higher self. I started letting my higher self (or soul) lead the way, while my ego and intellect became a useful tool serving my higher self (my *true* self). It felt as if God/Source/ The Universe itself was guiding me in my journey and leading me to different truths and realities.

So I didn't start my journey with much interest in ETs, UFOs, the paranormal, or any "spiritual" things like yoga, meditation, manifestation, psychic abilities, or crystals. I simply wanted to find Truth, and I was driven from the core of my being to find it. That drive is what led me to all of these things. I started connecting the dots between everything, and realized that essentially everything was a "piece of the puzzle" and it all intertwined and connected. At a certain point, I could finally see the "40-thousand-foot view" of reality and how everything fit together in the grand scheme.

After my awakening, I cringed thinking about how certain I was in my old beliefs, and how heavily programmed I was into my paradigm and belief system. "All I had to do was look around and seek with an open mind!" I thought. But I didn't look around. I didn't seek. Because I thought I already had all the answers. I didn't have an open mind, because my mind was already closed with programming. The beliefs and thoughts that I was programmed with told me what I was seeing, and what to believe about it.

Unless your mind and heart are open to all possibility, unless you can let go of your ego identifications, and you purely desire Truth above all else, then your searching is completely pointless and arbitrary. It means you don't actually *want* the truth. You just want what you *already* believe to be validated. You only want to find more evidence that further reinforces what you already believe to be true. A term for this is "confirmation bias." Confirmation bias is when you only seek out or accept the information that supports your preexisting beliefs. Any information that contradicts those beliefs is ignored, downplayed, or seen as illegitimate.

That's not seeking truth. That's seeking comfort and reassurance. Those are human needs, so it's completely understandable. But you should ask yourself, "Am I actually seeking truth, or am I merely seeking comfort and reassurance? Am I really just this physical body, or am I something greater? If so, what exactly am I afraid of?" Do you *actually* want truth, even if it happens to contradict things you currently believe and have tied your identity to?

As Gerry Spence said, "I would rather have a mind opened by wonder than one closed by belief." My mind used to be completely closed by belief, until the day I finally opened it with wonder and came alive.

Your true self is not a "human." You are so much more than that. There is actually no such thing as "death," and the *real* you could never be in any danger, so there actually is nothing to fear. There is no reason to cling to safety, which is not actually safety at all but just an illusion of it. When you realize you are *Infinite Consciousness* having a temporary experience as a human being, you no longer fear what anyone else thinks about you, says about you, or does to you. You stop clinging to your false egoic identity, the identity you *thought* you were, and all the things you thought gave you value. You stop clinging to false paradigms and beliefs that you developed throughout your life.

When you truly grasp THAT...then you are free. Then you are connected to Spirit, your *true* self, and you realize that any limitations or fears are merely mental programs and illusions. They aren't real. All that *is* real, is Infinite Consciousness...is Love...is that infinite energy that makes up everything. THAT is the real you.

David Icke has an amazing book of which the title says it all: "Infinite Love Is the Only Truth: Everything Else Is Illusion"

> You need to be willing to question everything, to stop and ask yourself, "Do I really know what I think I know, or have I just taken on the beliefs and opinions of others? What do I actually know. and what do I want to believe or imagine? What do I know for certain?" This one question—"What do I know for certain?"—is tremendously powerful. When you look deeply into this question, it actually destroys your world. It destroys your whole sense of self, and it's meant to. You come to see that everything you think you know about yourself, everything you think you know about the world, is based on assumptions, beliefs, and opinions—things you believe because you were taught or told that they were true. Until we start to see these false perceptions for what they really are, consciousness will be imprisoned within the dream state.
>
> The End of Your World
> Adyashanti

CHAPTER 2

The True Self vs. the False Self

"The most important kind of freedom is to be what you really are. You trade in your reality for a role. You trade in your sense for an act. You give up your ability to feel, and in exchange, put on a mask. There can't be any large-scale revolution until there's a personal revolution, on an individual level. It's got to happen inside first."
— Jim Morrison

"Only the truth of who you are, if realized, will set you free."
— Eckhart Tolle

"Nothing real can be threatened, nothing unreal exists. Herein lies the peace of God"
— A Course in Miracles

In this world, here in the third dimension in our unconscious state, we are easily susceptible to being programmed with all kinds of beliefs about who we are, what reality is, what we should or shouldn't do, what gives us value and worth, what we should or shouldn't care about, etc. etc. Until we start waking up out of this deep sleep and programming that the man-made systems of the planet put us in, we will go our entire lives thinking someone else's thoughts, believing someone else's beliefs, thinking that who we are is this physical body and our beliefs that were programmed into us by someone else, and our ego (in its perpetual fearful state) will cling on as tight as it can to all of these programmed identities that the world has given us.

When we think we are all of these things, then we cannot let them go because to let them go would equal death...or so our ego thinks. The ego (which can be called the false self) clings onto its identities and beliefs about who it thinks it is and what it believes about itself, the world, the nature of reality, because that's all the unconscious ego knows. What we don't realize is that the false self with its plethora of beliefs and judgements, isn't actually *you*.

During a TV interview, Bob Proctor (motivational speaker, author, and success coach) dropped this truth bomb on the world:

> "I found most people don't know who they are. They really don't.
> (Interviewer: What do you mean? I know my name, I know my age, I know...)
> Yeah that's not *you* though. If you ask the average person who they are, they'll give you their name. They'll say 'I'm Bob Proctor.' but I'm not. 'Bob' and 'Proctor' are two words. My parents gave them to me. They're called names, but it's not me, it's my name. Then somebody will say well *this* is me, but *this* isn't me either, it's my body. You never phone down here to the studio and say, 'Body won't be in today, it's sick.' We don't say 'am hand' or 'am leg.' We say *my* hand, *my* leg, *my* body, *my* name. Who am I? Well that's an interesting question. And I believe if a person will start to study that and look for the answer, they'll find it. See, I think we live simultaneously on three planes of understanding. We're spiritual creatures, we have an intellect, and we live in physical bodies. But, because we lack awareness or

understanding of who we are, we're totally locked into a physical world and we let things outside of us control us. 95% of the population are reacting to life. They're not really living at all."

Most people on the planet think they are their body, along with their ego, which is the false self they have identified with in their minds. They think they *are* their name, their personality, their beliefs, their job, their status in society, their money, the things they own, etc. etc. The false matrix, as I call it, encourages and reinforces this mindset. It rewards it. And it's constantly pressuring and seducing us to become more and more ingrained into it. To become more and more identified with a false self. It is constantly working to program us with a false self, with beliefs, and giving us things for our ego to feed off of and cling on to.

> "The Ego, however, is not who you really are. The ego is your self-image; it is your social mask; it is the role you are playing. Your social mask thrives on approval. It wants control, and it is sustained by power, because it lives in fear."
> — Deepak Chopra, *The Seven Spiritual Laws of Success*

Most people think the concept of freedom only has to do with external circumstances, or they are speaking of freewill where they are "free to choose," which you are. But who is the one choosing? Is it the *real* you, or is it the programmed false self? *True* freedom is internal. If you are living in fear then you are not free. You are a slave to fear. Most people on the planet are living in fear, whether they realize it or not. They fear what others think or say about them. They fear not having enough. They fear not being accepted. They fear being alone. They fear not being safe. They fear what the future may bring. They fear anything they don't understand. And probably the biggest of all: They fear death. Since they believe they are their body, and this one life is all they have, they are immensely afraid of death. But "death" is an illusion. There is no such thing as death. There is only energy changing forms and manifestations. What we perceive as "death" is actually just your eternal consciousness leaving the experience within the physical body. It's merely a transition. The body may "die" but the *real* you lives on.

> "Death can be viewed as a total illusion because you are dead already. When you think of who you are in terms of I, me, and mine, you are referring to your past, a time that is dead and gone. Its memories are relics of time passed by. The ego keeps itself intact by repeating what it already knows. Yet life is actually unknown, as it has to be if you are ever to conceive of new thoughts, desires, and experiences. By choosing to repeat the past, you are keeping life from renewing itself."
> –Deepak Chopra

The real you is fearless, powerful, and uncontrollable. It is anathema to any control system. That's why all governments, institutions and control structures greatly fear people awakening to their true selves, because sovereign beings who are awake and know who they truly are *cannot* be controlled.

> "Society does not allow it to happen, no society allows it to happen, because the real self is dangerous, dangerous for the established church, dangerous for the state, dangerous for the crowd, dangerous for tradition, because once a man knows his real self, he becomes an individual. He no longer belongs to the mob psychology; he will not be superstitious, and he cannot be exploited, and he cannot be led like cattle, he cannot be ordered and commanded. He will live according to his light; he will live from his own inwardness. His life will have tremendous beauty, integrity. But that is the fear of the society." — Osho

The truth is you are not just a human being. That's just the temporary experience you are currently having. You are *Infinite Consciousness* having a human experience. We are all that same One Infinite Consciousness experiencing the *illusion* of separation. As Albert Einstein said:

> "A human being is a part of the whole called by us universe, a part limited in time and space. He experiences himself, his thoughts and feeling as something separated from the rest, a kind of optical delusion of his consciousness. This delusion is a kind of prison for us, restricting us to our personal desires and to affection for a few persons nearest to us. Our task must be to free ourselves from this prison by widening our circle of compassion to embrace all living creatures and the whole of nature in its beauty."

You are not a human having a spiritual experience. You are Spirit having a human experience. You are a point of awareness in the mind of God, infinite consciousness dreaming that you are a human being.

> 'The Hindu says: "If God wished to hide, God would choose man to hide in." That is the last place man would look for God.
>
> The trouble with the masses of humanity today is that they are trying to become something that is already right within. We are seeking and searching everywhere outside ourselves for God, attending countless lectures, meetings, groups; reading innumerable books; looking to teachers and personalities and leaders, when all the time God is right within. If mankind will let go of the trying and accept that they are, they will soon be perfectly aware of the reality.'
> — Life and Teaching of the Masters of the Far East

"Your soul is not inside your body, your body is inside your soul. And what your soul is, is of course fundamentally the total universe."
— Alan Watts

"The total number of minds in the universe is one. In fact, consciousness is a singularity phasing within all beings."
— Erwin Schrödinger

CHAPTER 3

The False Matrix

There is a "world" that is overlaid onto the natural world. It's the world that is projected into our minds every day by all the pawns and machines of the system, and by our own unconsciousness. It is what I like to call the False Matrix. It's the false reality that many people believe is the only reality. This "reality" only truly exists in the mind, in the form of thoughts and beliefs in the minds of the people who buy into it and are programmed by it.

Two movies that are fantastic descriptions and metaphors for the False Matrix are *The Matrix* and *The Truman Show*. In both of these movies, there is a false version of reality that is overlaid onto, or held within, the *true* reality. It tricks its inhabitants into believing that the false reality is all there is. There is nothing else. No greater reality. Nothing outside of it at all. Whatever you do, do not look behind the curtain. Do not think for yourself. Do not question what you are told. Do not question authority. Just take the blue pill and stay asleep…

In The Matrix, Morpheus talks to Neo and attempts to get him to question "reality" and explains to him what the Matrix (false reality) is:

> "What you know you can't explain, but you feel it. You've felt it your entire life, that there's something wrong with

the world. You don't know what it is, but it's there, like a splinter in your mind, driving you mad."

"What is real? How do you define 'real'? If you're talking about what you can feel, what you can smell, what you can taste and see, then 'real' is simply electrical signals interpreted by your brain."

"The Matrix is everywhere. It is all around us, even now in this very room. You can see it when you look out your window, or when you turn on your television. You can feel it when you go to work, when you go to church, when you pay your taxes. It is the world that has been pulled over your eyes to blind you from the truth"
(Neo: "What truth?")
"That you are a slave, Neo. Like everyone else, you were born into bondage ... born into a prison that you cannot smell or taste or touch. A prison for your mind."

"You have to understand, most of these people are not ready to be unplugged. And many of them are so inert, so hopelessly dependent on the system that they will fight to protect it."
— Morpheus

In The Truman Show, the main character grows up and lives his entire life inside a fake TV show set, which he is led to believe is the real world. The fake world has programmed and conditioned him his entire life to not question it, to desire and cling to the things it wants him to, and to fear leaving his "town" (the false reality). At first he can't put his finger on it, but he starts to realize that something isn't right. Things seem very off. He begins to start pushing against things and going outside the lines of what he's been programmed with, and what the people in his life are constantly pressuring him to do. What really prompts him to start doing this is that he starts falling in love with a woman who he's not "supposed" to fall in love with. To me, this is symbolic that Love, and following your internal guidance system, is the way out of the false matrix.

He starts realizing that everything is trying desperately to keep him and this woman apart. So he starts defying his programs and the things everyone wants him to do. The more he does this, the more desperate the false reality gets, and the more and more he starts waking up out of it. It starts throwing everything it can at him to keep him locked inside the fake world. At first he lets his fear win, and he starts to go back into the "safety" of the world he's always known. But eventually he finds the courage to break free from the false reality.

Another great metaphor for the False Matrix is Plato's Allegory of the Cave, which tells the story of prisoners who are trapped inside a dark cave from birth. They can only see shadows on the wall in front of them, which they believe to be the only reality. One prisoner is freed and discovers the truth: the shadows are just illusions created by objects and a fire behind them.

As the freed prisoner adjusts to this new reality, they realize there is a whole world outside the cave. Initially blinded by the sunlight, they eventually see the true forms of everything and understand the world beyond the cave.

Plato uses this allegory to explain that the physical world we see is just a shadow of a higher reality. The journey out of the cave represents the quest for knowledge and enlightenment, as one moves from ignorance to understanding the true nature of reality.

The false world we are born into is the "cave" in which we are told is all that exists. There is a control system in place which is hell-bent on keeping us in that cave, keeping us in a trance-like state, never questioning or waking up out of the false reality.

The system needs us because we are its food and energy source. We are its generators, so to speak. It works by programming us with what it wants us to believe, how it wants us to think, and what it wants us to create. And then *we* are the ones that create it. We unconsciously think we're living our own autonomous lives, when in reality we are programmed and conditioned to think, act, and live in specific ways which only serve to feed into this system; one that does not serve nor care about us at all, but only uses us to power itself, fulfill its own agendas, and feed the entities running this machine. It wants to make us so entrenched in the system, and so hopelessly dependent on it, that we never wake up from its spell and see it for what it is. Because once we do, we are free, and it's Game Over for the system.

"We have to create culture, don't watch TV, don't read magazines, don't even listen to NPR. Create your own roadshow. The nexus of space and time where you are now is the most immediate sector of your universe, and if you're worrying about Michael Jackson or Bill Clinton or somebody else, then you are disempowered, you're giving it all away to icons, icons which are maintained by an electronic media so that you want to dress like X or have lips like Y. This is shit-brained, this kind of thinking. That is all cultural diversion, and what is real is you and your friends and your associations, your highs, your orgasms, your hopes, your plans, your fears. And we are told 'no', we're unimportant, we're peripheral. 'Get a degree, get a job, get a this, get a that.' And then you're a player, you don't want to even play in that game. You want to reclaim your mind and get it out of the hands of the cultural engineers who want to turn you into a half-baked moron consuming all this trash that's being manufactured out of the bones of a dying world."
— Terence McKenna

CHAPTER 4

My Awakening

"When one realises one is asleep, at that moment one is already half-awake."
— P.D. Ouspensky

"Awakening is not a thing. It is not a goal, not a concept. It is not something to be attained. It is a metamorphosis. If the caterpillar thinks about the butterfly it is to become, saying 'And then I shall have wings and antennae,' there will never be a butterfly. The caterpillar must accept its own disappearance in its transformation. When the marvelous butterfly takes wing, nothing of the caterpillar remains."
— Alejandro Jodorowsky

Not very long ago, I didn't believe in most of the things I now believe. Actually more than just belief, the things I now *know*. I never in a million years would have predicted that I'd be going to conferences dealing with topics such as UFOs, ETs, Spirituality, Metaphysics, NDEs, hidden information in history/science/health, etc...let alone be doing a podcast and writing a book on these topics, but here I am.

I call the year 2012 the year of my awakening. It was the first time in my life that I had truly started questioning my own long-held beliefs, truly started thinking for myself and doing my own research, and started expanding and "awakening" to so much more than I ever dreamed possible and to what I now know is the truer and greater reality that has been hidden from humanity for a very long time.

It was the year that I really first started to wake up to who I really was, become conscious of all the beliefs and programs I had installed, and for the first time ever, actually went on my own "Journey to Truth" and figured out what I actually believed for myself, instead of continuing to just believe things and have programs running that were given to me by someone else. I started questioning, examining, researching, and exploring literally everything, while using the "knowing" of my intuition and heart, to find Truth for myself. I explored information on the nature of reality, who I am in relation to the universe, what is really going on Earth and out in the universe...Do other intelligent life forms exist? Do other dimensions exist? Do we live more than just this one life? Do beings exist in these other dimensions? Did advanced civilizations exist on Earth long ago? Is there more going on than we are told? etc. etc. etc. I started asking myself all these questions and more. I wanted to find these answers for myself.

Up to this point in my life, I was a devout Christian. I believed all the dogmas that I was "supposed" to believe. I truly thought I already had the ultimate truth, that anything that didn't align with these beliefs couldn't possibly be true, and that there was no need to explore outside of my "box" because I thought that box WAS the truth. So therefore it was all I needed to know and believe. Why would I need to look outside of the box? All that could be found outside of it were lies...right?

All of a sudden, thoughts like these kept popping into my mind: "How do I really know these are the ultimate truths? I never actually formed these beliefs organically. They were just handed to me. I need to start researching." I'm not sure if this was my higher self, my guides, or my soul speaking to me. Regardless, it must've been Divine Timing for me to start waking up at that time. I'm so very grateful because it was the catalyst for my awakening, expansion and growth on a whole new level.

At some point it occurred to me: "Wait a second...these are beliefs about reality that were merely handed to me by someone else, and I was just told to believe them. I didn't actually form any of these beliefs organically on my own. How do I actually know these things are true?" "Well the Bible says these things and the Bible is the written word of God, so that's why" is what many Christians would say, and what I was taught to believe. Ok great! Then...how do we know the modern day Bible is the ultimate word of God? You can see where this is headed.

When you start thinking for yourself and questioning things that you previously just took someone else's word for, you start to realize that you actually don't know what you were so sure you knew. You realize that your beliefs (at least the majority of them) haven't actually been formed by truly seeking, searching, doing your own research and having your own experiences. They were just things you were just told to believe. You're told if you're a good Christian or [Insert Religion Here], and in order to be "saved," you have to believe and do X, Y, and Z. We also know you'll have some questions, so here are the pre-approved answers to those questions, which by the way we were just told by someone else, didn't really question or look into too much, and now we're handing them to you. And many of those answers essentially amount to "because God did it." Because to have an actual real honest answer would require actual real honest investigation and truth seeking, to which the vast majority of modern day Christians (and people in all the major religions) have never done for multiple reasons:

1. It isn't taught or encouraged at all, and usually discouraged in the form of "here are the answers and everything you need to know so there's no need to seek it on your own or do your own research."
2. You want to be "saved" and the fear of not being "saved" and going to Hell is so strong that you never stop to question or examine the beliefs in the first place. You never think: "Ok these people are saying this and it appears that the Bible might be saying this. Great. Let me look into all of this myself and figure out if these things are ACTUALLY true in the first place."
3. If you grow up in a very religious family like I did, your entire family holds these beliefs, and they usually pressure you to have them as well. Even if they don't, it can be way too scary for many people to go against the grain and religious beliefs of the rest of their family. Most of your friends are usually people with these same beliefs, and that just further reinforces the desire to hold onto those beliefs.
4. Your entire identity becomes tied into those beliefs. Essentially you think you ARE your beliefs. Therefore the thought of rigorously questioning them, finding them to not hold water or be accurate, and letting them go, is extremely frightening and can in fact feel like actual death.

The first thing I wanted to research was the concept of "Hell" and where it actually came from. I looked at all the times Hell was mentioned in the Bible and looked at the original Greek or Hebrew words that were translated into English as "Hell". To my surprise, literally NONE of the Greek or Hebrew words that were translated to "Hell" actually meant what we're taught as the concept of Hell: A place of eternal torment that souls go to when they die, or where demons reside.

There are four different words in the Bible that get translated into "Hell." The Hebrew word Sheol, and the Greek words Hades, Tartarus, and Gehenna. None of these words mean what we think of as "Hell." Here are the true meanings of these words:

The Hebrew word Sheol occurs 65 times in the Old Testament, and it means "the grave" (the place of the dead) or "the pit."

The other three Greek words:

Hades occurs 11 times in the New Testament and it is the equivalent of the Hebrew word sheol, so it also means "the grave" or "the pit."

Tartarus shows up only once in the New Testament in this verse:

2 Peter 2:4
For if God did not spare the angels who sinned, but cast them down to hell (tartarus) and delivered them into chains of darkness, to be reserved for judgment.

So it's saying it's a holding place for the fallen angels until their judgment. So it still doesn't mean the definition we're taught.

Gehenna occurs 12 times in the New Testament. Gehenna was the name of a spot in a valley located in Jerusalem called the Valley of Hinnom. It was used as the city dump where a fire was kept burning to burn up all of the city's garbage.

Christian theologians would argue that these terms are used as metaphors to make the point of "Hell," but strictly looking at the original text of the Bible, there is nothing that would indicate that this is the case. It's the concept of Hell that we've been taught, and then all of these words being translated as "Hell" that would give us this idea. So where did the concept of Hell come from?

It was actually a Pagan belief that is found in the writings of the ancient Egyptians, Greeks and Romans. When Rome essentially took over Christianity and made it the "official" religion (the word "Catholic" means universal. It was the Universal Church), they incorporated this concept into Christianity and used it as a perfect psychological tool of fear to control and suppress the consciousness of the masses. The Bible that we know today is a product of Rome and the Roman Catholic Church deciding what books should make up the Bible and excluding any that went against their narrative and control system. Of course they threw out all of the ones with the information and teachings of our own power, divinity, and many metaphysical concepts. The books of Enoch, Judas, Thomas, Mary Magdalene and others were all excluded. The "powers that be" simply could not have the masses learning any empowering truths about themselves and the universe. Anything that went against the "official" doctrine and narrative had to be removed or mistranslated to keep people in a state of fear, guilt, shame, and servitude. The last thing the control system wants is for humanity to wake up to who they really are.

I also later learned that the word Elohim that occurs throughout the old testament is actually a plural word, and the correct translation of that word is actually the "Shining Ones," who came down from the heavens. That definitely sounds a lot more like Extraterrestrials to me than it does "God." So that was the next big mistranslation I found, and I went on to discover many more.

At the point when I learned that the whole concept of "Hell" was a complete lie and fabrication used to control the masses, not only did that destroy the whole central Christian teaching of needing to accept Jesus as our Lord and Savior to be saved from Hell, but it caused me to question *everything* I had believed and been taught. I thought, "If that isn't true, then what else isn't true? And more importantly, what IS true?"

Suddenly my tiny dogmatic box had been blown apart into a million pieces. I went through a short period of feeling lost as my entire belief system and religious identity was destroyed. I no longer knew who I was or what was actually true. It was my "dark night of the soul" as many have termed it. Luckily, I was so passionate about finding truth that this process was very short lived, and my desire for truth and excitement and fascination with what I was finding propelled me on my new journey. It felt like a massive weight was lifted from me, and I felt more free and alive than I ever had in my entire life.

Suddenly I went from thinking I knew the ultimate truth, to now being open to all possibilities and free to explore on my own what the truth actually is, who I am, what is the nature of reality, and what actually exists in the universe. I was so excited to explore that I just went down every rabbit hole of information that I came across. The most intriguing topics to me were the so called "conspiracy theories" or "fringe" subjects, such as the concept of a global elite controlling the world and a dark force working through them (I had already slowly started becoming aware of this at this point), UFOs and Extraterrestrials and life existing all over the universe, and the nature of the Soul, Consciousness, and Spiritual Truths.

YouTube videos were my main source of awakening and learning, and at this time the censorship of Youtube was much less than it is today, and there was an immense amount of "conspiracy," extraterrestrial/UFO, and spiritual/metaphysical videos available at that time. Searching many topics would mostly result in great quality videos. Today when you search many topics on YouTube you'll get mostly mainstream news clips, big youtube channels giving extremely watered down and/or false information, or hit pieces or "debunking" videos on the topic.

I was absolutely fascinated with the information I was coming across. I was taking in and exploring everything I found that fascinated or intrigued me. It was like taking in information through a fire hose. I couldn't get enough of it. The first few people I came across with information that truly intrigued and resonated with me were David Icke, David Wilcock, Dolores Cannon, Steven Greer, and Alex Jones. Shortly after these I came across Project Camelot (Kerry Cassidy and Bill Ryan interviewing various insiders and experiencers), Jordan Maxwell, Max Spiers, Jim Marrs, Bashar (Darryl Anka), Barbara Marciniak, Gregg Braden, Abraham Hicks, Old Coast to Coast episodes with Art Bell, and many more. I remember watching interviews and presentations by different ET contactees and experiencers such as Travis Walton, Billy Meier, Whitley Strieber, Alex Collier, and others. I remember watching Bob Lazar interviews and Phil Schneider videos. There was a YouTube channel I watched called Spirit Science. I watched the documentary Zeitgeist and was blown away. I was absolutely fascinated by all of this information. I started buying books by Dolores Cannon, David Wilcock, David Icke, and others.

In the Spring of 2012 when I was 25 years old, I moved in with my good friend Jake. We were in the beginning stages of forming a band, as we were jamming around and writing songs. I had just quit my previous band and was excited to start one that was more of the style I was into, which was anything in the vein of Indie Rock, Alternative, Punk or Post-hardcore. We were very influenced by bands like Fugazi, Sonic Youth, Radiohead, Sunny Day Real Estate, At the Drive-In, Unwound, Jawbox, The Appleseed Cast, HUM, Deftones, Manchester Orchestra, Pedro the Lion, The Pixies, Dinosaur Jr., The Cure, and many more.

Jake and I both grew up in Christian families, and when

we met were both Christians. We both started questioning things and leaving the "Christian box," but went in completely opposite directions. While I was curious and open to exploring new ideas, Jake was leaning towards not believing in God or anything spiritual. I noticed this change in him from our talks. Though I went through a phase of uncertainty, I still had the "knowing" that there was more to reality, like souls, a spirit world, and a greater intelligence behind everything.

Jake, on the other hand, was moving away from believing in anything beyond what we can see and touch. He thought stuff like souls or an afterlife didn't exist because there "wasn't any proof." Our chats showed how differently we were thinking. We agreed that some Christian teachings didn't add up, like the idea of Heaven and Hell being the only options after death. But when I brought up things like reincarnation or aliens, Jake would just dismiss it.

Even though I understood where he was coming from, I was on my own journey. I was so fascinated by what I was finding and felt the truth of it deep in my soul. But it was frustrating because Jake didn't want to hear any of it. None of my friends, Christian or not, were interested in these deep conversations either. So I felt pretty lonely and isolated in my journey.

Over the next five years, I continued in my personal "Journey to Truth" until one day I finally had the strong urge to connect with other like-minded people. That's when I finally decided to attend my first conference.

CHAPTER 5

Eclipse of Disclosure

In August of 2017 I attended my first UFO/Metaphysical/ Spiritual conference, called Eclipse of Disclosure. It was held in McCloud, CA, a small town very close to Mt. Shasta. As the name of the conference suggests, it was held during the solar eclipse of 2017. It was a brand new conference with about 400 people attending, and it featured some amazing speakers including Laura Eisenhower, Niara Isley, Dr. Michael Salla, Clifford Mahooty, Jay Weidner, Corey Goode, Justin Deschamps, Eric Raines, Jordan Sather, and others. They used the town's Dance Hall as the venue for the speakers.

About a month or so before the conference, on the conference's Facebook group, a few people were saying where they were from and where they were traveling from. I posted a screenshot of the GPS directions for my trip from St. Charles, MO (close to St. Louis) all the way to Mt. Shasta. Yes, I drove all the way there from St. Louis. I love driving on long road trips, it was cheaper, and I just wanted the adventure of driving rather than flying. A woman named Chastity commented on my post and said she was driving from Wichita, Kansas, and suggested that we follow each other there since our paths joined up in Kansas. She was driving to the conference in a van with her four children (what a brave woman). So we met up in Salina, KS and followed each other the rest of the way to Mt. Shasta.

It was a three day trip, but it was so beautiful driving through Colorado, Utah, and California. When we finally reached Northern California, after driving through Nevada, suddenly the landscape turned lush green, beautiful, and mountainous. I was in awe of the scenery as that last stretch through Northern CA was the most beautiful part of the drive.

We finally reached the small town of McCloud, found the sign for the conference and parked at the campground area. It was in a huge field next to the logging mill. As soon as we got there I could feel the amazing energy of the Shasta area.

I was looking at the mountain and I noticed some red lights hovering around it. I kept looking at them trying to figure out what they were. I hadn't had any UFO sightings up to this point, so I was excited to see some "unidentified" objects or lights in the sky. I thought, "I can't believe I just got here and I'm already seeing UFOs. This place really is special." Each night we saw various numbers of UFOs or lightships in the sky.

After getting our tents set up, we started walking around the campground area. We heard a drum circle and we joined in. Someone handed me a Djembe drum and I played it for a bit. So at this point in time I didn't know what sage was. I was standing around just watching the drum circle, and this girl who was kind of dancing and waving her sage stick around, suddenly handed me the sage stick. I had no idea what this was at the time and didn't know what to do with it, so I just stood there holding the burning sage bundle like an idiot (haha). She then came up to me and was like, "wave it around like this," and showed me how to wave it around. I went "Ooooh thanks!" I was still a newbie and ignorant of many "spiritual" things at this point in time.

Before the conference, I remember thinking, "David Wilcock should be speaking at this event. Why isn't he listed as a speaker?" At that time the big show on Gaia that myself and so many people were fascinated by was "Cosmic Disclosure." The show consisted of David interviewing Corey Goode about his experiences in a secret space program, and it was what brought my awareness to both Corey and the SSP information. At that point in time, David and Corey had basically become a duo, were always booked at the same conferences, and often spoke together. So I naturally just assumed David would be speaking since Corey was. It turned out that David was asked to speak, but was not able to do any more conferences for the year. So I was a little disappointed about that, but it didn't matter because there were so many fantastic speakers. More than that, just hanging out with so many amazing like-minded people who were on the same wavelength in such a beautiful and magical place was by far the best part of the conference.

Every single night I saw at least a handful of UFOs or light ships in the night sky, which I wasn't used to at the time. On Sunday night they had an official "skywatch" where there was a pair of military grade night vision binoculars that we could look through. A line formed for people to take turns using the night vision. I saw one UFO through the night vision, and followed it along as it went, but I saw at least about 5 other UFOs with my naked eyes. The skywatch went on pretty late, and around about 2am, Jimmy Church announced to everyone that William Tompkins had just passed away. Most knew and respected William Tompkins and were very saddened by the news.

The next day was the big Solar Eclipse, which was about 90% totality for us in the Mt. Shasta area. We were all given glasses to look at the eclipse, and we did a powerful and energetic meditation during it at 11:11am. It felt like a massive activation to me, and many others said the same. That day a few of us had realized that William Tompkins technically passed away right at the start of the Eclipse. We all agreed there was no way that was just a coincidence.

I ended up going on a hike at McCloud Falls (beautiful waterfalls and hiking area) with a different group of people every day of the conference. On the last day I went with a group of some new friends, and during the hike one of them pulls out a bag of psilocybin mushrooms (psychedelic mushrooms) and offered them to us. I had never taken "shrooms" yet at this point and was curious to try them. I just pinched some out of the bag having no idea how much it was, but it seemed like the proper amount. A few of us took some and we continued on the hike. I knew it would take a bit to kick in, but I was expecting it to happen at some point on the hike, which it never did. It ended up taking about 2 hours to take effect, and by the time it did I had completely forgotten I had taken them.

When the hike was over and I was hanging out back at the campgrounds, a new acquaintance asked me for a ride into Shasta because he wanted to meet up with some people there, and I said sure. By this point I had completely forgotten that I had taken the mushrooms almost 2 hours ago and they still hadn't kicked in yet. It was about an 18 minute drive into town. So I dropped him off and started heading back to McCloud. As soon as I started driving I felt the mushrooms kick in. I just thought "Ooooh no, this is not good! I totally forgot about the mushrooms!" I realized I had two choices now. One: I turn around and park in a parking lot somewhere in Shasta and ride this out there. It was about 8 or 8:30pm, so that would mean I would be there all night and miss everything going on back at the campgrounds, and probably have to sleep in my car. Or Two: I keep driving, concentrate REALLY hard, and pray that I make it back to McCloud safely. Apparently I was dumb enough to choose option two. I remember it being intense the whole way, but I just mustering up all of my will to focus and concentrate on driving. Cars were passing around me because I was going too slow. Apparently my guides were protecting me because I somehow made it back to the campgrounds alive without crashing.

I was now having a full-out mushroom trip! I remember just being super blissed out and feeling so much love. I felt absolutely amazing! I was still able to talk to people and have conversations, but people could definitely tell I was on something (haha). It felt like I was in a waking dream state, where everything was kind of hazy and fluid. There was a drum circle going on. I stood to listen and take it all in for a while. I also remember having these constant epiphanies of truth like "Everything is One and connected" "Love all that actually exists" "We are all eternal beings of pure Source energy" etc.

When the conference was over, I was so filled with love and gratitude for the experience and for the amazing connections I made, but at the same time I was so sad that it was over and I had to go back home. I was tearing up a lot that morning and started crying during the drive.

I remember having the strong feeling that what I had experienced at that conference was how life was meant to be. There was a pervasive love, joy, and deep sense of connection among everyone there. Living in a loving community among the beauty of nature is how life is *supposed* to be. Many people have spoken about the ascension and the "New Earth." Dolores Cannon spoke on this topic often because of information she would receive through QHHT sessions with her clients. I knew that what I had experienced was a little glimpse of New Earth, a small preview of the amazing future humanity is moving towards.

My UFO Sighting Back Home

A few months after the conference in my hometown of St. Charles, MO, I had my most profound UFO experience still to this day. I was hanging out with a recently made new friend who happened to be spiritual and into ETs and UFOs as well. We were hanging out around Main Street in St. Charles sometime around 6pm. It was January so it was already dark. All of a sudden, right in front of us in the night sky we saw three lights moving around the sky. From different areas, all three lights slowly came together and locked into a formation resembling Orion's Belt. The lights were all at different levels of brightness, and they were all fluctuating in intensity. They stayed in the Orion's Belt formation for about 3-4 minutes, then slowly drifted apart in different directions and then faded away. We were just staring at the lights for a bit when we asked each other, "Are you seeing this?" Fortunately, I was able to get a cell phone video of the event.

Screenshot from my video of the sighting. The dimmest light doesn't show up on the video.

I got the strong feeling that the beings on the ships were our Star Family that either one or both of us were connected to, and have spent many other lifetimes with. They were showing up to say "Hello" and let us know they're here and watching over us. So why the Orion's Belt formation? My best guess is because it's the most recognizable star formation, they were using it to show us that they were beings from the stars in a way that we were sure to understand.

CHAPTER 6

We Are Not Alone

"We are not alone in the universe. They have
been coming here for a long time."
— Edgar Mitchell

"If you think, out of ten billion suns in the Milky Way,
that this speck of dust, this emerald with the yellow
sun in the outermost corner of God's mind, is the
only planet to host life, you need a vision!"
— Ramtha, *UFOs and the Nature of Reality*

"The cosmos is populated much more than the common person
has any inkling of, or any idea about. The cosmos is extremely
populated and well-traveled and utilized. The area of our home
planet is more populated in what would be called 'inhabited'
planets. There are more inhabited planets per sector of space.
In other words, it's a crowded place there. It really is."
— Dolores Cannon, *Keepers of the Garden*

"I'll tell you what I've concluded: We are not alone, and we have never been alone. We have had an intimate interrelationship with advanced intelligence from somewhere out there, and it's not just time and space as we know it. I'm talking about different dimensions as well. The human race has had a continual intimate interrelationship with advanced extraterrestrial intelligence from the beginning of our history."
— Command Sergeant Major Robert Dean

The Milky Way galaxy contains between 100 to 400 billion stars. Each of these stars potentially has its own galaxy. Imagine that for every grain of sand on Earth, there are about 10,000 stars in the universe. Among these stars, around 5 percent are similar to our Sun, meaning there could be around 500 quintillion Sun-like stars. Some of these stars may have planets in their habitable zones, where conditions could support life similar to Earth. If even just 1 percent of stars have Earth-like planets, that could mean there are about 100 billion billion of them out there. For every grain of sand on Earth, there could be a hundred Earth-like planets in the universe. In our galaxy alone, there could be about a billion Earth-like planets. Even if only a small percentage of these planets have life, there could be a vast number of inhabited worlds. And if a fraction of those have intelligent civilizations like ours, there could be millions of them in the universe, with thousands potentially in the Milky Way. These numbers challenge the idea that Earth is unique and isolated in the cosmos. Considering the age of the universe, there could be civilizations much older and more advanced than ours, with capabilities far beyond our current understanding.

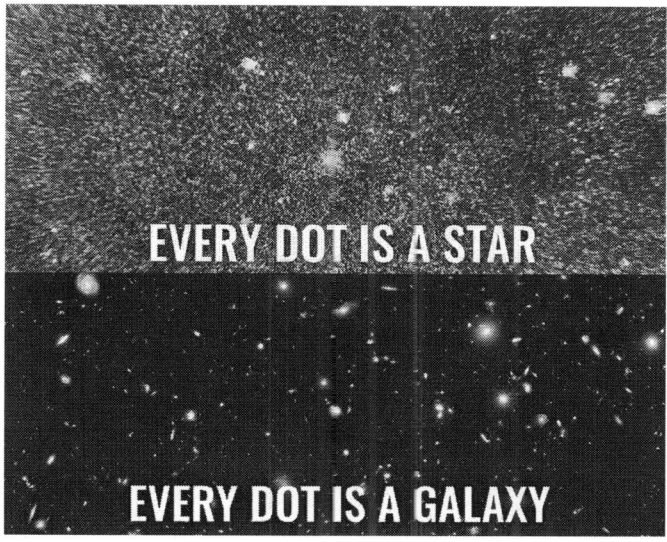

Along my journey I've come to realize that we are *absolutely* not alone in the universe, and that there are an infinite number of diverse beings and intelligences in the multiverse, throughout multiple densities and dimensions.

The evidence shows that we humans are *ourselves* ETs. Our genetics are a mixture of various extraterrestrial species, and through our DNA we are energetically connected to those star races. Many people, including Andromedan contactee Alex Collier, have claimed that human beings are very unique, and are in fact considered "genetic royalty" throughout the galaxy.

Many of us have had multitudes of incarnations as various ET races and different types of beings. If we feel very connected to a specific race, it's most likely because the majority of our incarnations have been as that species or within that specific star group.

We are all eternal souls and infinite consciousness having experiences as different beings on various planets. There ultimately is no such thing as "solid matter" or "death", because in reality everything is just energy, frequency, and vibration. Essentially all that exists is Infinite God Energy/ Consciousness which is going out and organizing in different ways and vibrating at different frequencies in order for consciousness to have different experiences. We are all a part of this infinite consciousness. There is no separation. All is One. That is the ultimate truth I've learned throughout my journey.

So then where do ETs and UFOs fit into this picture? Through our growth in technology, knowledge and understanding as a species in the last seven thousand years, we've come to realize that the universe we live in is vast and enormous beyond what most of us can even comprehend. On top of that, even our mainstream science has found out that at least 12 dimensions exist. So are we supposed to believe that in all of that vastness and all of those other dimensions, there is no other life? How exactly does that make any sense whatsoever?

As Carl Sagan said: "The universe is a pretty big place. If it's just us, seems like an awful waste of space."

It would be a massive waste of space, if it was just us. But the universe doesn't waste. It is perfectly efficient, and infinitely intelligent, abundant, and creative. Also, time doesn't actually exist. All that truly exists is the Zero Point Eternal Now. Here in third density, we are having the *experience* of space and time in order to be able to have certain types of experiences.

As we perceive things to be happening in time, the Universe and all life within it is ever growing, expanding, and evolving. So it would make no sense whatsoever if there was only ONE species existing on only ONE planet in only ONE solar system in only ONE galaxy, in only ONE dimension.

Some people believe in the existence of ETs throughout the universe. Some people are adamant that "ETs are all demons!'

Some people will say that they're not all demons, but they are all interdimensional beings that are either benevolent or malevolent, and could be called angels and demons. Some people will tell you they believe ETs do exist, but they've never interacted with humanity and there's no chance of us finding them anytime soon. Many people become locked into a belief system which then everything else has to fit inside that box for them to understand it and for it to not threaten their own beliefs. Many people want to believe everything seemingly paranormal or mysterious going on is all one specific thing, or fits into one specific box.

What I've learned and awakened to on my journey is that the answer is almost always "All of the Above." Physical 3D extraterrestrials do exist. Higher dimensional beings also exist. Some of them are more evolved (service-to-others) and some of them are more regressive (service-to-self), and the terms "angel" or "demon" are and can be used to describe these beings. Many UFOs are actually advanced secret military and government craft (often using technology gained or reverse engineered from ETs), but many UFOs are in fact extraterrestrials or higher dimensional beings. It's not just one or a couple of these things. It's "All of the Above."

Some people don't believe any other intelligent life forms exist other than humans, because they weren't told about it in school, from academia, from the government, or from any other perceived "authority." In fact, many people are told definitively that no other life forms exist and "There is no evidence!" And so many people are programmed to believe this. The people who claim that "there is no evidence," are merely repeating what they've been told, and only believe that because they haven't had any experiences or seen any evidence, although they haven't truly looked very hard, if at all for the evidence. "There is no evidence" is a conclusion that is come to using confirmation bias, looking at what the "official" sources say, which means heavily controlled, programmed, and/or propaganda-based sources of information: mainstream media, governments or militaries' official statements, and mainstream academia. What exactly do they mean by "evidence"? Do they really expect the very people who have a vested interest in covering up UFOs and the existence of extraterrestrial life to fully and officially come out and say "ETs exist and they are here!"? People who say this do not understand, nor accept, that governments and militaries have been playing an active role in suppressing any and all evidence for many decades.

In reality, there are such enormous mountains of evidence that it's mind-blowing and absolutely ridiculous that anyone on the planet is still believing the nonsense that we are actually alone. There are numerous people who at one time didn't believe ETs were real, or that they've been to our planet. These individuals then had their own personal experiences that changed their minds and lives forever. When you do proper investigation, listen to the experiences of numerous ET contactees, and/or have your *own* personal experience with extraterrestrials, then the truth becomes immensely apparent that ETs exist both on our planet and throughout the universe.

> "There are many other species, and humans don't understand that. But we like the humans. They are a part of us, and they discover that when they leave their body. If they knew this they would behave differently. They're very lovely. They mean well, and they all have this love in their heart, and we just want them to love from their heart. And if they love from their heart, they won't create these things that occur."
> — Dolores Cannon, *The Three Waves of Volunteers and the New Earth*

CHAPTER 7

Contact in the Desert

In the summer of 2018, my friend Chastity and I decided to attend Contact in the Desert together. If you're not familiar, Contact in the Desert is the world's largest UFO conference (it's been referred to as the Woodstock of UFO conferences) that is currently held in Indian Wells, CA (close to Palm Springs). It used to be held in Joshua Tree, CA. The year we attended was the first year they had moved the conference from the Joshua Tree Retreat Center to the Renaissance Hotel in Indian Wells. I remember some people that year were calling it "Contact in Beverly Hills." It was a massive conference with about 4,000 attendees that year. It was at this point where I realized that the huge conferences in hotels are not really my thing, though I'm glad I got to experience that conference one time. I feel like I would've liked the old Joshua Tree Retreat Center location more, but still it would've been too big for my tastes. I prefer the smaller, more intimate conferences that are more in nature, like Eclipse of Disclosure.

Me, Chastity, Sarah and Laura Borgatta with
famous UFO abductee Travis Walton

That being said, I still had a great time, and saw some amazing speakers including Michael Tellinger, David Wilcock, Nassim Haramein, Michael Salla, Laura Eisenhower, James Gilliland, Jason Quitt, and Linda Moulton Howe. I got to meet Travis Walton and talk to him for about 45 minutes. He was super nice and genuine. I didn't get to catch John DeSouza's talk, but I remember talking to both him and Jason Quitt at their merch tables. I bought both of their books, "The Extra-Dimensionals" by John DeSouza, and "Forbidden Knowledge" by Jason Quitt, which are both outstanding books. I attended Corey Goode's "intensive" during which they showed us an extremely bare-bones, first draft of the documentary *Above Majestic*.

Chastity and I had met and made friends with a couple ladies there who were from Omaha, NE. We ended up hanging out with them a lot during the conference. They both had bought tickets to a CE5 (Close Encounters of the Fifth Kind, a term popularized by Dr. Steven Greer, referring to human-initiated contact with extraterrestrial beings or spacecraft through conscious and intentional communication protocols), but they decided that they didn't want to go, and gave us their tickets. So we attended the CE5 (my first ever), did the group mediation with everyone, and we saw a few ships.

A friend who I would meet later on, who goes by the name Alara Sirius, while attending Contact in the Desert in 2019 (the very next year, which I did not attend) actually captured footage of a TR3B (Black triangle UFO) along with another "lightship" while outside during the conference. She claims she saw a big bright light moving in the sky, and was able to get a cell phone video of it. It wasn't until later when she was reviewing the footage that she noticed there was a black triangle craft, or TR3B, in the sky with the lightship. She claims that she didn't see the TR3B with her naked eye, but was only filming the bright light. She was shocked to find the TR3B craft show up in the footage as well.

Screenshot from Alara's video of the lightship and TR3B craft

In the Summer of 2018, shortly after the conference, I ended up moving to Wichita, Kansas to live with my friend Chastity. We had become good friends over the past year. I was really wanting to move, and Chastity was needing help with some things, so I decided to move in and help her out. We had so many amazing conversations during that time. One night I'm pretty sure Chastity saved us all from a tornado that very nearly missed our house when she started doing energetic protection.

CHAPTER 8

Meeting a Soul Brother

The next conference I attended was Dimensions of Disclosure on August 17-19, 2018. This was essentially the "sequel" to Eclipse of Disclosure, and it was put on by the same people as the first event. They moved the event this year from Mt. Shasta to Loveland, Colorado. It was held at a beautiful ranch, called Sunrise Ranch, in Loveland. It had many of the same speakers as EOD, along with some new speakers, including David Wilcock (he made it this time!), Corey Goode, Emery Smith, Dr. Michael Salla, Niara Isley, Laura Eisenhower, Bridget Nielsen, Clifford Mahooty, Justin Deschamps, Dr. Sam Osmanagich, Jordan Sather and many more. This is the conference where I first met Tyler, and was the connection which led to the formation of our podcast.

One day while I was outside talking to people, Tyler and his dad Jim (Tyler was there with his dad, which I thought was so awesome) were standing around with me in the same circle of people talking. At this point I hadn't gotten their names or learned anything about them. As the circle of people started to disperse, they told me they were about to go on a hike and asked if I wanted to go with them. I said "sure!" and the three of us went on our own little hike on-site of the ranch. As we're hiking, either Tyler or his dad Jim asked me "So Aaron, where are you from?" I said "St. Louis," expecting the usual "Ah cool," or "Hmm…what state is that in again?". Instead they responded "Oh nice, we're from St. Louis too!" "No way! That's awesome!" I said. I was super excited to have met a couple new local friends (though I was living in Kansas at the time) at a small conference in Colorado. What are the chances?! I just happened to be talking to Tyler and his dad at the exact moment when they were about to go on a hike, and got invited along. Looking back this was definitely a Divine synchronicity. The Universe brought the three of us together at the exact right time.

At this conference, I remember seeing both Roger Richards and Niara Isley again and giving them hugs. I also met and hung out a bit with Matthew Mournian, Justin Deschamps, Simon Esler, and Renee Armenta. I remember Renee Armenta, myself, and a couple other people did this little drum/instrument circle at one point, which was very powerful.

I attended the CE5 during this conference as well. It seemed that almost everyone attending the conference was there. I remember at some point afterwards, I found Tyler and his dad, and they were all excited talking about these giant blue orbs that they saw during the CE5. They said that no one else (including myself) saw them because they appeared in a completely different place than where everyone was looking.

After the conference was officially over, I stayed the next day and hung out with the few people who were still at the ranch. Matthew Mournian was there and he offered me a Tarot reading, which I gladly accepted. In hindsight, the reading he gave me was absolutely spot on. It told me something was about to collapse or end, with the tower card, but that something new and amazing was about to begin. This is exactly what happened shortly after the conference. Two months later, I ended up leaving the band I was in at the time. I started being verbally attacked by a couple of the band members over things they didn't like that I was sharing on my personal Facebook account, which was the straw that broke the camel's back. The band had already lost its steam and become much more burdensome than fun by that point. But then three months later, a new exciting endeavor took its place when Tyler and I started Journey to Truth Podcast.

CHAPTER 9

Journey to Truth Podcast

A few months after the conference, I traveled back to visit my family back in St. Louis. Tyler, his dad and I made plans to meet up and get lunch. Tyler and I were chatting about how we both want to start some kind of project, whether it be a YouTube channel, write a book, or something else as a forum to cover disclosure and truth-seeking topics. I suddenly remembered the suggestion my friend Kalyn had made to me a few months prior. She said that I should start a podcast, because she felt there weren't enough podcasts out there within the disclosure/awakening community. So I brought up the idea and said "What if we do a podcast?" I don't remember exactly what Tyler said. All I remember is that it just clicked and we both felt like "Yes, that's it. Let's do it." Since neither of us at the time were very used to or comfortable being on camera, the idea of an audio podcast (which is what it started out as) rather than doing something on video was very appealing to us. And the idea just seemed really fun. We could have amazing conversations, record them, and throw them up on the internet for whoever cared to listen. We honestly just thought it sounded like a lot of fun. We had no expectations whatsoever, nor did we have any future plans or goals for it. We were purely just "following our highest excitement," as Bashar always teaches. We were really just living in the present and taking things as the Universe was laying them in front of us.

We then immediately started planning out how we were going

to go about this whole podcast thing. We had to come up with a name for the podcast. At the time, I had a Facebook group called "Journey to Truth," which Tyler and I were both regularly posting to. And the story of how *that* name came to be, is because I was posting in my friend Chastity's Facebook group "The 3D Journey to Truth," and when she decided to end the group, I asked her if I could use the name "Journey to Truth" for my own group. So, since Tyler and I were both active in my Journey to Truth group on Facebook, it just made sense for us to call the podcast "Journey to Truth Podcast," and we both really liked the name.

We decided that we were going to do it once a week, and try to stick to that schedule. We wanted to have as many guests on as possible, so we figured we'll reach out and try to get on as many people as we can, and then the rest of the weeks we'll just have the show be the two of us. Little did we know that we'd end up having a guest on the show *every single week*, minus one week early on when we had a last minute cancellation.

In preparation to start the show, Tyler and I each reached out to a handful of people we'd met at conferences. To our excitement, every single person we reached out to agreed to be a guest on the show, and we were just like "Whoa this is so cool! It's actually happening!" I remember we hadn't even recorded the first episode yet and we already had the first 6 weeks of guests lined up.

We wanted to do an audio podcast, but neither of us at the time could figure out how to do that, and it just seemed way easier to make a YouTube channel and upload everything there. So that's what we did.

We made a short promo video and shared it out all over Facebook. The next day, we recorded our very first episode with Tyler's dad, Jim, as the guest. We used Zoom and recorded what was essentially a three-way phone conversation between the three of us. We shared it out on Facebook, which was the only social media platform we were using to promote at the time. Early on, the podcast transitioned from audio only to video, which everyone seemed to like better so we stuck with that.

A couple months later in April, Tyler attended a conference in Hawaii called "Cosmic Waves," which was put on by Joan Ocean in collaboration with Corey Goode. While there he met Laura Eisenhower, who agreed to do a show with us. We were both fans of Laura and were super excited to be having her on the show! Since that time we've become good friends with Laura, and I believe she holds the record for most appearances on the show. She recently released her phenomenal book *Awakening the Truth Frequency*. I can't recommend it enough. In it she tells her entire story and all the information and knowledge that she's gained throughout her life.

Tyler and I attended ECETI ranch for the first time in July of 2019 for the summer conference that year. ECETI stands for Enlightened Contact with ExtraTerrestrial Intelligence. It is a ranch in southern Washington run by James Gilliland. Because of the vortex created by Mt. Adams (the nearby mountain) and the sacred land there, it is a massive hotspot for UFO, ET, and spiritual activity.

Every night during the skywatches we'd see so many craft in the sky that we'd usually lose count. We were absolutely dumbfounded by how many UFOs we would see in the sky every night. We would also regularly see lights appear and disappear on the mountain. If you go to ECETI, you are basically guaranteed to see UFOs.

During the conference, Tyler had a Sasquatch encounter (one of many) where he was awoken in the middle of the night by a loud *WHACK* on the tree next to his tent, followed by two stomps and a deep grunt, clearly none of which came from a human. My tent was right next to his by the way, and I didn't wake up or hear any of this. The next morning when he told me this, we saw a giant stick laying next to the tree which we both knew for a fact was not there the night before. That day when Tyler was out walking, he asked for confirmation of the experience being a Sasquatch. As soon as he asked that in his mind, a rock came from the direction of the trees and hit him in the leg. He looked and there were no people anywhere near where the rock came from. When he told James Gilliland the story, James said that they love throwing rocks. So we both knew that was the Sasquatch confirming it was them.

In 2020, when the world was shutting down from the pandemic, things started to speed up for us and the podcast really started to take off. We started filming for our Cahokia Mounds documentary that year, though it got put on hold until we were able to finish it last year. That's also the year when the censorship online really started ramping up, and we first started being majorly affected by it.

Tyler and I went on to attend many other conferences, and we started getting asked to be a part of some conferences. We were asked to be a part of a conference called Camp Disclosure (held close to Asheville, NC) where we did what we called an "Experiencer's Lounge". We had a canopy tent set up as a hang out area, and anyone who wanted, we filmed them sharing about any profound ET, UFO, or spiritual experience they've had. After the conference, we compiled them all together into a video and uploaded it to our YouTube channel. We've done our "Experiencer's Lounge" at multiple conferences since then.

In 2022, we put on our very own conference for the first time called the Secret Space Conference in Grafton, IL. It dealt with the topic of the Secret Space Program, and many SSP experiencers whom we'd had on the show spoke at the event, along with a few non-SSP people. The conference was a success beyond what we imagined, and everyone loved it so much that we put on another one the following year called Journey to Truth Conference. We are now about to do our third one this year, called Rebels of Disclosure Conference, and we plan to continue doing an annual conference for the foreseeable future.

We started the podcast having absolutely no idea what we were doing, and having absolutely no expectations whatsoever. We never dreamed we'd be doing our own conferences and documentaries. We were just having fun and following our highest excitement. The Universe has truly been guiding and supporting us since day one, and it's almost felt as if we jumped into a river that we've been flowing in ever since. The amazing people we've met, the experiences we've had, the people we've been privileged to have on the show, and the opportunities that continue to come our way have been a bigger blessing than we ever thought possible. We're so incredibly grateful for everyone who has supported us and for everything that has come from Journey to Truth Podcast.

CHAPTER 10

A Divine Soul Connection

In early 2021, I became involved in a long-distance relationship with a girl who lived in Portland, Oregon. That summer, I relocated to Portland to be with her, but the relationship lasted only another four months. After the end of the relationship, I was living with my good friend Scott. I loved Scott and the couple other roommates I was living with, but I wasn't enjoying Portland quite as much anymore with the extremely long rainy season. I thought about moving back to St. Louis sooner, but it must have been Divine guidance that led me to stay in Portland until later the next summer, because that's when something amazing happened.

By June of 2022, I had decided I was moving back to St. Louis at the beginning of August. There is an annual summer conference in Mt. Shasta which is put on by Rob Potter. About three weeks before the conference, I decided to attend it and bought my ticket. Since Portland is only about six hours from Mt. Shasta I knew I could easily drive to the event. If I had moved back to the Midwest any earlier I likely would not have attended, as it would've been much more expensive with plane tickets.

I shared an AirBnB with my good friend Barry and three other friends. Lowell Johnson was leading a hike on Saturday, but it was already sold out by the time I found out about it. Barry was going on the hike and asked me if I could give him a ride to the meet up spot. That morning, he knocked on my door before my alarm went off, and said that our mutual friend Miriam decided to back out of the hike last night. He asked if I wanted her ticket. So I ended up going on a hike that was already sold out.

When we arrived at the meetup spot, that's when I first met Amanda, the girl that would become my now life partner. We both experienced a powerful energetic and soul level connection that changed both of our lives.

Our first picture together from the hike

57

Here is Amanda's testimony of what happened from her personal perspective:

'Serendipity – Jumping Timelines

After processing intense pain from having my husband absent for so many years, my life seemed to be in flow. I had done the work to love myself more. As I did this and embraced the feelings that I deserved a partner that was more present, things shifted and he was home more. Our respect for each other started to grow. Mr. J had found more balance. I accepted what was and the manner in which I loved him, and was willing to make it work. We had built a beautiful life together. Still there was a piece of me that felt melancholy at times, a longing and homesickness that I never could shake.

Shortly after, everything blew up. I had been called for a few years to return to Mt. Shasta. So when my friend Deb mentioned going to a conference there, I quickly jumped on board. Deb is a tiny spitfire of a woman. Although close in age to my mother she has a youthful spirit and is a powerful Craniosacral and Polarity practitioner. She practices homeopathy too, and honestly, I do not know where I would be without her! She has taught me so much about how to keep my system clear and have healthy boundaries. The tools and lessons she has taught me through a work called RYSE has helped me to strengthen my system and care for it as an empath. I can always count on her to be honest with me and guide me even when it is hard to hear. She is a beautiful balance of tough and loving.

Mt. Shasta is an extremely powerful place and every time I visit, I come home changed. We flew into Sacramento and drove to the mountain. It was lovely meeting unique and like-minded individuals. I found it difficult to sleep because of the time change. Deb and I had signed up for the Lowell Johnson hike on the Saturday of the conference. That morning, I was up early contemplating all we may experience. Lowell has an incredible story of his journey into Telos and Inner Earth. My guidance in prayer was to say yes to everything that day.

At our meeting point, we greeted others and made plans to carpool to a few stops on our way up to the trailhead for our hike. Two women were headed towards our car to join us when out of nowhere they stopped dead in their tracks and walked the other direction. Deb looked confused and motioned that we still had space to two guys, Barry and Aaron, who jumped into the backseat of our car. Barry was likable, friendly, and full of light and stories. I can best describe him as a gentle, clumsy, funny guy with a big heart. Aaron was quiet, calm and there was a peaceful presence and depth about him. He had made the decision to come to the conference a few weeks before, and the hike was already sold out. One of his Airbnb mates had decided to give up her ticket the night before. So bright and early, Barry knocked on Aaron's door to pass on the news.

We first stopped at the Gateway Peace Garden to enjoy the view of the mountain and to walk a beautiful labyrinth made of flowers. Our next stop up the mountain was a wooded area, I believe Lowell said it was near a vortex point. We stopped to prepare ourselves for the mountain and make an offering. I became more curious about Aaron. He was kind and offered me water. Deb had told me he had a podcast as an aside, but I had never seen or heard of it.

At the top, we hiked up a rocky trail to a large rock that looked like it could be a doorway or entrance into the mountain. I immediately felt drawn to the rock. I stood and sat up against it and it was as if there was a magnetism that held me pressed up against the stone. I could sense others on the other side of this stone and I felt as though they were helping me. I specifically felt energy flowing through my third eye.

Once the rock released me, I listened to a few of Lowell's stories before I went up to sit in a nook in the rocks. An older woman named Penny Ann joined me and we had a magical, emotional moment when she and I held onto her Lemurian crystal. To this day I am unsure what happened in that moment. I only know that something powerful happened between us and that crystal. I am humbled and grateful for her kindness and the experience.

When I returned we snapped a few pictures and I noticed Aaron observing me. We posed for a picture together and Penny Ann said, "Is this your husband?" I said "No, but I feel like I know him!" "Well perhaps in another life," she chuckled. On the trip back down the mountain, Aaron and I talked about our lives. I spoke about my children and family. He told me about starting the podcast. It felt like time stood still. We were in our own vortex. Somehow it took the others way longer to get down the mountain. At this point we realized we had lost Barry. Somehow in his wandering he ended up miles down the mountain. He needed a ride up to meet us. It was bizarre and we referred to him as "Lost in the Portal Barry" for the rest of our time in Shasta.

We rode down the mountain and parted ways. I found myself looking for him back at the conference location and when we crossed paths, he and Barry invited Deb and I to dinner and a sky watch that evening with a group. We sat together staring up at the sky and sharing more about our lives. When the night was closing, we hugged our new friends. I hugged Aaron and was like "woah." At that moment I heard one of the women with us let out an "awe."

I could not sleep at all that night. I was overwhelmed with feelings of gratitude for having the opportunity to meet such an amazing soul, and also felt extreme pain because I didn't think it was likely that I would ever see him again. I was in total denial about what I was feeling... Deep down I knew that the homesick feeling I had dealt with for much of my life was gone in the moment we embraced. I'd had strong friendship soul connections before and I was wrestling with myself, trying to convince myself that this was the same thing.

Deb and I went over to the conference to watch some speakers around midday and met up with Aaron. People kept stopping Aaron and I, saying things like "wow," "what a spark/connection," and asking how and how long we'd known each other. Aaron sat next to me during an Alex Collier talk. The intensity of the connection just continued to build. I felt completely unhinged. His arm grazed mine and I had to leave the talk for a break. It was too much for my system to handle.

Deb and I had planned to start our drive to Sacramento once the speakers had wrapped up. Aaron and I took a short walk on a trail near the headwater. I felt ridiculous. I was asking him, "Do you feel this?!" It was completely unnerving. At one point on the walk, we stopped and embraced. I have never in my life experienced anything like what overcame me in that moment. I could feel every chakra in my body responding and the only thing I can think to call it is a Kundalini activation. Aaron started to tremble and his heart was beating so hard I thought it might leave his chest. My body was covered in goosebumps in response to his touch. We went back to this place a year later and it still holds an energy signature from this moment.

Deb and I decided to stay and grab dinner before our drive to Sacramento. Aaron and I could not eat anything, and my whole sensory/neurological system was in complete overload. As we got into the car drove away from him, I looked at Deb and said, "WHAT THE &#%! WAS THAT?!" She just laughed.

The flight home was rough. I was in total agony. Deb was dosing me with homeopathic remedies for grief and shock to help ease my pain. For weeks I could barely eat and I had constant vertigo. Soon after that trip I decided that not exploring this connection was scarier than anything I would have to walk through to make the changes required in my life. Not making changes meant denying my truth. It wasn't fair to anyone involved. Once you know this level of connection, you cannot unknow it. I felt like a piece of myself that had been missing was returned. Knowing this was the beginning of the end of my marriage no matter what I chose. So two weeks later, I told Mr. J that I had a huge shift and extreme clarity that I no longer wanted to be in the marriage.

It was one of the hardest things to walk through. The pain felt by Mr. J and my children was heartbreaking, but the level of clarity I had in knowing that this was the right choice helped me to hold strong. I knew that what I was about to unlock about myself was a place that Mr. J would not be willing to go. Our resonance had distanced so much over the years that we couldn't even sleep peacefully near each other. Our soul contract was up; we had each grown as far as we could in the marriage and the dynamic needed to change.

The trials after this moment were intense. Many in my family did not respond well, were extremely triggered, passed judgment and chose sides. I lost close friendships, and years later there is still distance with some immediate family. You see, truly loving someone means supporting them, even when you don't understand or agree. I learned how to create healthy boundaries and how to express needs during this time. I had been so disconnected from myself that I didn't even know what my needs were. I was extremely private, and they made assumptions. I chose to use discernment more than anything to protect my children. I knew no one would understand. How could they? I honestly couldn't even understand it! At the end of the day, I fell in love in an instant. It wasn't something I could control without health consequences. All I could do was surrender.

Mr. J is my family and a soul I had experienced many lifetimes with. Love is described with one word in the English language, but in reality there are many types of love. The affection I felt for him was more like that of the love I have for my son or even a brother. Mr. J really stepped up as a father during this time. His engagement with the children was amazing and he really made up for a lot of lost time, especially with our son. I believe we continue to grow through our shared partnership in parenting two very special souls.

Meeting Aaron was a catalyst for changes that needed to happen in my life. I had no intentions or expectations of pursuing a new relationship. At the very least, meeting Aaron illuminated that I was not supposed to be in my current relationship. I had been compartmentalizing parts of myself to make things work in my marriage. I had abandoned myself in this because of fear of change. I didn't know what path my relationship with Aaron would take, all I knew was that meeting him was the most powerful thing I have ever experienced. Aaron was a constant support. He has this ability to "see" people. He understands their trauma and just holds this beautiful heart energy. It was so painful for him to witness everything I had to walk through and the lives it impacted. I am so grateful for the support and safety he created for me and even though our journey was challenging to start, we felt divinely supported.'

"Trusting the universe means surrendering to the flow of life and embracing the unknown."
— Alan Watts

Since that day, Amanda and I have had the privilege of going on some incredible trips together. We went on a trip to Egypt in the Spring of 2023, which was led by Kerry Cassidy and Maria Wheatley. That year we also visited Chaco Canyon and Ship Rock in New Mexico, where Amanda in particular had some incredible experiences.

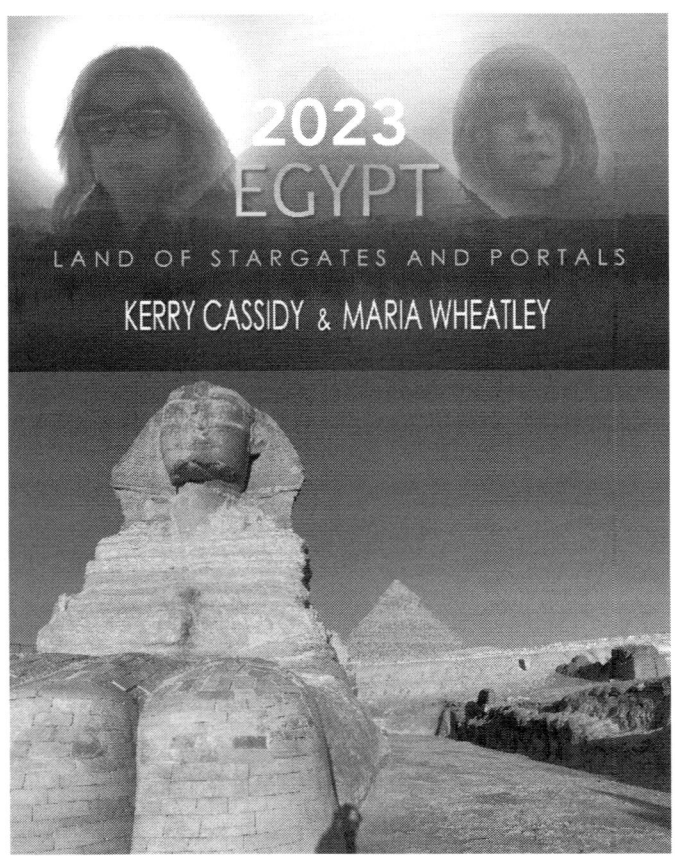

Pictures from Chaco Canyon and Ship Rock:

Ship Rock

Amanda:

'I had never heard of Ship Rock but if I have learned anything over the last year it is that visiting sacred places brings me so much joy. We are changed when we go to these high energy places filled with ancient knowledge. I like to think I bring it home with me into my world and to the people with whom I cross paths! So when our friend Nikki, aka Nikkiana Jones, offered to take us on an adventure to Ship Rock we were all in.

We arrived just before dusk. Ship Rock stood out like a bold castle in the peach and blue sky on the arid, rocky terrain. Our first stop was to see a long rock wall that led up to the Ship Rock. They claim this was formed from lava, but is lava formed from rocks with a mortar looking substance between them? Does lava have perfectly cut out circular holes naturally cut into it? We took some time to scale to the top of the wall and take some fun pictures.

Further up the road as we approached Ship Rock, Nikki pointed out a place that looked like it could be a stargate. We finally got close to Ship Rock at dusk. At 1583 feet high it feels nearby way before you are upon it. I stepped out of the car and thought I might fall over. The energy of this thing was so powerful it took me a minute to adjust. Once I felt steady all I could focus on was touching the side of the ginormous rock. The power and energy of this place fueled me and I took off uphill full speed in my dress and black and pink New Balance sneakers. Our friend Joaquin followed close behind. Aaron somehow managed to make the climb in flip flops!

When we reached the rock it was almost dark. I used to run

marathons but I was nowhere near being in that kind of shape when I decided to make this uphill long sprint. I stopped at the top and placed my hand on the textured warm rock and felt my heart pounding, my lungs burning and my ears ringing from the intensity of the effort. I caught my breath and enjoyed the high before climbing back down. At this point, it was very dark and difficult to see. Fear started to try to take hold and the thought of snakes being hidden in sporadic bushes caught me for a minute. Joaquin was close behind and he must have sensed my unease, he began making noises that magically seemed to calm me. He would just intuitively let out a call when I was starting to freak out to disperse the fear and it helped me to focus on my footing while making the steep descent.

Once I made it down and found my love's arms, we stopped to observe the sky. I felt something stir within me, a call, a familiarity. At this point, 3 ships moved towards us and then stopped and just hovered there. We could see the lights and they held this position for quite some time. My friend Shavon looked at me with wide eyes and said, "they are here for you." Deep down I knew it. She had a sense that they were pushing our contract by coming so close at that moment, but that they knew I needed to know they were there. It was a beautiful and humbling experience with some of my favorite people.'

CHAPTER 11

Guidance from the Universe and Connection to Spirit

"The universe is filled with infinite possibilities and potential, if we only trust in its power to guide us."
— Deepak Chopra

"The universe is always conspiring to help us, if we only trust its wisdom."
— Ralph Waldo Emerson

"Intuition goes before you, showing you the way. Emotion follows behind, to let you know when you go astray. Listen to your inner voice. It is the calling of your spiritual GPS system seeking to keep you on track towards your true destiny."
— Anthon St. Maarten, *Divine Living*

I now feel and know that I'm connected to and one with God/Source/Spirit. I will often get "downloads" or messages from Spirit, where I will suddenly just know something or have a strong intuitive feeling. Usually it's whatever I need at that time or in that moment. I get intuitive feelings and nudges all the time to either do, or not do something. I will often have synchronicities happen where the Universe will either confirm that I'm on the right track, or it's the Universe putting something in my path to get me to follow it and take the next step.

When you're on your mission and living from your true authentic self, the Universe will constantly be giving you signs and synchronicities to let you know you're on the right track, to help guide you, and to provide the next step for you to take in your journey. In her book *Signals from My Soul*, Julia Marie tells her story of awakening and all the synchronistic things that happened to her as she's been divinely guided by Spirit throughout her life. She talks about how the Universe is constantly communicating with us and guiding us, and what happens when you start following its guidance:

> "I was consciously unaware of why I needed to be there, but I surrendered to whatever the Universe asked of me. I always remind myself the Universe does not waste energy and that I will know what I need to know when I need to know it, and not a moment sooner."

> "Spirit continues to push the limits of my concept of my Soul. The first story taught me we often hold energy from lifetime to lifetime until we express it. The second story taught me our souls are multi-dimensional in their make-up, which means I am multi-dimensional too, and so are you."

> "We all have this connection with Spirit, and we can learn to respond to the input from our Soul's senses. It takes practice, persistence, and observing how our unique connection works."
> — Julia Marie, *Signals from My Soul*

In his book *The Surrender Experiment*, Michael Singer tells about his journey of allowing God/Spirit/the Universe to guide him. He talks about how making the decision to let go of his ego-driven desires and surrender to the Universe's guidance led him to a life filled with magic, abundance, fulfillment, and spiritual growth that he never dreamed possible. Singer's story emphasizes the power of letting go of the ego's desires and trusting in Divine Intelligence to guide one's path.

As he would let go of his ego and instead follow the guidance of the Universe, his life became more and more filled with joy, abundance, success, peace, and spiritual growth beyond what he could ever imagine. He talks about how he decided to relinquish control over his life (his ego's control) and surrender to the Universe as it put people and events in his path. Every time he followed what was put in front of him it would synchronistically lead him to amazing things that he never possibly could have imagined. In the opening paragraph of the book, Singer states:

> "Life rarely unfolds exactly as we want it to. And if we stop and think about it, that makes perfect sense. The scope of life is universal, and the fact that we are not actually in control of life's events should be self-evident. The universe has been around for 13.8 billion years, and the processes that determine the flow of life around us did not begin when we were born, nor will they end when we die. What manifests in front of us at any given moment is actually something truly extraordinary—it is the end result of all the forces that have been interacting together for billions of years. We are not responsible for even the tiniest fraction of what is manifesting around us. Nonetheless, we walk around constantly trying to control and determine what will happen in our lives. No wonder there's so much tension, anxiety, and fear. Each of us actually believes that things should be the way we want them, instead of being the natural result of all the forces of creation."
> — Michael Singer, *The Surrender Experiment*

We are all constantly co-creating with the Universe. It always has amazing things in store for us, but in order for those to happen it needs us to trust it and let go of control of how things play out. Our egos tend to want to control every little thing that happens to us. We tend to *think* we want something, when in fact we don't even know what we actually want, because it's better than we can even imagine. The Universe has infinitely greater wisdom, knowledge, and perspective than our small 3D selves, and once we start connecting to it and surrendering to its guidance, our lives will become magical and fulfilling beyond what we can ever possibly imagine.

How I still react to all the synchronicities in my life because the universe's magic never gets old

CHAPTER 12

The Control System

"When we give our minds and our responsibility away, we give our lives away. If enough of us do it, we give the world away and that is precisely what we have been doing throughout known human history. This is why the few have always controlled the masses. The only difference today is that the few are now manipulating the entire planet because of the globalization of business, banking and communications. The foundation of that control has always been the same : keep the people in ignorance, fear and at war with themselves. Divide, rule and conquer while keeping the most important knowledge to yourself."
— David Icke, *The Biggest Secret*

"Your image and sense of social consciousness only knows what the conspiracy of civilization has told you and no more. You have literally been taught to disbelieve anything other than that. You have 'learned' to destroy anything other than the way society wants you to view God."
— Ramtha, *UFOs and the Nature of Reality*

The False Matrix is in place for one reason: Control. And to keep this control they have to create a false illusionary world that we constantly feed into. They create a hierarchical structure full of compartments, and then each compartment is essentially manipulated by the ones above them and are only told what they need to know to operate and fulfill their mission. At the very bottom of the pyramid is the over 99% of humanity who is made to power this entire system, all the while not even realizing they are in a control slavery system, let alone that they have been manipulated into creating and powering it. Jordan Maxwell was well aware of this control system and the false reality it sells to humanity, and he talked about how the systems of the world are not what they appear to be:

"Nothing in this world works the way you think it does. Nothing. Governments do not operate the way you think they do. Banks do not do what you think they do. The police department is not here for what you think it is. Nothing in your world works the way you think it does. There's a far higher, bigger picture going on on the Earth for at least 7,000 years of human history that we modern day people really just don't relate to. All we know is what we live with today, but never suspecting that the institutions of power, banking, education, the military industrial complex of the world has taken hundreds of years to develop."
— Jordan Maxwell

For thousands of years there has been a control system in place on this planet that has been manipulating humanity for its own power, control, and self-serving agendas. It has suppressed and hidden the truth and greater reality from humanity for millennia. Over these many years, there have been people in power and "behind-the-scenes" forming groups, institutions, and secret societies, and conspiring together to manipulate and control the population. These people and the overall umbrella of control have been referred to by many different names: the Deep State, the Cabal, the New World Order, the Illuminati, the Dark Controllers or as I have recently begun saying more often, the Control System, which I prefer because it simply describes exactly what's going on. It's an organized system, and it seeks to control humanity at all costs.

There have been so many people over the years who have seen and experienced the Control System firsthand, in different ways, at different levels, and to various degrees, and have been attempting to wake up humanity to its reality, including David Icke, Jordan Maxwell, William Cooper, Michael Tsarion, Freeman Fly, Alex Jones, Max Spiers, Kerry Cassidy, Bill Ryan, Barbara Marciniak, Robert Dean, Dr. Michael Salla, John Lear, Jim Marrs, Benjamin Fulford, Cathy O'Brien, Phil Schneider, David Wilcock, Brad Olsen, Brooks Agnew, Alfred Lambremont Webre, Richard Dolan, Steven Greer, Fritz Springmeier, Stewart Swerdlow, Sean David Morton, Laura Eisenhower, Tony Rodrigues, Niara Isley, James Gilliland, Michael Jaco, Robert David Steele, Michael Tellinger, William Tompkins, Len Kasten, Mark Passio, Leo Zagami......the list goes on and on and on......

Even some US Presidents have become aware of the control system in some aspect or to a certain degree, and have attempted to warn humanity. They've alluded to aspects of the control system in various speeches.

John F. Kennedy gave a strong warning to the world in his speech on April 27, 1961:

"The very word 'secrecy' is repugnant in a free and open society; and we are as a people inherently and historically opposed to secret societies, to secret oaths and to secret proceedings...For we are opposed around the world by a monolithic and ruthless conspiracy that relies primarily on covert means for expanding its sphere of influence-- on infiltration instead of invasion, on subversion instead of elections, on intimidation instead of free choice, on guerrillas by night instead of armies by day. It is a system which has conscripted vast human and material resources into the building of a tightly knit, highly efficient machine that combines military, diplomatic, intelligence, economic, scientific and political operations."

Dwight D. Eisenhower did as well in his Farewell Address:

"We face a hostile ideology-global in scope, atheistic in character, ruthless in purpose, and insidious in method. Unhappily the danger it poses promises to be of indefinite duration. To meet it successfully, there is called for, not so much the emotional and transitory sacrifices of crisis, but rather those which enable us to carry forward steadily, surely, and without complaint the burdens of a prolonged and complex struggle-with liberty at stake. Only thus shall we remain, despite every provocation, on our charted course toward permanent peace and human betterment.

...

In the councils of government, we must guard against the acquisition of unwarranted influence, whether sought or unsought, by the military-industrial complex. The potential for the disastrous rise of misplaced power exists and will persist.

We must never let the weight of this combination endanger our liberties or democratic processes. We should take nothing for granted. Only an alert and knowledgeable citizenry can compel the proper meshing of the huge industrial and military machinery of defense with our peaceful methods and goals, so that security and liberty may prosper together."

Ronald Reagan talked about an "alien threat" and an "alien force" that is among us:

"In our obsession with antagonisms of the moment, we often forget how much unites all the members of humanity. Perhaps we need some outside, universal threat to make us realize this common bond. I occasionally think how quickly our differences worldwide would vanish if we were facing an alien threat from outside this world. And yet, I ask you, is not an alien force already among us?"

President Woodrow Wilson talked about it:

"There is a power so organized, so subtle, so complete, so pervasive, that they had better not speak above their breath when they speak in condemnation of it."

Even Thomas Jefferson warned about it:

"Single acts of tyranny may be ascribed to the accidental opinion of a day. But a series of oppressions, begun at a distinguished period, and pursued unalterably through every change of ministers, too plainly proves a deliberate systematic plan of reducing us to slavery."

This system of control and the beings behind it go far beyond and far deeper than mere human political structures and institutions, though those play a role within their system. These controllers are beings that usurped the planet thousands of years ago and have been manipulating humanity ever since, though that is all changing now as the awakening of humanity progresses.

How the System Operates

"The Central Intelligence Agency owns everyone of any significance in the major media."
— William Colby, former CIA director

"We'll know our disinformation program is complete when everything the American public believes is false."
— William Casey, former CIA Director

*"**Media:** Keep the adult public attention diverted away from the real social issues, and captivated by matters of no real importance.*
***Schools:** Keep the young public ignorant of real mathematics, real economics, real law, and REAL HISTORY [WC emphasis].*
***Entertainment:** Keep the public entertainment below a sixth-grade level.*

Work: *Keep the public busy, busy, busy, with no time to think; back on the farm with the other animals."*
— Milton William Cooper, *Behold a Pale Horse*

"Mass beliefs in the power of outside authorities are firmly entrenched in your psyche; they are strong and old, and somewhat like a redwood forest they too can be felled very, very quickly, raising many questions about the truth of who you are and why you place your trust outside yourself."
— Barbara Marciniak, *Path of Empowerment*

"When you buy into any version of fear, it can become your experience because your molecules are intelligent and your energy responds to the predominant feeling in your being. The focus of your mind is exactly what gives the orders to create what you experience."
— Barbara Marciniak, *Family of Light*

The Control System operates by programming and steering our consciousness in various ways that keep us psychologically conditioned and programmed to feel, think, believe, and act in ways that only serve to feed the system and keep us suppressed, in fear, and at a very low energetic vibration. The controllers operate by telling us who we are, what to think, feel, and do, and put in front of us the version of reality that they want us to create, and then we are manipulated into creating it for them. So ultimately we are the ones who have actually been making the system work, we've just been conditioned and manipulated into doing it. David Icke lays out how it works:

> "The reason we are so controlled is not that we don't have the power to decide our own destiny, it is that we give that power away every minute of our lives. When something happens that we don't like, we look for someone else to blame. When there is a problem in the world, we say

'What are they going to do about it.' At which point they, who have secretly created the problem in the first place, respond to this demand by introducing a 'solution' - more centralisation of power and erosion of freedom. If you want to give more powers to the police, security agencies and military, and you want the public to demand you do it, then ensure there is more crime, violence and terrorism, and then it's a cinch to achieve your aims. Once the people are in fear of being burgled, mugged or bombed, they will demand that you take their freedom away to protect them from what they have been manipulated to fear. The Oklahoma bombing is a classic of this kind, as I detail in ...And The Truth Shall Set You Free. I call this technique problem-reaction-solution.

Create the problem, encourage the reaction 'something must be done,' and then offer the solution. It is summed up by the Freemason motto 'Ordo Ab Chao' -order out of chaos. Create the chaos and then offer the way to restore order. Your order. The masses are herded and directed by many and various forms of emotional and mental control. It is the only way it could be done."
— David Icke, *The Biggest Secret*

In SunBow's book *The Sasquatch Message to Humanity*, information is channeled from a Sasquatch Elder named Kamooh about the history of our species and planet, and what these controllers have been doing:

"The new uncivilization that ruled your world had been banned from the Star Council, which left from our home-planet until a later evolutionary leap. Those same powers serving the lower lords are still keeping this Earth enslaved today, through a combination of means including control of the information, mind programming, staged events and a series of advanced technologies. They want you to forget how they took over the control of your home-planet and destiny through illegitimate means, and have kept your people enslaved, making you more and more dependent on new technologies.

They want you to forget the Divine Law and Cosmic Order that we have protected with our Star ancestors, with whom we have kept in contact. As a proof of their dominion, the lower lords want you to keep destroying our home-planet, which is not their home, and that they have invaded for their own selfish interests and powers. Since they have laid the basis and frames of your known civilizations and have set the stage for most major events influencing your collective consciousness and destiny, to push forward their agenda of global control, all of your people have fallen under their material and psychic enslavement to some extent and level, none has been left untouched by their detrimental influence."
— Sasquatch Elder Kamooh channeled through SunBow, *The Sasquatch Message to Humanity*

This control system on the planet goes back thousands of years. All the way back to the times of Atlantis and Lemuria (Mu). The beings at the top of this control system are "service to self" and do not have empathy like we do. These beings are not human, and in fact despise humanity. They have been enslaving, using, and feeding off of humanity for a very long time. The very top of the pyramid of control are non-corporeal entities, who could be called demons or demonic entities. The Gnostics referred to them as the Archons. They are very powerful but very low vibrational entities who exist outside of our dimension. The main proxy race of beings these Archons work through on Earth are the Draco Reptilians (distinct from other types of Reptilians, many of which are more benevolent).

In David Wilcock's book *The Ascension Mysteries*, he shares information told to him by a Cabal/Illuminati insider (which perfectly lines up with other information and what many other insiders have said) about the Draco Reptilians and how they operate:

> "The next major incursion was of the Draco, or what the Law of One refers to as the Orion Confederation. According to Jacob, this is a group of six different reptilian humanoid species...The Draco 'master race' traveled throughout the galaxy, looking for other humanoid groups that evolved out of reptilian life. Everywhere they found this life, they infiltrated, mixed their DNA together with them, and brought them into their Empire.
>
> The Draco feed off the energy of fear, sadness, depression, selfishness, narcissism, anger, hatred, and jealousy. They are utterly dependent upon this energy for their survival. The Cabal calls this 'loosh,' and directly associates that word with Lucifer. Hence they have a saying, 'Give Lucius his loosh.' As outrageous as this must sound, the Draco are ultimately controlling the Cabal.
>
> Many of the Cabal's actions do not seem to make any sense. Why would they want to destroy so many people's lives and keep us all in terror and depression? The answer is that this generates loosh for the Draco, according to Jacob, Bruce, Corey, Pete, and all the others. Most interesting, Jacob told me that if everyone on Earth were happy for even one day, such as in some kind of globally inspiring event, the Draco would be utterly defeated. Furthermore, their own time-viewing technology shows their downfall is a certainty as we ascend. They are doing everything they can to try to stop it, but every plan they have made has been foiled."

The Draco infiltrated our planet long ago, interbred with humans to create the ruling bloodlines, kept their own hybrid "proxies" in power, and have been manipulating, abusing, feeding off of, and enslaving humanity for thousands of years. There is obviously a physical 3D aspect to this control system (including corporations, political systems, institutions, and media), but that is *by far* not the only layer to this. The extraterrestrial, spiritual and metaphysical aspects make up the deeper layer of the control system, and they rely on our consciousness and energy as their food source, and to create reality on their behalf.

If the Reptilians or the Archons could lock us down into a permanent full-on enslavement on their own, they would've done so a long time ago. The reason they haven't yet is because they can't unless *we* allow it to happen and give our consent. So for a long time the Cabal has been doing what David Icke refers to as the "Totalitarian Tiptoe." This is essentially where they have to implement their control and enslavement through gradual steps, so as not to awaken humanity to what is really going on.

They also continually implement a method of "Problem-Reaction-Solution." This refers to how the controllers will create a problem, so that there will be a desired reaction from the population, that then allows them to implement their "solution," which is the thing they wanted to do all along, they just needed an excuse and our consent to do it. Of course, we would never do these things if we consciously knew what we were doing or what was *really* going on, so they have to trick and manipulate us into it. The only way they can accomplish this is if the majority of humanity is sound asleep and operating in an extremely unconscious state. That's why they work so hard to keep us suppressed, in fear, fighting each other, and at a low level of consciousness. The second enough of us raise our consciousness and frequency, their whole game comes crumbling down. This is already well underway and humanity *is* awakening.

When you start to find out the truth of what's been going on for so long on the planet, it can be overwhelming to many people. It can send some into a spiral of fear, anxiety, and hopelessness. The terms "black-pillers" or "doomers" have been used to describe people that get trapped in this state after learning about the dark realities of the control system and what they've been doing. This is understandable because it does appear terrifying and even hopeless from a very limited and surface-level point of view. But *that* is the trap. That's exactly what the system *wants* you to buy into. They don't want us to wake up to the reality that *you and I* are the ones with all the power, and are creating and manifesting this reality we live in. We are infinite conscious energy having a human experience. We are *always* creating with our energy, and we can either consciously create or we can unconsciously create. When we're unconsciously creating, we are merely acting out programming that's been instilled into us by someone else or by our past experiences. These are programs do not serve us, and only keep us enslaved. They force us to continually feed into and perpetuate fear, lack, and suffering.

When you wake up and realize that there *is* nothing to fear because, while the body can be killed or enslaved, nothing can kill or enslave the soul. Nothing can kill or enslave infinite consciousness. When you raise your level of consciousness, you naturally lose fear. When you lose fear (False Evidence Appearing Real) the system loses all its power and leverage over you. The whole game of the control system ultimately comes down to fear, which is the main energetic tool they use to control the masses. As Barbara Marciniak writes, "Your power ends where your fear begins."

"Many millions of people have proved to themselves that thought creates reality by using their intuition to tap into the non-physical and invisible energies that permeate time and space and all of existence. Reality is built in the mind. Those who attempt to steal or seal off your mind have known about and hoarded these secrets for a long, long time. Liberating knowledge is not taught in your schools. You are dissuaded from the truth, so it is no great wonder that the major issue rising to the surface in so many lives involves repressed expression—basically, dealing with and healing feelings of fear about owning your truth on a personal, global, and galactic scale.

The current fashion in Western civilization promotes doubters and skeptics who are recognized and rewarded for their worrisome speculations. And because of an ancient ingrained fear of the body and its wisdom, people can no longer tell the difference between what they are told is the truth and what makes sense to them. This collective denial has now achieved a critical mass, and ages of emotionally toxic debris are rising to the surface to be identified and safely released. From a bigger picture of reality, the people of Earth are emerging from an amnesiac-like state of collective shock, which has blocked the influx of spiritual knowledge into the human gene pool. And while it is quite obvious to many that 'you create your reality,' the vast majority of humans still need to be awakened from the unconsciously controlled trance of powerlessness that they voluntarily took on."

— Barbara Marciniak, *Path of Empowerment*

The lies that we've been told are so numerous, their scope so vast, and they've been told to us for so long, that it is extremely difficult for many people to even begin to question them or to wake up and see them for what they are. Many people have become completely overtaken by the programming and the lies.

Carl Sagan said:

"One of the saddest lessons of history is this: If we've been bamboozled long enough, we tend to reject any evidence of the bamboozle. We're no longer interested in finding out the truth. The bamboozle has captured us. It's simply too painful to acknowledge, even to ourselves, that we've been taken. Once you give a charlatan power over you, you almost never get it back."
— Carl Sagan, *The Demon-Haunted World: Science as a Candle in the Dark*

The Nazi Joseph Goebbels explained how it works:

"If you tell a lie big enough and keep repeating it, people will eventually come to believe it. The lie can be maintained only for such time as the State can shield the people from the political, economic and/or military consequences of the lie. It thus becomes vitally important for the State to use all of its powers to repress dissent, for the truth is the mortal enemy of the lie, and thus by extension, the truth is the greatest enemy of the State."

The system is absolutely *terrified* of us waking up to the truth of what's really going on, to who we really are, and most importantly to the fact that we don't need them or their system. The reality is that *we* are the ones with all the power and we can easily create a much different reality than *their* reality. The system works tirelessly to keep us asleep, and to keep us programmed and continually feeding into it. They do not have the ability to create the control system themselves, they being so few and we being so many. They have to trick and manipulate us into creating it for them. When we stay programmed, in fear, and in an unconscious state, we are easily played and manipulated by the system. But it doesn't have to be this way. The moment we wake up and take our power back, is the moment the system loses all its power, the power that *we have been giving it all along.*

In his book *Infinite Love is the Only Truth, Everything Else is Illusion*, David Icke explains how the system operates:

"Societies are not structured to be 'better for people' or any other life form. That's not the idea. They are designed to serve the Matrix, full stop, end. When you observe what we call society from the perspective of the virtual-reality game, and understand its agenda, you can see the method in the apparent madness we call 'life'. The Matrix is a multi-dimensional, self-powered, free energy machine. The definition of free energy is something that produces more energy than it needs for itself. It is like your computer taking electricity from the plug for its own needs while somehow using that to produce energy for the whole house. The Matrix is a system which manipulates consciousness trapped within its vibratory illusions to generate the energy that fuels the system. That energy is fear and its related emotions."

In her book *Path of Empowerment*, Barbara Marciniak lays out how the control system manipulates our consciousness through orchestrated events and information coming from the media through our electronics:

"For many decades a very controlled and corrupt media has been directing the attention of the masses by uniformly reporting on a state of managed chaos, which is scripted and staged to produce mental confusion and fatigue. The relentless reporting and rehashing of catastrophic and traumatic events, with images of despair and destruction repeatedly planted into the minds of the viewers, create supreme states of anxiety and are, in reality, a form of psychological warfare. Authorities play with truths, half-truths, deceptions, and lies to render you hopeless, feeling it is pointless to do anything— this now passes as 'the news,' and it can rule your life.

When millions of people focus their attention upon listening to the same words, seeing the same pictures, and hearing the same descriptions, tremendous energy is generated and a massive thought-form is created. Thought-forms are vibrational blueprints that hold instructions for manifesting reality. The media captures your attention and then programs your imagination, essentially canceling out your unique creative drive to manifest your own reality as well as your desire to know yourself. You have been conditioned to believe that all you need to know can now be found in the wonderful world of electronic boxes and the information and entertainment they hold. When 'the news' is slanted toward a message of continuous war, a state of despair and a sense of hopelessness are created. A paralysis of power takes hold because you become convinced that the only reality is what is described and prescribed by the authorities in the box. Reality is created and produced by each and every one of you, and those seeking to control the world have kept this knowledge a well-guarded secret."

In *Bringers of the Dawn*, she talk about what is currently happening on the planet as these beings are starting to lose their food source, and are desperately trying to maintain their control:

"As the frequency of fear begins to diminish upon this planet, many activities will be promulgated to bring about an increase in fear because those who live off the fearful frequency will be losing their nourishment, their food. They will make an attempt to reinstate that frequency before they change their nourishment to the new frequency of love. The Lizzies have set Earth up with devices that can broadcast and magnify the emotional turmoil on this planet. That turmoil is sent to them, and it sustains them in some way."

The reason these controllers have to do *so* many things and go to *such* great lengths to control us and keep us suppressed, is because they know how powerful we are, and they are absolutely *terrified* of us waking up to that power and stepping into our sovereignty. Alec Zeck writes:

> " 'They' would not attempt to dumb us down, indoctrinate us, poison us, sicken us, keep us in fear, divide us, threaten us, keep us attached to their systems, infiltrate our movements and organizations with bad actors, keep us stuck, and keep us believing that 'they' have authority over us if they weren't fully aware that each of us possesses immense power and the ability to create our own reality and to negate any of 'their' agenda upon recognizing and acting upon it.
>
> That is the first requirement to prevent 'them' from having any further effect; each of us must recognize our own power and take radical ownership of our own thoughts, feelings, beliefs, and actions and no longer blame 'them' for what we can fix collectively by taking ownership individually."

The magicians behind the curtains. They know that Human consciousness co-creates reality based on what the mind believes to be true and real. This process is amplified when instilled in the collective consciousness of the masses. THEY are projecting what THEY WANT into YOUR MINDS so that you build it for them.

So how did we get here? There are many details to the story of exactly *how* it happened. To put it simply, at some point in time humanity fell into a deep sleep and completely forgot who we were, what our true nature is, and lost our conscious connection to Spirit. We forgot the fact that we are all connected to God/Source/Spirit, each other and the planet. Egoic and power hungry humans began wanting power over others, and many people became so immersed in fear and separation that they supported and reinforced these hierarchical systems of control. The negative or "service-to-self" beings simply took advantage of us in our state of amnesia, fear, and vulnerability.

In reality, what we experience as "evil" or "negative" beings, are essentially just beings who are "lost in the game" so to speak. The so-called force of "evil" isn't really a force at all. The frequency and energy of Love is the only true power source in the universe. It is the energy that makes up *everything*. So "evil" or "darkness" could be thought of as essentially "not Love." Meaning, it is still made up of the energy of Love, but it has completely forgotten that and become "lost." It is merely the result of a blockage, absence, or an unconsciousness of Love. "Evil" is committed by beings who hold a tremendous amount of fear and pain within themselves. Instead of healing, they project their fear and pain onto others in the form of violence, abuse, and control. It's essentially just an extreme version of seeking control over the external environment. People only seek control of their outer environment when they feel extremely insecure and out of control on the *inside*. The more fear you hold within yourself, the more extreme actions you will take in attempting to control everything outside of you.

> "Yes, but negative is an illusion. Negative and positive are both construction material. Negative is evolutionary catalyst. D: But you know humans consider something negative as being bad. C: They should reword it to evolutionary catalyst. We have been given on purpose these catalysts for evolution. These things that appear negative... these things are on purpose."
> — Dolores Cannon, *The Three Waves of Volunteers and the New Earth*

Love is the only thing that can ever overcome "evil," because Love is the only true power that exists. As Martin Luther King Jr. said: "Darkness cannot drive out darkness; only light can do that. Hate cannot drive out hate; only love can do that."

We overcome "evil" with Love. We choose Love over fear. When we *become* Love and live from that place, then "evil" or "darkness" will cease to have any power over us because we no longer *give it* any power.

All that being said, we still must *acknowledge* the current manifested reality, and not stick our heads in the sand in an attempt to avoid anything "negative" or "dark." When you do that, you're actually telling the Universe that you're extremely afraid of those "negative" and "dark" things, and therefore those things have power over you. You're also telling the Universe that you need *more* of those things in your reality so you can learn to face and overcome those fears, and finally take your power back.

When you're in resistance to what is, you're actually *feeding* the very things you think you are avoiding. The Universe says, "Oh you're in fear of these things? Cool, here's more of them!" And it will do that until you reach the point where you're no longer holding any fear or resistance to those things. Think about what God/Source/Love/Infinite Consciousness would do. I'll use the phrase Infinite Consciousness here, but you can replace it with any one of those words. Would Infinite Consciousness run and hide from things? Would Infinite Consciousness stick its head in the sand and try to avoid things? Would Infinite Consciousness run from anything "negative" because it's worried it will be overcome by it or create more of it if it merely acknowledges it? Would Love do any of those things? Of course not. Love is *fearless*. Love faces things boldly because it has no fear. Well guess what...THAT is who you really are! When you finally wake up to THAT fact, then it's Game Over. You can still experience temporary moments of fear or anxiety, as they are completely normal human emotional responses, but you no longer *dwell* on them or are overcome by those energies. You no longer hold fear in your system. That's when the parasitic beings and energies that feed on fear and operate on that frequency, no longer have *any* power over you whatsoever, because you've now taken your power back.

CHAPTER 13

Creating a Reality that Serves Us

"Our deepest fear is not that we are inadequate. Our deepest fear is that we are powerful beyond measure. It is our light, not our darkness that most frightens us. We ask ourselves, 'Who am I to be brilliant, gorgeous, talented, fabulous?' Actually, who are you not to be? You are a child of God. Your playing small does not serve the world. There is nothing enlightened about shrinking so that other people won't feel insecure around you. We are all meant to shine, as children do. We were born to make manifest the glory of God that is within us. It's not just in some of us; it's in everyone. And as we let our own light shine, we unconsciously give other people permission to do the same. As we are liberated from our own fear, our presence automatically liberates others."
— Marianne Williamson, *A Return to Love*

"Our strategy should be not only to confront empire, but to lay siege to it. To deprive it of oxygen. To shame it. To mock it. With our art, our music, our literature, our stubbornness, our joy, our brilliance, our sheer relentlessness – and our ability to tell our own stories. Stories that are different from the ones we're being brainwashed to believe.

The corporate revolution will collapse if we refuse to buy what they are selling – their ideas, their version of history, their wars, their weapons, their notion of inevitability.

Remember this: We be many and they be few.

They need us more than we need them.

Another world is not only possible, she is on her way.
On a quiet day, I can hear her breathing."
— Arundhati Roy, *War Talk*

"Where Love is there also is unity, harmony and the peace
of Love's balanced rhythms in a united world. Where hate is
there follows the degeneracy of disunity as night follows the
day. That is the lesson which unfolding man has still to learn.
Until he learns that simple lesson of power which comes from
giving of service to his fellow man instead of taking from him
against his will, his civilizations will disappear in their own man-
made chaos, one after another, until he learns that lesson."
— Walter Russell, *A New Concept of the Universe*

"We cannot solve our problems with the same
level of thinking that created them."
— Albert Einstein

"There is an extremely powerful force that, so far, science
has not found a formal explanation to. It is a force that
includes and governs all others, and is even behind any
phenomenon operating in the universe and has not yet
been identified by us. This universal force is LOVE."
— Albert Einstein

The second we start waking up, raising our consciousness and frequency, taking our power back and reclaiming our sovereignty, the control system will cease to exist, because we have been the ones feeding it and sustaining it the whole time. It has been our own unconscious creation. We've been asleep at the wheel and completely unaware of what was happening. When we stop feeding into the system and instead use our attention and focus to manifest a reality that we actually want, one that is coming from our true authentic selves, then everything will change. We don't need to "fight the system." That's a big trap that the system wants you to fall into. When you're focusing all your energy into fighting the system, what you're actually doing is further feeding into and reinforcing it. David Icke talks about this in his book *Human Race Get Off Your Knees: The Lion Sleeps No More*:

> "The system wants you to riot in response to its injustices and so many are duped into this. They want an excuse to bring in a fully-fledged police state all over the world and those who riot in their desperation (instigated invariably by agent provocateurs) are just the excuse they are looking for...The only way to stop all this is not to react as they want us to, with violence and hostility to both the State and each other. How many violent revolutions have led to just another tyrannical regime to replace the one that fell? It has to be so because what is destroyed by violence will be replaced by the same energy. Eternal Consciousness in awareness of itself doesn't riot; it is not violent and it doesn't loot."

The system wants you to fight it. It needs you to take the bait and fall into that trap, so that it can continually have the energy it needs to sustain itself, and the excuses to do everything it wants to do. It needs to continually keep humanity under its spell. In order to do that, it needs you to feed it energy, otherwise it ceases to exist. Remember: Energy flows where attention goes. Therefore it needs to fully capture your attention.

In an interview, Max Spiers (MILAB experiencer) talks about the nature of the consciousness behind the control system and how it operates:

> "This particular consciousness stream that is controlling the planet at the moment is vampiric in nature. It's a

'taking' energy. It's not a 'giving' energy. It doesn't have a central source. It cannot self-sustain. It has to take from others...The vampiric consciousness that is here has created religions, or sport, or philosophies...They don't care particularly which one you follow or which one you attach to, as long as you attach to one of them. It's like an octopus. So there's a central point. The strands come out, but they all lead to the same center point, which is a black hole essentially that is pulling energy from people in any way. And they particularly like any of the religions because that's precious energy that's given away like that. Even a lot of the big music gatherings that go on are set up ritualistically. So they don't care whether you're cheering or whether you're booing. It doesn't really matter, as long as you're doing it strongly. It's all ritualistically done to pull energy from the people. And then they gather that energy, harvest it, and use it then to manifest the false reality that we're living in. Because they can't create reality. They don't have the creative spark themselves, but they do know how to manipulate the ones that do have it...They've hijacked the subconscious of the real creators, and now we're stuck in this false reality mess."

In her book *Bringers of the Dawn*, Barabara Marciniak talks about why these beings feel like they have to control and feed off of us:

"The new owners of this planet had a different appetite and different preferences than the former owners. They nourished themselves with chaos and fear. These things fed them, stimulated them, and kept them in power...They rearranged your DNA in order to have you broadcast within a certain limited frequency band whose frequency could feed them and keep them in power.

...

The creator gods who have been ruling this planet

have the ability to become physical, though mostly they exist in other dimensions. They keep Earth in a certain vibrational frequency while they create emotional trauma to nourish themselves. There are some beings who honor life before everything else, and there are also beings who do not honor life and do not understand their connection to it.

Consciousness feeds consciousness. It is hard for you to understand this concept because you feed yourself with food. The food for some beings is consciousness. All food contains consciousness at some point in its own development, whether you fry it, boil it, or pick it from the garden; you ingest it to keep yourself nourished. Your emotions are food for others. When you are controlled to bring about havoc and frenzy, you are creating a vibrational frequency that supports the existence of these others because that is how they are nourished."

So how do we stop feeding these beings and this control system? How do we create a different reality? By stepping into and maintaining our *own* authentic frequency, instead of staying stuck in the frequencies they want to keep us in.

Barbara Marciniak says in her book *Family of Light*:

"Everything changes when you start to emit your own frequency rather than absorbing the frequencies around you, when you start imprinting your intent on the universe rather than receiving an imprint from existence."

We will start manifesting a much different reality when we start to focus our energy and conscious intent towards creating our own system, one that actually serves us. The control system will become completely obsolete and fall away on its own when we stop feeding into it. When we say "No more! We're done. We're not buying what you're selling. We're not letting you dictate our lives and state of being anymore. We're the ones in charge here and we're no longer playing your games. We're sovereign beings, we're taking our power back, and we're going to create the reality that *we* choose to create."

Barabara Marciniak writes in *Bringers of the Dawn*:

> "You will begin to hold, keep, and maintain a certain frequency and then to live it. Identity as frequency is the sum total of your physical, mental, emotional, and spiritual bodies broadcast as electronic pulsations. As you live your frequency, you affect everyone, every place you go. That is what you are doing now."

We came here to be a part of the dismantling of the old system, and the birthing of the new world. Not the "New World Order" that *they* want us to create, but the beautiful new world that we are consciously co-creating. David Icke lays it out beautifully:

> "The real motivation for being 'here' is to both experience, and make a contribution to, the exposure and dismantling of the Control System that has held this reality in servitude for thousands of years...This reality has been hijacked and it can be un-hijacked if only we will redefine our self-identity from powerless to All-Powerful, from little me to the All-Knowing 'I'. This is the biggest challenge of all because everything comes from that shift in self-awareness. Once you open to that level of self you no longer need to ask, 'What do I do?' You know. You no longer have to summon the courage to do the right thing, you just do it. Making that shift is vital to what has to be done...When we awaken to the truth of who we are, the world looks very different and so do the challenges that are put before us, or we put before ourselves. Move your point of observation and everything changes. Try it. Try ceasing to identify who you are with your body, your name and the reflection in the mirror. Try seeing those things as experiences and not who you are. Try observing your life and the world from the

perception of the real you – eternal Consciousness, All That Is, Has Been and Ever Can Be."
— David Icke, *Human Race Get Off Your Knees: The Lion Sleeps No More*

When we stop letting the outside world completely dictate and program who we think we are, what we do, and how we feel, we can then find and strengthen our *true* authentic frequency. We can then discover our *true* selves, and step into our sovereignty, where now *we* are the ones having an impact on the world instead of letting the world impact and program us. As Barbara Marciniak writes in *Bringers of the Dawn*:

> "The whole planet has been controlled in such a way that you have been taught and trained from the time you first arrived here that you are not in control of your own reality. You have been taught that everything is circumstantial and that everything depends on something you have no say in. This is wrong! You are the one who controls your DNA.
>
> You have complete control over everything. Until you discover that and believe it, you are subjected to whatever anyone else wishes to do to you in this free-will zone. And, in your innocence, you have been exposed to things that have allowed your DNA, your intelligence, and many other things to be controlled."

When multiple individuals come together and meditate with a focused intent, it can have an amazingly powerful effect on reality. This is known as "mass meditation." The Maharishi Effect is a scientifically verified proof of this concept.

In 1975, Maharishi Mahesh Yogi talked about humanity moving into a new era of science and enlightenment. Scientific studies revealed that in communities worldwide where just one percent of the population practiced Transcendental Meditation, the trend of increasing crime rates reversed, indicating a surge in order and harmony. This phenomenon demonstrated the impact of collective consciousness on societal well-being. Nearly 50 rigorous scientific studies conducted over 25 years validate the unique benefits of the Maharishi Effect on nations. These studies employed strong research methods, including time series analysis, to control for cyclical trends in social data. The harmony created by the Maharishi Effect not only improves the well-being and unity within a nation but also has a broader impact, promoting better international relations and decreasing conflicts worldwide.

We are creating our reality all the time, whether we realize it or not. Once we wake up and realize this fact, the old system will fall away, and we will naturally start to consciously create a beautiful new reality. We are in the process of doing this right now. We are waking up to our true nature, our true power, and we are reclaiming our sovereignty.

> "You do not realize the power of your own mind. By focusing on the reality you desire, you can create it. Your energy is scattered. Once you learn how to focus and direct it, you are capable of creating miracles. And if the power of one man's mind is that powerful, think of the power of group mind once it is harnessed. The power of the focusing of many people's minds is not only multiplied, it is squared."
> — Dolores Cannon, *The Convoluted Universe - Book Two*

CHAPTER 14

The Conscious Universe, Divine Matrix and Heart-Based Creation

*"As above, so below, as within, so without,
as the universe, so the soul…"*
— Hermes Trismegistus

*"The universe is a fractal. Whatever energy signature
we carry will be repeated infinitely, again and
again… until we change that vibration."*
— Paige Bartholomew

*"The basic laws of the universe are simple, but because our
senses are limited, we can't grasp them. There is a pattern in
creation. If we look at this tree outside whose roots search
beneath the pavement for water, or a flower which sends its
sweet smell to the pollinating bees, or even our own selves
and the inner forces that drive us to act, we can see that we
all dance to a mysterious tune, and the piper who plays this
melody from an inscrutable distance—whatever name we give
him—Creative Force, or God—escapes all book knowledge."*
— Albert Einstein

With a grounded energy, focused mind, and pure intent, we
can and will create a beautiful reality based on Love. The more
we do this, the more the old reality based on fear will disappear
and fall away, and the reality we are consciously creating will

begin appearing. The more we focus our energy towards a desired reality, the more that desired reality will appear.

This is commonly referred to as the "Law of Attraction." It is a fundamental law of the Universe which in a nutshell is this: You attract the people, things, and circumstances that are a match to your thoughts, feelings, and overall frequency. Though a more accurate way to describe this would be that whatever you hold inside of you will be mirrored in the external world.

Gregg Braden explains how this mirroring works:

"It's less about attraction, and more about a mirroring... Our own science now is telling us that there's a field of energy that underlies all physical reality. In 1944 the father of quantum theory, Max Planck, identified this field and he called it the matrix. That's where this term came from. What we're now beginning to understand is that when we create the feelings of what we choose to experience in our lives–everything from conscious choices of the perfect relationship, or abundance in our lives, or the healing in our bodies, or the healing in the bodies of our loved ones–that those feelings are creating the patterns of magnetic and electrical field in our hearts that are literally rearranging the stuff of this quantum soup, this quantum essence, allowing the pattern of what we have claimed in our hearts to become manifest in the world around us. So it's less about attracting, from a scientific perspective, and more about consciously creating the template within us, knowing that the stuff of the universe will congeal around that template in the world around us to simply mirror/ reflect what we've claimed."

"Life is a mirror and will reflect back to the thinker what he thinks into it."
— Ernest Holmes

Nassim Haramein elaborates on how the "Law of Attraction" really operates, and that many people are missing a huge piece of how it works:

> "There is a concept that a person can create their own reality. This concept is only partially correct because it is generally discussed in a one-way manner i.e., a person sending a message to the field with a request/intention/prayer desiring an outcome. This is only ½ of the loop. The wave you're sending is the feed-forward part of the loop. You need to realize that the wave coming back is the feed-back which is the rest of the universe creating its reality and responding to you. The universe (Planck Field or "the Divine") interacts with the rest of humanity and your creation and the universe gives you a result that is a combination of everyone's feed-forward waves. If a person could create a reality exactly the way they wanted it, a few things would happen: 1) you would be the only one in it because everybody else would be creating their own. It would be very lonely. 2) you'd also be bored within seconds since you had everything you wanted. What happens is that you put your intention out into the field and you stay open to what comes back, realizing it's going to get modified for the highest evolution of the whole. This unexpected feed-back gives you empathy for yourself and others. You might not get exactly what you expected but now you're learning from the experience. The totality of everyone's learning is how the universe learns about itself."

> "The world around us is nothing more and nothing less than a mirror of what we have become from within."
> — Gregg Braden

There is also a false version of this that gets propagated. Many people think the Law of Attraction is essentially like a spiritual "Amazon Prime," where they can just get a bunch of cool stuff from the Universe if they make a vision board and constantly think about having the things they want, or rather that their ego *thinks* it wants or needs. People who are operating from a place of unconscious ego and are steeped in materialism love this idea, because they think it'll give them all the stuff that their ego thinks it wants and needs. The universe is not interested in appeasing your unconscious ego by giving to you all its superficial material desires. That being said, please do not hear what I'm not saying. Having money and material things is not bad at all. It's actually fantastic! Money is just a form of energy and abundance, and we need money in the hands of as many higher consciousness beings as possible right now. But when money and things start "owning" you, that's when there's a problem. The universe is trying to bring you to a place of Love, Truth, and "service-to-others." For some people, owning more/nicer stuff and having a ton of money is just going to take them *further* away from Love, Truth, and being "service-to-others." It is true that what shows up in our reality is what we focus on, but this is an immature, unhealed, and false version of what is actually going on here.

We must remember that there is a Divine Intelligence that is the foundation of the universe, and everything is connected to everything else. So when we are creating, we must be connected to the will of God/Source/Divine Spirit so that It is creating through us. We (our ego) may *think* we want or need something, but if that thing is not actually going to serve us or the people around us, then the Universe is going to have different plans. We might end up getting the superficial things our ego wants, but it won't truly fulfill us, and often it will only intensify our pain or misery. It's like the saying goes: "Wherever you go, there you are." If you don't deal with what's going on inside of you, the same external circumstances will keep manifesting, and having more/nicer things or a better job will never heal you or change your internal state on its own.

We also cannot create the reality we prefer by avoiding or resisting the currently manifested reality, or whatever shows up in your life. Whatever you resist, persists. When you say "Noooo don't talk about that negative thing even though it's a currently manifested reality!" You're actually in resistance to and therefore *feeding into* the very thing you think you're "not manifesting." You're in resistance to what is. You can't spiritually bypass your way to enlightenment or a preferred reality. You go have to feel it to heal it. The way out of the currently manifested reality is to acknowledge it for what it is and then focus our energy towards what we want, but that DOESN'T mean we can't ever talk about it and bring the darkness to light. A master does not fear the dark or the "negative" but faces it and transmutes it.

So how do we start creating the reality that we actually want to create? Simply start following your highest excitement and your highest passion. Figure out what makes you come alive. What brings you *the most* excitement. And this can change from moment to moment. Figure out what your highest excitement is in this now moment, and go do that. Then be on the lookout for signs and synchronicities that the universe brings your way, and follow them.

Bashar (channeled through Darryl Anka) puts it well:

> "The sensations you refer to as passion, excitement, love, creativity and inner peace are your physical body's 'translation' of the frequency of your core signature vibration. In other words, your true, essential being. Anytime you align with that core frequency through your beliefs, emotions, thoughts and reinforcing actions, you 'propel' your consciousness through the specific series of frames that produce the space-time experience of living more and more on your preferred version of Earth."

The Divine Matrix and the Conscious Universe

Many people believe that the universe is some lifeless mechanistic thing outside of us, where everything is completely random, we have no connection to the things around us or each other, and that we must fight and struggle with each other and the universe to live and survive. This is usually coupled with a belief that the five-sense physical reality is all that exists, and that there is no higher power, order, or spiritual world beyond what we can see, touch, smell, taste, and hear. All of this could not possibly be further from the truth. The truth is that the universe is not only alive and conscious, but that every single thing within the universe is alive and conscious as well. Everything within the universe is connected, and the true nature of the universe is not of competition, but of cooperation and harmonious relationship.

There is SO much more going on than the tiny speck of all that exists known as the 3D physical reality. There is a spiritual reality beyond what our five senses can perceive, and it is always connected to, influencing, and manifesting what goes on in this physical reality. We are all conscious participants and creators in the universe. It's our job to create. We're always creating whether we realize it or not. We can either do it consciously or unconsciously. We can either create a "Heaven on Earth" reality that serves us and all other life, or we can create a 'hell on Earth" reality that is full of pain, suffering, and disconnection. It's completely up to us. We're in charge. Every second we are making choices with our thoughts, feelings, words, and actions to either be loving and constructive to the people and things around us, or to be in disharmony and be destructive to the people and things around us. Most importantly, this includes ourselves. When we cultivate self-love, we naturally radiate that love out to everything around us, and therefore help in creating a beautiful reality based on Love. When we do not have self-love, we cannot possibly give what we do not have ourselves, and we then think, feel, and act out of a place of pain and fear. This causes destruction and disharmony within ourselves and the world around us. It all comes down to the self and our inner state of being.

In his book *The Divine Matrix*, Gregg Braden says:

> "Ancient spiritual traditions remind us that in each moment of the day, we make the choices that either affirm or deny our lives. Every second we choose to nourish ourselves in a way that supports or depletes our lives; to breathe deep and life-affirming breaths or shallow, life-denying ones; and to think and speak about other people in a manner that is honoring or dishonoring."

> "Both science and mysticism describe a force that connects everything together and gives us the power to influence how matter behaves—and reality itself—simply through the way we perceive the world around us."

> "The universe is conscious and alive, and everything within it is conscious and alive as well. You might've heard the phrases 'As above, so below,' or 'As within, so without.' What these statements mean is that we are all conscious fractals of the great conscious fractal universe. There is a Divine structure to the universe, and what we observe on a small scale is reflected on a larger scale. Our state of being on the inside is constantly being reflected on the 'outside.'"

When you observe nature and the universe, you'll notice the same patterns repeat over and over and everything seems to be mirrored, from the smallest things to the biggest. From the micro to the macro. This is because we live in a fractal universe. So...what is a fractal? A fractal is a design or pattern that repeats itself endlessly. No matter how much you zoom in or out, the same pattern and general structure appears over and over again, and any part looks similar to the whole. Fractal patterns show up continuously throughout nature, including trees, rivers, coastlines, mountains, clouds, seashells, leaves, crystals, lighting, snowflakes, and more. Your own body is a fractal, along with your body's respiratory system, circulatory system, nervous system, and brain.

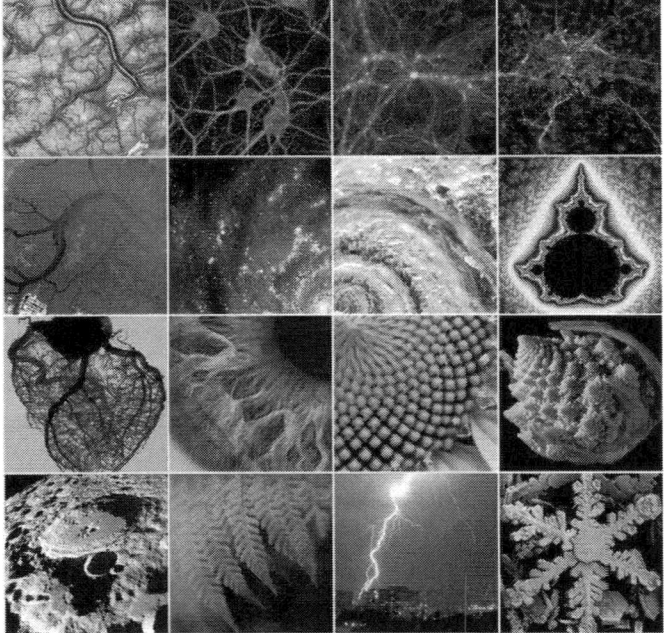

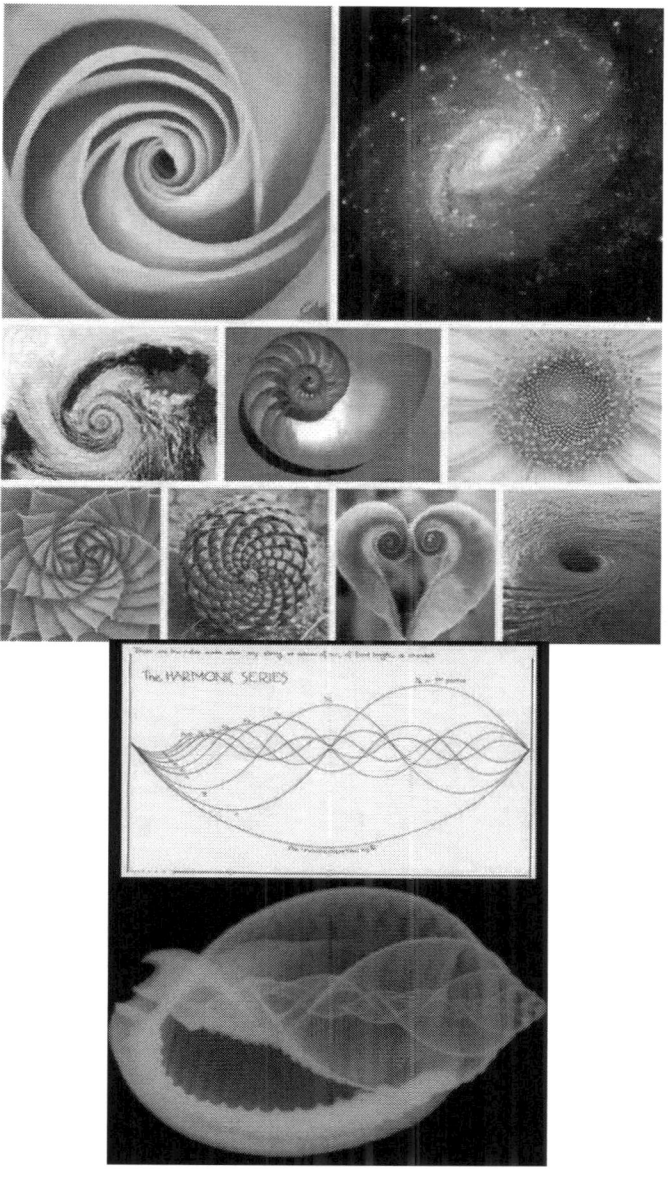

Great Pyramid of Giza

Parthenon

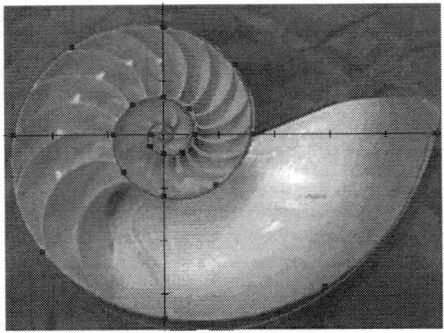

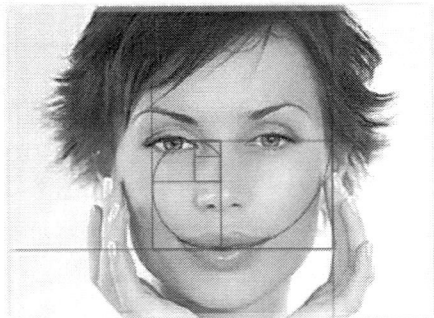
Human Face

The universe is not only fractal in nature, but it is structured within Sacred Geometry. Therefore we see Sacred Geometry and Sacred Geometric fractal patterns show up throughout the universe. The repeating pattern of the Phi Ratio (also known as the Golden Ratio or Golden Mean) shows up repeatedly throughout the universe. The Phi Ratio derives from the Fibonacci Sequence, which is a series of numbers where each number is the sum of the two preceding ones: 0, 1, 1, 2, 3, 5, 8, 13, 21, 34, and so on.

Not only can we see the sacred geometrical structures and patterns of the universe throughout creation, but sound frequencies actually hold sacred geometrical structures which we can see through something called "cymatics."

Cymatics is the study of visible sound and vibration. It explores how sound waves can create patterns and shapes in different mediums, such as liquid, powder, or solid surfaces. The term "cymatics" comes from the Greek word "kyma," meaning wave, and was coined by Hans Jenny, a Swiss scientist, in the 1960s.

Cymatics demonstrates how sound frequencies can affect matter, often producing intricate and symmetrical geometric patterns. These patterns emerge when sound waves pass through a medium, causing it to vibrate at specific frequencies. Different frequencies generate different patterns, and changes in frequency or amplitude can alter the patterns formed.

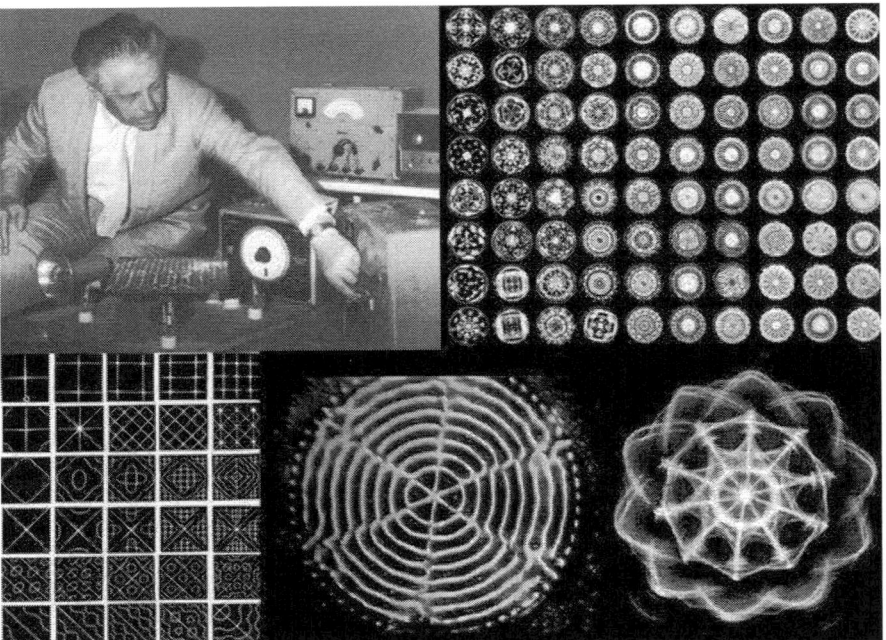

In "Cymatics, the universe and sacred geometry," Chris-Anne writes:

> "These patterns echo the fractals that are the base of all life. In sound waves, we can see the sacred geometry that holds the secrets of the nautilus shell, the spiral patterns of fiddleheads, the fibonacci patterns that you find in the middle of a sunflower.... and the spiral galaxies like our own Milkyway.

> Think about chakra drawings, tibetan mandalas and the sacred geometric patterns in DaVinci's work. They are supposed to encapsulate some of the blueprints for creation... and all life follows these patterns. From atoms to cells to the mathematical ratios that create crystal structures... life follows these patterns.

> And now we can see that sound does too. It's fascinating."

Everything is made up of energy, and all energy vibrates throughout a range of frequencies. As energy vibrates it forms into Sacred Geometrical patterns and structures. There is nothing that isn't vibrating energy. Nikola Tesla put it simply when he said, "If you want to find the secrets of the universe, think in terms of energy, frequency and vibration."

German physicist and founder of Quantum Theory, Max Planck, found that there is an intelligence force that holds all matter together through vibration:

> "All matter originates and exists only by virtue of a force which brings the particle of an atom to vibration and holds this most minute solar system of the atom together.
> We must assume behind this force the existence of a conscious and intelligent mind. This mind is the matrix of all matter."
> — Max Planck

This is exactly what all the ancient texts and ancient cultures were telling us thousands of years ago, and what all the indigenous tribes and cultures have known for thousands of years. They all talk about an infinite and omnipresent field of energy that everything is connected to. The Taoists call it the Tao. The Hindus call it Brahman. Christians call it God. It wasn't even a question of whether this Divine Matrix field existed. They *knew* it existed. They tapped into it and experienced it firsthand. This is exactly what Remote Viewers are doing. They are able to tap into this field to view and experience any location in the Universe. Shamans have been tapping into and gathering knowledge from the Divine Matrix for thousands of years.

> "All things are connected. Whatever befalls the earth befalls the sons of the earth. Man did not weave the web of life; he is merely a strand in it. Whatever he does to the web,

he does to himself." — Chief Seattle

In the ancient Hopi prophecies, they mention the "web of creation" that connects all life. They say that after the destruction of the First World, emerging into the Second World, the Spider Grandmother spun a web of creation through which all things were connected and could exist.

The ancient Buddhist texts talk about how the great god Indra created the web of creation:

> "Far away in the heavenly abode of the great god Indra, there is a wonderful net – Indra's Net – which stretches out indefinitely in all directions. The artificer has hung a single glittering jewel at the net's every node, and since the net itself is infinite in dimension, the jewels are infinite in number."
> — THE AVATAMSAKA SUTRA, the jewel net of Indra

There was an experiment done at the University of Geneva in 1997, in which they took a single photon and broke it into two separate photons. They then put the two photons into a chamber, and used fiber optic cables to send each photon seven miles away in opposite directions from the starting point. They then manipulated one of the photons, and at exactly the same time, the other photon would behave identically. They used atomic clocks which showed that the time between the changes of each photon was zero. They happened instantaneously. This experiment proves that Einstein's theory of relativity is false. The theory of relativity says that nothing can travel faster than the speed of light. This experiment showed that particles remain energetically linked even when they become physically separated. It proves that everything is connected through Quantum Entanglement.

All beings throughout the universe, who are at a certain level of advancement and evolution, understand the concept that everything is One and that everything is connected through Quantum Entanglement. They utilize this concept, and have developed their innate abilities and/or technology to both communicate and to travel throughout the universe. This is how things like telepathy, extra sensory perception (ESP), and psychic abilities are possible. This is how Remote Viewing works. This is how our intuition works. This is why Karma exists. Separation, either through time or space, is an illusion. There is no separation.

Atoms are 99.9999999% empty space, and the rest is pure energy. If all that space disappeared, the entire universe would fit into the size of a single green pea. All of the matter and energy in our universe was once a single point that then expanded outward, and it is all still connected through Quantum Entanglement.

There was an experiment done in 1909 by British physicist Geoffrey Ingram Taylor, known as the "double-slit" experiment. This experiment showed the wave-particle duality of matter and energy, and proved that our consciousness actually affects reality itself.

In the double-slit experiment, they shot a single electron towards a barrier with two slits in it. When they observed the electron, it would go through one of the two slits as a single electron, and hit a single point on the other end. When they were not observing the electron, a wave-pattern would show up on the other end. This showed that when the electron was not being observed, it would travel as a wave. It would only "lock into" a single particle when observed. This experiment shows what the ancients already knew thousands of years ago, that reality exists as an infinite field of possibility until we observe it and "lock in" one of those possibilities into physicality, and that our consciousness affects everything we experience.

Gregg Braden says this about the experiment:

> "This is one example of the kind of behavior that scientists simply have to call 'quantum weirdness.' The only explanation here is that the second opening has somehow forced the electron to travel as if it were a wave yet arrive at its destination just the way it began: as a particle. To do so, the electron has to somehow perceive that the second opening exists and has become available. And this is where the role of consciousness comes in. Because it's assumed that the electron cannot really 'know' anything in the truest sense of the word, the only other source of that awareness is the person watching the experiment. The conclusion here is that somehow the knowledge that the electron has two possible paths to move through is in the mind of the observer, and that the onlooker's consciousness is what determines how the electron travels."

Our modern day science is starting to discover what the ancients knew and told us a long time ago: That everything is connected to everything else, that everything affects everything else, and that we are conscious creators in a conscious universe.

> "We know that we are living and conscious beings. We are surrounded by a wealth of biological life. We appear to be separate from everything else around us, but we are connected by the hidden energy in the quantum realm that flows through and creates all matter. All life on Earth is ultimately the fruit of this universal seed, if this new model is correct. Therefore, the seed must have all the ingredients needed to make biological life and consciousness. The seed itself must be alive and intelligent. Everything we need to make intelligent civilizations like the ones we now see on Earth would be contained within the seed. That means the ingredients to make intelligent life are cosmic in nature,

and sentient life may very well have flowered throughout the universe. This also means that life could have an energetic component that would not require any physical biological material to exist. The energy itself is alive, forming what I call the 'Source Field'—and all matter in the universe is part of a living cosmos.

If you have already read *The Source Field Investigations* and *The Synchronicity Key*, then you have seen extensive scientific proof to support these assertions. The cosmos is not a void of darkness peppered with unthinking blobs of gas burning away with nuclear fusion. The universe is alive, aware, and intelligent. It is designed to make biological life. The codes that make DNA, proteins, and cells are directly written into the laws of quantum physics."

— David Wilcock, *The Ascension Mysteries*

God Consciousness Energy

All energy actually manifests from the "Zero Point," or from the nonlocality of God/Source/Infinite Consciousness, and this energy crystallizes as everything we perceive in the physical third dimension. This God energy manifests the illusion of time and space in order to give us the ability to have specific types of experiences. It appears to take "time" to do or create something, and we need the "space" to do it in. It's the illusion of separation that allows us to have these experiences and interactions with each other and everything around us. Time and space are actually both a singular manifestation known as Spacetime, and it is just that: a manifestation.

The infinite God Consciousness energy that makes up everything is called many different things, all referring to this same energy: Scalar, Chi, Prana, Orgone, Tachyon, Zero-

Point Energy, etc. This is superluminal light energy that travels trillions of times faster than conventional light. This energy emanates from the centers of galaxies, spirals and fractalizes outward, and ends up coagulating into what is perceived as physical matter. Our own bodies and DNA are fractal antennas for this God Consciousness energy. The energy forms a "cosmic web," influencing matter and creating a holographic universe. Pyramids are structures that act as powerful antennas that capture and rebroadcast this energy in a toroidal field. Our own bodies are fractal antennas which channel and rebroadcast this energy. Volcanic minerals and other substances which are filled with monoatomic elements, such as ORMUS (monoatomic gold) and Shilajit, enhance the reception of this energy and can increase the health and growth of plants, animals, and human beings.

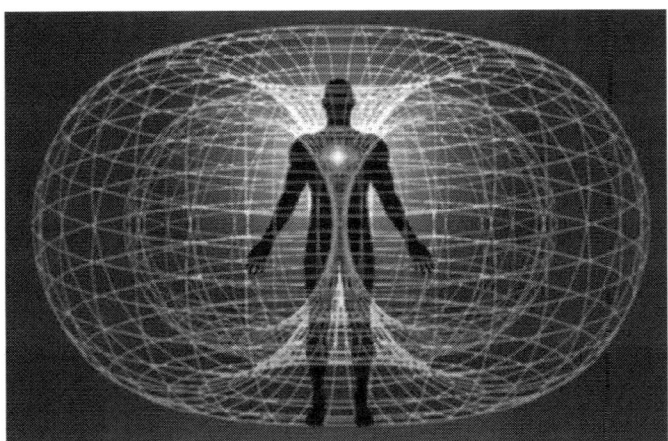

God consciousness energy flows outward from the Zero Point in a toroidal shape, or a torus field. We all have an energetic torus field, which is the electromagnetic field of energy that encompasses our physical body. It's also known as our Aura or Energy Field. Everything has consciousness, and everything has a toroidal energy field. So not only do you and I have an energy field, but animals, plants, trees, rocks, mountains, structures, and even the planet itself all have a toroidal energy field. This field contains information which is constantly communicating with and affecting everything it touches. So just being around someone, you are having an effect on them and they are having an effect on you, through each others' energy fields. You don't even have to speak a word to have an effect on the world and environment around you. Your energy is already doing that constantly, and you are affecting the planet itself just by being here. People can feel your energy, and it's affecting them on a deep energetic level whether they realize it or not. Dolores Cannon used to talk about this:

"They have been described as antennas that unconsciously channel energy onto the Earth. They do not have to do anything; they just have to be. Their energy affects everyone they come into contact with."

"They have told me many times that when we go someplace, we leave a part of our energy there and we influence more than we can ever imagine."
— Dolores Cannon, *The Three Waves of Volunteers and the New Earth*

"You'll become a beacon and the light spreads far and wide. Many see it and are attracted to it. And they will flock to you like a moth to a candle. Even though they have not been aware or interested before, now they see they want to be a part of it."
— Dolores Cannon, *The Convoluted Universe - Book Five*

The Power and Intelligence of the Heart

When you are centered in your heart, you are connected to the energy of Love, which is Source energy and intelligence. The mind is a useful tool and is fantastic for getting us around this 3D environment, but beyond that it is extremely ignorant. It is where our ego/personality lives, and if we are disconnected from our heart, and therefore from Love/Source energy, then we are operating from a place of extreme ignorance and disconnection. When we connect to our Heart, we are connected to and operating from a place of Love and Oneness. We are then connected to our Higher Self, and are in alignment with God/Source/Divinity.

The intelligence and energy of our Heart (or Higher Self) is far greater than that of our mind, especially when we are operating solely from the mind. Modern science has discovered that every human heart has approximately 40,000 specialized cells which create a neural network in the heart. These are brain-like cells in the heart that are called sensory neurites. Scientists discovered that these cells think, feel, and remember, completely independently of the brain. So the heart is actually a brain that thinks, feels emotions, and stores memories completely independently of the cranial brain. The heart also generates the strongest electrical and magnetic fields in the body. The heart produces an electric field that is about 100 times stronger than our brain, and a magnetic field that is about 5,000 times stronger. Why this is so important is because the physical world is made of both electrical and magnetic fields of energy. As Gregg Braden states:

> "Our own physics books now tell us, if we can change either the magnetic field of an atom, or the electrical field of the atom, by doing that we literally change that atom. We

change the stuff that our bodies and this world are made of. And it appears now that the human heart is designed to do both. To change both the electrical field and the magnetic field of our bodies and our world, and they do so in response to the emotions that we create between our heart and our brain."

When we sync our brain with our heart, that's when the magic happens. We can then use our will and our intent to consciously create, by thinking the thoughts of what we want to create, and feeling in our hearts the feelings that correspond to those thoughts. When our hearts and our minds are synced up and in harmony, we then are able to have a powerful effect on our own bodies, and the field of reality itself, or the Divine Matrix.

"The heart has the most powerful electromagnetic field within the human energy field and there are more nerves going from the heart to the brain than going the other way. The latter is indicative of a sparkling truth that has been long forgotten – the brain is not the focus for intelligence within the body – the heart is."
— David Icke, *The Perception Deception - Part One*

When we start to live from the heart, and from the space of Love rather than fear, we will start to attract things that are in the same resonance as the energy of Love, and repel things that in the resonance of fear, or any of its subcategories such as hate, depression, guilt, shame, lack, etc. You will be absolutely floored at the amazing synchronicities that start to happen and the amazing people, things, and opportunities that the universe brings to you when you stop living from a place of fear and start living from a place of gratitude and Love.

In one of his talks, David Icke lays this out:

> "When you think you're a victim, the victim vibe goes out, the victim circumstance goes in. When you say "Hey, I'm not a victim. *I'm* in control of my life. *I've* created these circumstances I don't like, therefore I can create circumstances I do. At that point the victim mentality is gone. Victim circumstances stop being attracted, and suddenly people come into your life who are just the people you need to get you out of the circumstances you don't like. And if you don't realize what's happening, and most of us don't at the time, we say "Oh my God mate I was so lucky! This fella came into my life at just the right time and this person...I couldn't believe it! Amazing luck." No. You pulled them in because your state of being had changed, and you synced with what you needed to get out of that situation. We are *so* in control of our destiny it's unbelievable. And yet billions are persuaded they're not, and therefore they create a very different reality. If we're in fear, we can attract a reflection of fear. But when we omit love, we create a very different energy, therefore we create a very different reality."

We will manifest a beautiful reality, both individually and collectively, when we start living from the Heart. When we step out of fear and move into the energy of Love. Love is not just the most powerful force in the universe, it is the *only* force in the universe. The more we align ourselves with and step into the frequency of Love, the more powerful we will be and the more conscious we will become.

"Love is the most powerful force in the world. If people tell you that the opposite of love is fear, it is not so. Love just is. Love has no opposite. Remember that, dear one. Love has no opposite. Love just is. It is the answer to everything. Everything."

— Dolores Cannon, *The Convoluted Universe - Book Two*

CHAPTER 15

Advanced Civilizations and Extraterrestrials in Ancient Times

There is an enormous amount of evidence that points to the existence of advanced civilizations on Earth, going back many thousands of years. There is much evidence suggesting extraterrestrial beings were here in ancient times as well.

All over the world there are ancient cave drawings, artifacts, hieroglyphs, petroglyphs, and geoglyphs depicting extraterrestrial-like beings as well as UFOs or spacecraft. UFOs appear in many historical artworks. Many ancient megalithic structures seem to be a kind of ancient space port, such as Baalbek and Puma Punku. There are massive geoglyphs that can only be discerned from high above the earth, such as the Nazca lines in Peru and the Serpent Mound in Ohio. There are many ancient pyramids and structures that align with specific stars and are in the layout of constellations.

More than 300 elongated skulls have been discovered in Paracas, Peru, many dating back to almost 3,000 years ago. Some of them still have hair on them. Brien Foerster, along with many other scientists, archaeologists, and investigators, have studied and tested many of these skulls and determined that they are absolutely not human. The most conclusive proof of this has been through DNA testing, critical differing features, and the fact that there have been elongated skulls found of infants and fetuses. There was also the "Starchild" skull found that was studied by researcher and author Lloyd Pye. There were 25 differences found between the Starchild skull and a human skull. Twenty five!

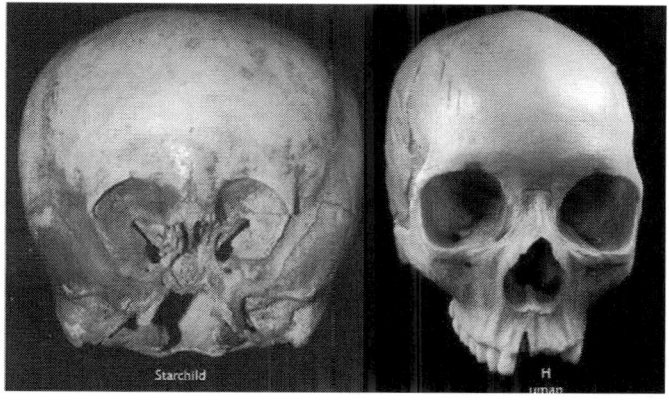

There is tons of evidence of advanced technology existing in ancient times. There are massive megalithic stones that were somehow mysteriously set into place. Many of them are etched or cut with a precision that cannot be replicated today. There are massive and intricate pyramids, temples, and structures that cannot be built or replicated today. The great pyramids in Egypt are massive and intricately constructed, using immensely heavy stones which came from hundreds of miles away. In Japan, they made a failed attempt in building a pyramid at one fifth the size of the Great Pyramid. We cannot even come close to replicating these structures today, yet we are expected to believe that somehow primitive civilizations built them!

Nancy Thames lays it out well:

> "1. Pyramids are not tombs; no mummy has ever been found inside the pyramids. All mummies were found in the Valley of the Kings.
> 2. How do you cut 20 ton blocks of granite with extreme precision and lift them one on top of the other, in the "King's Chamber", with WOODEN RAMPS !!
> 3. Let's say wooden ramps were used; you need to cut down a whole forest in order to provide wood to move 2.3 MILLION blocks of huge stones. Where is the evidence for that wood?
> 4. There is not a single hieroglyphic text that says ancient Egyptians built the pyramids.
> 5. How many "slaves" or workers do you need to quarry, cut and lift 2.3 MILLION stones? Where do you find people who can laser cut and lift huge tons of granite?
> 6. How do you position the whole pyramid to face true north, 4000 years ago when the builders "didn't know about the WHEEL" ? (That's the bias of mainstream egyptologists).
> 7. The top of the pyramid is a quarter of an inch off center (base of the pyramid); that's after placing 2.3 million blocks of stone. When you divide that tiny margin of error by 2.3 million stones, the accuracy at which the stones were placed is unparalleled and has never been done by modern architects with all modern technology.
> Conclusion: 90% of Human history was buried by time, the other 10% is written by the victors.
> There was advanced technology that has been suppressed to benefit those in power and their agendas at the time. Too many clues remain to ignore."
> — From Nancy Thames in her Facebook group "Time For Disclosure/We Have Never Been Alone/We Are the

Disclosure!"

Nikola Tesla believed that the Great Pyramids of Egypt were giant energy transmitters. He designed his Tesla Towers after studying the Pyramids.

TESLA KNEW WHAT THE EGYPTIAN PYRAMIDS WERE

IN 1905, TESLA FILED A PATENT IN THE U.S. TITLED "THE ART OF TRANSMITTING ELECTRICAL ENERGY THROUGH THE NATURAL MEDIUM," OUTLINING DESIGNS FOR A SERIES OF GENERATORS AROUND THE WORLD WHICH WOULD TAP THE IONOSPHERE FOR ENERGY COLLECTIONS. HE BUILT A TOWER FACILITY KNOWN AS THE TESLA EXPERIMENTAL STATION IN COLORADO SPRINGS AND WARDENCLYFFE TOWER OR TESLA TOWER ON THE EAST COAST THAT SOUGHT TO TAKE ADVANTAGE OF THE EARTH'S ENERGY FIELD. HE MAPPED THESE ENERGY FIELDS AFTER RESEARCH INTO THE INNER WORKINGS OF THE PYRAMIDS, AND BEFORE IT WAS FULLY DISCOVERED TESLA KNEW THERE WOULD LIKELY BE PYRAMIDS ALL OVER THE EARTH.

The Yonaguni Monument, found under the ocean off the coast of Yonaguni Island in Japan, consists of rock formations which are clearly man-made structures, with angular rocks arranged like terraces, steps, and pillars. This appears to be an ancient submerged city or temple complex, and it had to have been built many thousands of years ago when the area was above sea level.

There is much evidence to suggest that Machu Picchu in Peru was built by an advanced civilization and/or by extraterrestrial beings due to the site's advanced architectural features, incredible precision of its construction, mysterious origins, and its layout and design which align with celestial bodies and energetic ley lines.

There are structures whose stones are so precisely fit together that you cannot fit a thin piece of paper between them. Many stones appear as if they were melted and then solidified into place. The Al-Naslaa Rock in Saudi Arabia is over 4,000 years old and appears to have been laser-cut in half.

There are many out-of-place artifacts (OOPArts) that have been found all over the planet, which are objects that seem to be out of their expected time period or place, and often depict advanced machinery suggesting the existence of advanced ancient civilizations. One of these is the Antikythera mechanism, which is an ancient Greek analog computer that appears to have been designed to track celestial movements, including the positions of the sun, moon, and planets, as well as to predict eclipses and other astronomical events. One of the best OOPArts revealing ancient advanced civilizations is the Klerksdorp spheres, which are small spherical objects that were found in 3-billion-year-old pyrophyllite that have three parallel lines inscribed along their equator. These are clearly not just natural formations, but had to have been made and carved by intelligent beings.

Michael Tellinger is a researcher who has made significant discoveries related to ancient civilizations and human origins. He has focused much of his work on Southern Africa, particularly in Mpumalanga, South Africa, where he has identified ancient ruins and artifacts. One of his most significant findings is "Adam's Calendar," a stone circle structure that he claims is the oldest man-made structure on Earth and may have functioned as an astronomical calendar. Tellinger has also found many stone circles in the region, and suggests that they were part of an interconnected network used for energy generation and distribution by an advanced ancient civilization.

Atlantis and Lemuria

There are many people who talk about the ancient civilizations of Atlantis and Lemuria. Much of the information about these ancient civilizations came through the famous psychic Edgar Cayce. Cayce described Atlantis as a highly advanced civilization with sophisticated technology, including energy crystals and flying machines. He said that Atlantis reached its peak around 10,000 to 12,000 years ago but ultimately sank into the ocean from cataclysms. Cayce indicated that remnants of Atlantis could still be found beneath the waters of the Atlantic Ocean, particularly near the Bahamas and the Caribbean. In 1968, the "Bimini Road" was discovered off the coast of the Bahamas, validating Cayce's information.

He also talked about Lemuria which was another ancient civilization that existed in the Pacific Ocean region, predating Atlantis. Lemuria was described as a spiritually advanced society that focused on the development of psychic abilities and spiritual knowledge. Like Atlantis, Lemuria's downfall was due to a series of cataclysmic events, which included the sinking of landmasses and the shifting of tectonic plates. Cayce said that there was interaction between Atlantis and Lemuria, and that both civilizations traveled between each other and exchanged knowledge. He said that some people from Atlantis reincarnated later on to play significant roles in other civilizations, including ancient Egypt.

UFOs and Advanced Craft in Ancient Times

Various ancient civilizations, including the Egyptians, Mayans, and Sumerians, depicted flying objects and beings in their artwork, hieroglyphs, and texts. For example, the Egyptian Pharaoh Thutmosis III reportedly witnessed "fiery disks" in the sky around 1440 BCE, as documented in the "Annals of Thutmose III."

The book of Ezekiel in the Bible describes a vision experienced by the prophet Ezekiel around 593 BCE, which absolutely appears to be an encounter of a UFO and higher dimensional beings. Ezekiel describes seeing a "whirlwind" and a "wheel within a wheel" in the sky, accompanied by strange creatures and bright lights.

In ancient Indian texts such as the Vedas and the Mahabharata, there are references to flying machines called "vimanas" used by gods and ancient warriors. These descriptions include detailed accounts of aerial battles and advanced technological capabilities.

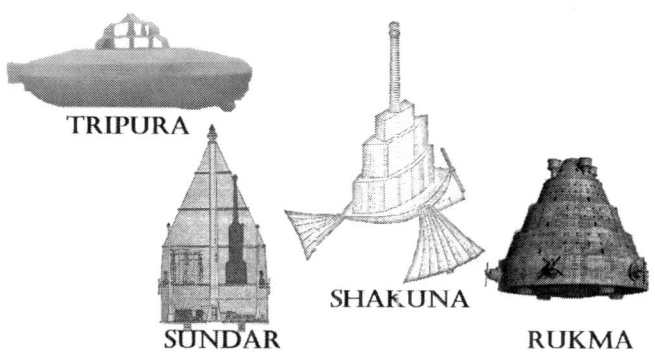

The Dogon tribe of Mali, West Africa, possesses knowledge of the star system Sirius that has puzzled researchers. The Dogon are said to have knowledge of Sirius B, a companion star to Sirius A, which is invisible to the naked eye. It appears that the Dogon's knowledge may have been passed down through ancient contact with extraterrestrial beings.

CHAPTER 16

UFOs

*"The evidence points to the fact that Roswell was a real incident
and that indeed an alien craft did crash, and that material was
recovered from that site. We all know that UFOs are real. All we
need to ask is where do they come from, and what do they want?"*
–Edgar Mitchell

*"The evidence is overwhelming that Planet Earth is being
visited by intelligently controlled extraterrestrial spacecraft."*
–Stanton T. Friedman

There is now a different term being widely used as well: UAP, which stands for Unidentified Aerial Phenomenon. This new term is basically an attempt to get away from the ridicule, stigma, and "laugh factor" of the term UFO, and to bring more legitimacy to the reality of the subject to the public, scientific establishment, and world governments. I totally understand the motive there, and there are honest people with pure intentions who are using this term. That is fantastic and I say more power to them. I also think there are factions of the Control System that are using this new term in their attempt to control the narrative around UFOs and ETs, which goes in line with the controlled partial disclosures, or "limited hangout" that they are attempting to corral the public into. I will only be using the term UFO, because I do not believe we need to pander to any government, academic, or scientific establishments, or even the greater public. What we need is for an awakening of humanity to happen. It already is happening. We don't need to play these games of trying to convince the world and "sell" the fact that UFOs are real. More and more people are taking their power back and thinking for themselves. We no longer need "authority" figures or institutions to tell us what is or isn't true or legitimate.

The term "UFO" stands for Unidentified Flying Object. It first started being used in the 1950s to describe reports of unknown objects observed in the sky that defied conventional explanation. Before the term UFO became more popularized, the term "flying saucer" was most widely used. That term came from the misunderstanding of the famous UFO sighting of pilot Kenneth Arnold, when he described the objects as moving "like a saucer if you skip it across the water." His account was widely publicized in newspapers, and the term "flying saucer" suddenly entered popular culture to describe UFO sightings. The term UFO was coined by the United States Air Force in the early 1950s. Project Blue Book was created on March 25, 1952, by the United States Air Force, who recruited the American astronomer and professor J. Allen Hynek as a consultant for it. Project Blue Book was established to "investigate" UFO sightings reported by civilians and the military. Except what it was *really* about was to come up with a "logical explanation" to give the public about all these flying objects they were seeing. They already knew exactly what they were. They just didn't want the public to know, or to start realizing that these things are real, to start investigating them or demanding answers from the government/military, and to realize "Hey! We're not alone in the universe!"

To J. Allen Hynek's dismay, he realized he wasn't at all tasked to investigate UFO sightings. He was actually hired to help cover them up, and to explain them away to the public. Hynek started out as a skeptic who didn't believe UFOs or ETs were real. So when he was tasked with investigating UFO sightings, he actually *did* expect to find perfectly logical explanations for all of them. He expected to be able to explain them with science or as some form of natural phenomena. In some cases he was able to do just that. In many of them, he was not. He eventually started realizing that many of the UFOs could not be explained by science or as anything known. These seemed to be operated by an intelligence, and appeared to be advanced beyond our knowledge and technology. He eventually turned into a believer in the UFO phenomenon and that many UFOs are of extraterrestrial origin.

In April 1953, Hynek wrote this in the Journal of the Optical Society of America:

> "Ridicule is not part of the scientific method, and people should not be taught that it is. The steady flow of reports, often made in concert by reliable observers, raises questions of scientific obligation and responsibility. Is there ... any residue that is worthy of scientific attention? Or, if there isn't, does not an obligation exist to say so to the public—not in words of open ridicule but seriously, to keep faith with the trust the public places in science and scientists?"

In a 1985 interview, Hynek was asked why he changed his opinion. He said, "Two things, really. One was the completely negative and unyielding attitude of the Air Force. They wouldn't give UFOs the chance of existing, even if they were flying up and down the street in broad daylight. Everything had to have an explanation. I began to resent that, even though I basically felt the same way, because I still thought they weren't going about it in the right way. You can't assume that everything is black no matter what. Secondly, the caliber of the witnesses began to trouble me. Quite a few instances were reported by military pilots, for example, and I knew them to be fairly well-trained, so this is when I first began to think that, well, maybe there was something to all this."

Stories, depictions, and documentation of extraterrestrials, interdimensional beings, and UFOs have been around for as long as our documented history goes. UFOs and ETs show up in essentially all of the ancient texts, they show up in every religious text, they are depicted in hieroglyphs, petroglyphs, cave drawings, ancient artifacts, historic art pieces, and are a part of almost every indigenous culture's teachings and tribal history.

U.S. AIR FORCE AIRCRAFT IDENTIFICATION CHART

Mystery Airships

In the late 1800s, particularly in the United States, there were numerous reports of mysterious airships or unidentified flying objects in the skies. These sightings, often referred to as the "mystery airship wave," occurred primarily between 1896 and

1897 but continued into the early 1900s.

Witnesses described the mystery airships as large, cigar-shaped or cylindrical objects equipped with lights, propellers, and sometimes wings. Some accounts mentioned portholes, steam engines, and even crews of humanoid occupants visible inside the craft. The airships were said to move silently or emit a low humming noise as they flew.

Thousands of people across the United States reported seeing these mystery airships. Newspapers of the time were filled with accounts of sightings by ordinary citizens, farmers, and even prominent figures.

Foo Fighters

During World War II, many Allied pilots reported seeing mysterious objects in the sky they termed as "foo fighters". They were described as glowing orbs, balls of light, or other unidentified aerial objects that appeared to be under intelligent control. They often exhibited erratic movements, such as rapid acceleration, sudden stops, and sharp turns, which seemed to defy the capabilities of known aircraft. Pilots from both the Allied and Axis powers reported encounters with foo fighters during combat missions and reconnaissance flights. These encounters occurred primarily at night but were also reported during daytime operations. Foo fighters were often observed flying in formation with aircraft or trailing them at a distance. At first, both the Ally and Axis pilots and militaries thought that these things must be some form of advanced secret weapon of the enemy. Eventually it became clear that it wasn't anything from either side, but was some other phenomenon entirely.

(And yes, this is where Dave Grohl got the name for his band.)

Kenneth Arnold

The first widely famous UFO sighting in modern times happened in 1947. Amateur pilot and businessman Kenneth Arnold claimed to see nine unknown objects flying near Mount Rainier while flying from Chehalis to Yakima, Washington. He estimated the objects' speed at several thousand miles per hour. He told the reporter that they moved "like saucers skipping on water." This got misinterpreted in the report as the objects being saucer-shaped, and hence the term "flying saucer" was coined and became the popular term for unknown flying objects until later on when the term "UFO" became popularized and more widely used.

Cape Girardeau, MO UFO Crash

One of the earliest reported UFO crashes occurred in Cape Girardeau, Missouri, in April 1941. According to some accounts, Reverend William Huffman was called to administer last rites to alien occupants of a crashed saucer-like object. When Huffman arrived at the crash site he found three creatures, two of which were already dead. Soon after, the U.S. military arrived at the crash site, threatened everyone into secrecy, and confiscated all the evidence.

Paul Blake Smith, author of *MO41: The Bombshell Before Roswell*, had these things to say about the Cape Girardeau crash during a news interview:

> "When he got there [pastor William G. Huffman], he got the shock of his life. There was no cylindrical airplane with wings or propellers. There was a round silver disc that was broken open, and there was debris...metallic shards in the field that had set fire to the field"

> "One of them was apparently still alive, still breathing as Reverend Huffman knelt over this creature. And they were about three and a half to four feet tall. Your typical Greys as we would call them today, with big black eyes and long, thin arms and legs, and the creature expired in front of him"

> "Everyone was told, do not talk about this. This is a matter of national security. It didn't happen," he said "Getting hard evidence for this has been like trying to nail JELL-O to the wall. It's very frustrating."

The Battle of Los Angeles

The Battle of Los Angeles, also known as the Great Los Angeles Air Raid, occurred on the night of February 24-25, 1942, during World War II. There were mysterious unknown objects or craft hovering over Los Angeles, California, that triggered a massive anti-aircraft barrage and caused widespread panic.

The incident started around 2:00 AM on February 25, 1942 when air raid sirens sounded, and the military launched a massive barrage against the unidentified objects. Over 1,400 rounds of anti-aircraft artillery were fired over Los Angeles, creating a barrage of explosions and gunfire that lasted for several hours. The craft moved very slowly and did not make any attempt at evasion. No known aircraft at the time could survive the impact of a single anti-aircraft shell.

Over half a million people witnessed the event, of which many described hearing explosions and feeling the ground shake from the barrage. People reported seeing smaller ships circling around the main craft. Many witnesses reported to the LA

Times that the shells exploded in rings around the craft.

The morning after the incident, the military held a press conference to address the event. They claimed that the anti-aircraft barrage had been triggered by a "false alarm" or "war nerves," suggesting that the unidentified objects may have been weather balloons, Japanese aircraft, or enemy reconnaissance balloons launched from submarines off the California coast.

In his book *Selected by Extraterrestrials Volume 2*, Former Naval Intel Officer William Tompkins tells what he believes really happened that night:

> "I surmised that there was a massive interplanetary mothership orbiting our planet that was from somewhere out in the galaxy. The mothership had disembarked hundreds of smaller landing-type vehicles with a totally unknown mission onto planet Earth. Just observing our inability to work out our differences and our inability to get along with each other concerns the ETs. Hostilities and wars seem to be our history that they must have observed for thousands of years. They were not here to take us over, but to investigate our insane dropping of atom bombs, and even more importantly, to determine who was giving us such a bad time. The Nordic Navy knew that the Reptilians had been mind-controlling us for a long time. Also, nuclear weapon technology is a big red flag and a no-no out in the galaxy."

> "They were still in shock from watching huge mother ships half a night, the largest mass sighting ever recorded. There were hundreds of massive 'naval space battle fleet ships' flying, or some even parked for over an hour at only 8,000 feet above them. That was unbelievable to all who saw them. Yes, these important witnesses were aware of the alien existence influencing the German SS, but this was the

United States!

This massive naval space armada was obviously from out in this part of the Milky Way Galaxy. And for some reason, a possible threat to us? The space vehicles were under aircraft fire from our naval battleships, cruisers, aircraft carriers, destroyers anchored in the Long Beach Harbor and even navy ships in drydock in San Pedro naval base. Also, the Army anti-aircraft guns of the Coast Artillery. Collectively: overnight they used up all their ammunition. Everyone could see continuous explosions on the spaceships' hulls.

Let's put this in perspective, don't forget: several alien civilizations from way out there have been watching our inability to not prevent wars for hundreds of years. SEVERAL! Unbelievable: for five hours maybe a hundred spaceships from another sector of our galaxy penetrated our air space. Just two months earlier, while watching the Germans bomb Britain, the spaceships of course had watched the Japanese Pearl Harbor attack from space and were now aware of our military situation. Their home base at a remote star's planet had seen the Japanese planes attacking our navy and dispatched this armada of force to evaluate our threat situation."

UFO Crashes Before Roswell

Other than the Cape Girardeau crash in 1941, there are other UFO crashes that happened before the Roswell incident. There is a section in Len Kasten's book *Secret Journey to Planet Serpo* where he discloses two other pre-Roswell UFO crashes:

"Roswell was not the first incident. We now know that there were at least two other crashes of alien craft in, or near, the United States prior to July 1947. The U.S. Navy retrieved a disc in the Pacific west of San Diego in 1941. Better known was the spectacular crash in the Plains of St. Augustin, southwest of Socorro, New Mexico, on May 31, 1947. The alien craft was resting on its roof and still smoking when the military arrived. Four aliens were on the ground—three alive and one dead. Bob Shell, the former editor of Shutterbug magazine and a military cameraman assigned to film the scene, reported that each of the live aliens was tightly grasping a box and making shrieking noises. He said that they looked like 'circus freaks.' Two of the three surviving aliens were injured and died within three weeks, at which point the cameraman was called upon to film an autopsy of one of the creatures in Fort Worth, Texas. This ultimately became the famous 'Santilli autopsy film.' As can be seen in the film, these aliens appeared almost human, although smaller, and had six fingers and toes on their otherwise human-looking hands and feet. The alien craft and bodies were taken to Wright-Patterson Air Force Base near Dayton, Ohio.

So the military already had experience with this type of event before Roswell. Given this experience, we can reasonably conclude that Army procedures for dealing with crashed alien craft were in place before Roswell, and that the Pentagon had established a policy to not reveal these events to the press if they had any military implications."

Roswell Ufo Crash

Disk Craze Continues

Army Disk-ounts New Mexico Find As Weather Gear

FORT WORTH, July 9—(AP)—An examination by the Army revealed last night that a mysterious object found on a lonely New Mexico ranch was a harmless high-altitude weather balloon—not a grounded flying disk.

Excitement was high in disk-conscious Texas until Brig Gen. Roger M. Ramey, commander of the Eight Air Forces with headquarters here cleared up the mystery.

The bundle of tinfoil, broken wood beams and rubber remnants of a ballon was sent here yesterday by army air transport in the wake of reports that it was a flying disk.

But the general said the objects were the crushed remains of a Ray wind target used to determine the direction and velocity of winds at high altitudes.

Warrant Officer Irving Newton, forecaster at the Army Air Forces' weather station here, said "we use them because they go much higher than the eye can see."

NOT A FLYING DISC—Major Jesse A. Marcel of Houma, La., Intelligence officer of the 509th Bomb Group at Roswell, New Mexico, inspects what was identified by a Fort Worth, Texas, Army Air Base weather forecaster as a ray wind target used to determine the direction and velocity of winds at high altitudes. Initial stories originating from Roswell, where the object was found, had labelled it a "flying disc" but inspection at Fort Worth revealed its true nature. (AP Wirephoto).

LOST PURSE HOLDING DIAMONDS IS FOUND, BUT MONEY MISSING

Somewhere in Corsicana Wed-

The Roswell UFO crash is by far the most well known and widely discussed UFO incidents in modern times. It occurred in 1947 close to Roswell, New Mexico, and initially involved the US military announcing the discovery of a "flying disc" on a ranch near Corona, NM. However, they swiftly retracted their statement, attributing the debris to a weather balloon. This event having anything to do with extraterrestrials was denied and ridiculed by the US military and government. Upon deep investigation, it becomes clear that the military did in fact cover up the retrieval of an extraterrestrial spacecraft and the bodies of alien beings during the Roswell incident. There were recovered materials, ET bodies, and one living extraterrestrial that were transported to the base at Area 51 and other locations such as Wright-Patterson Air Force Base in Ohio.

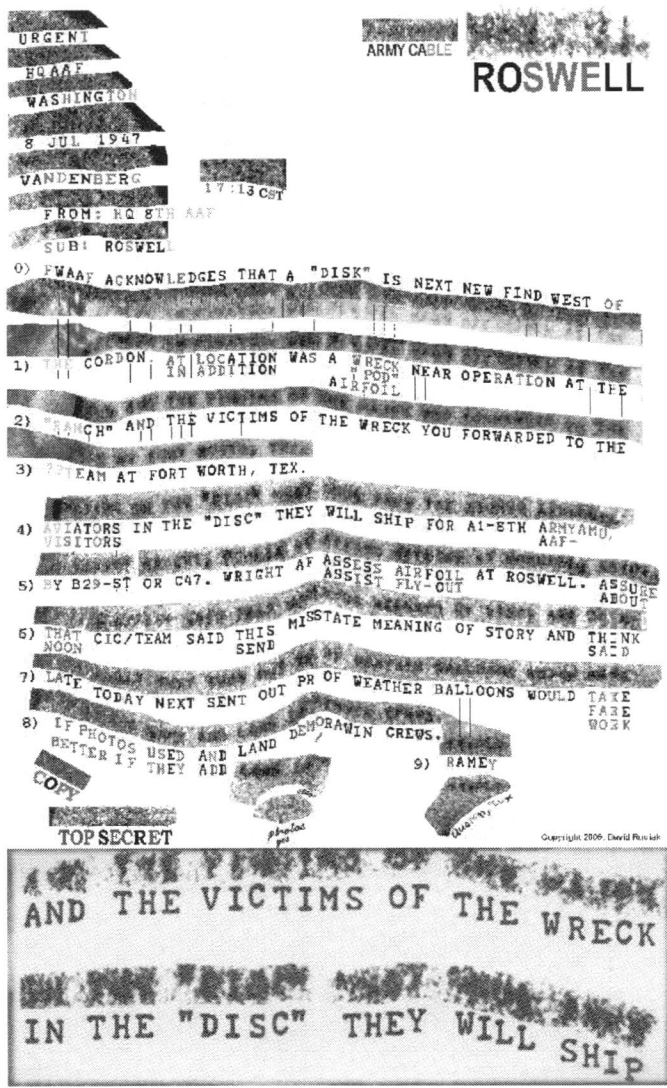

URGENT

HQ AAF

WASHINGTON

8 JUL 1947

VANDENBERG 17:13 CST

FROM: HQ 8TH AAF

SUB: ROSWELL

ARMY CABLE ROSWELL

0) FWAAF ACKNOWLEDGES THAT A "DISK" IS NEXT NEW FIND WEST OF

1) THE CORDON. AT LOCATION WAS A WRECK NEAR OPERATION AT THE IN ADDITION "POP" AIRFOIL

2) "RANCH" AND THE VICTIMS OF THE WRECK YOU FORWARDED TO THE

3) ??TEAM AT FORT WORTH, TEX.

4) AVIATORS IN THE "DISC" THEY WILL SHIP FOR A1-8TH ARMYAMU, VISITORS AAF-

5) BY B29-ST OR C47. WRIGHT AF ASSESS AIRFOIL AT ROSWELL. ASSURE ASSIST FLY-OUT ABOUT

6) THAT CIC/TEAM SAID THIS MISSTATE MEANING OF STORY AND THINK NOON SEND SAID

7) LATE TODAY NEXT SENT OUT PR OF WEATHER BALLOONS WOULD TAKE FARE WORK

8) IF PHOTOS USED AND LAND DEMORAWIN CREWS. BETTER IF THEY ADD

9) RAMEY

COPY

TOP SECRET

Copyright 2006, David Rudiak

AND THE VICTIMS OF THE WRECK

IN THE "DISC" THEY WILL SHIP

"All I could do is keep my mouth shut. General Ramey's the one who told the news man what it was and to forget about it. It was nothing more than a weather observation balloon. Of course we both knew differently."

–Jesse Marcel, From: In Search of... - UFO Cover Ups - Season 5: Episode 1

In 1978, Stanton Friedman conducted an extensive interview with Jesse Marcel about his experiences at Roswell. Marcel provided detailed testimony about his involvement in the recovery operation, describing the debris he saw and handled at the crash site.

During the interview, Jesse Marcel described the debris recovered from the Roswell crash site as being unlike anything he had ever seen. He mentioned finding metallic foil-like material that was incredibly lightweight and flexible, as well as thin, I-beam-like structures with strange hieroglyphic-like markings.

UFO researcher and investigator Richard Dolan sums up the coverup with this statement: "The Roswell case is just one of many instances in which the US military baked it, the press served it, and the public ate it."

A year before his death in 1997, Colonel Philip J. Corso released his book "The Day After Roswell". In the book Corso claims that he was involved in the handling of debris recovered from the Roswell UFO incident. He says that this debris was of extraterrestrial origin and that it led to significant technological advancements, including fiber optics, integrated circuits, and night vision technology. Corso suggests that these advancements were the result of reverse-engineering alien technology recovered from the crash site.

In his book *Secret Journey to Planet Serpo*, Len Kasten tells about what happened:

> "In 1962, Colonel Corso was given the job of seeding American industry with the objects found in the Roswell disk. He got this assignment from his boss, General Arthur Trudeau. At that point, he had no way of knowing about the events that had transpired in the fifteen intervening years

since the crash. That information was so secret and highly compartmentalized that even President Eisenhower didn't have the whole story. Only MJ-12, the super-secret advisory committee empaneled by President Truman knew all the details. All Corso knew was that the intriguing pieces of equipment picked up at the crash site displayed technology very far in advance of anything we knew about. His job was to quietly turn that technology over to the scientists and corporations that were best positioned to understand it and to use it as a springboard to perhaps copy it and develop it further. In that role, he was a 'lone gunman.' He didn't have the clearance to learn about what had happened since 1947. He just had to assume a civilian-like aspect, and to silently insert these objects into American R&D, and then disappear. So it is not surprising that, when he wrote his book in 1997, he still believed that the aliens known as Ebens were hostile and a potential threat to the United States and the planet. It's an incredible testament to just how effectively the compartmentalization and secrecy machinery functioned that, even fifteen years later, an Army general and colonel had no inkling about the fact that we had been hosting those aliens at Los Alamos Laboratories and Area 51, and had already successfully back-engineered an Eben flying disc!"

CHAPTER 17

Invasion of Washington and ET
takeover of U.S. Government

T here were a series of UFO sightings over Washington DC from July 12 to 28, 1952. They were accompanied by radar contacts at three separate airports in the area. Jets were scrambled to go after these unknown craft, but the craft easily outran and evaded them.

President Truman demanded answers, and a person from the Air Force's Project Blue Book was sent to D.C. Before anyone could truly investigate the incident, the Air Force quickly held a press conference in an attempt to explain what happened and put the situation to rest. They claimed that the radar blips were caused by "temperature inversions" and the visual sightings were simply meteors, stars, and city lights. Even Project Bluebook later on dismissed the official "temperature inversion" explanation, and labeled the sightings as "unknown." The radar operators also rejected the official Air Force explanation as they confidently knew the difference between temperature inversions and true objects being picked up by radar.

Radar controller Harry Barnes stated:

> "Inversion blips are always recognized by experts, we are familiar with what weather conditions, flying birds, and [other] such things can cause on radar.

> Temperature inversions on radar are typically weak returns and move at a slow ground speed. These blips were distinctly clear, reported as a very good return, solid and often traveled at unbelievable speeds."

Not only were the objects caught on multiple radar, but two airline pilots and a newsman saw unknown lights in the sky that same night.

Capt. S.C. (Casey) Pierman of Detroit, piloting Capital Airlines Flight 807 described what he saw as "falling stars without tails". Pierman said "In my years of flying I've seen a lot of falling or shooting stars...But these were much faster...They couldn't have been aircraft. They were moving too fast for that."

Up to this point, almost all UFO sightings had happened in more rural or sparsely populated areas. These craft clearly wanted to be seen, and especially by the US government. It appeared as if they were letting the US government know they could occupy its most restricted air space and there was absolutely nothing they could do about it.

Some insiders and researchers have said that these were actually Nazi craft, and not extraterrestrial. People like William Tompkins, Dan Cooper (SSP experiencer), Dr. Michael Salla, and others say that these were actually the Nazis (Nazi/Draco alliance) putting on a show of force and dominance, and forcing the United States into an unconditional surrender.

Here's what Michael Salla says about what really happened with the Washington Flyover in his book *The US Navy's Secret Space Program and Nordic Extraterrestrial Alliance*:

> "This strategic action, together with what both Tompkins and Goode described as a Nazi fly over of Washington DC in the summer of 1952, led to subversive agreements with the Eisenhower administration. Goode says these agreements were a 'silent coup':
>
> During the 1950's and after they [NAZI's] had successfully infiltrated and subverted the Military Industrial Complex and major Corporate heads they had effectively won control of the direction of not only the BreakAway Civilization Programs but also the mainstream government and financial system. It was a very effective and silent coup that gutted what was once the American Republic and turned it too into a Corporate Entity with each of us being 'Assets' with our very own serial numbers.
>
> Both Tompkins and Goode say that the Navy played catch-up for several decades with the more advanced German/Nazi space program. It was only in the early 1980's that Solar Warden became operational with its first spaceship deployments in what would ultimately lead to eight space battle groups. Tompkins asserts that the key to the Navy finally succeeding in its efforts was the covert assistance provided by Nordic extraterrestrials, who offered highly

advanced engineering expertise to help design and build the future space battle groups, despite Nazi-Reptilian sabotage efforts."

Eisenhower ET Meetings - Agreements made with ETs

There is a narrative that has been propagated by many in the UFO community that president Eisenhower supposedly made a deal and "sold us out" to the Greys. Upon further research that narrative is not accurate at all. First off, presidents do not carry the power that most people think they do. They are essentially just middle managers within a system where the true power and control hides behind the scenes, is completely unaccountable to the US government (within which they have their agents and people under their control), and does not in any way, shape, or form answer to the President. This is how things have been in the US government at least since the time of Truman's presidency. President Eisenhower had a rude awakening when he ran into this secret control system. There are at least 35 levels of clearance *above* the President of the United States. The real power and control lies far above the President.

On the evening of February 20, 1954, while Eisenhower was on vacation in Palm Springs, California, he suddenly disappeared and went missing. This was not something that happened at that time, where a US President just goes missing and not a single person knows where they went. The Associated Press even put out a wire saying that he died in the middle of the night! And literally two minutes later they retracted it and said "Oops, we made a mistake." Eisenhower then showed up at church the next morning. It's obvious that something happened to him that night that was not normal, and that they didn't want the public knowing about.

So what really happened? There are multiple insiders that say and information that points to what actually happened. There was a deal made with the Greys that allowed for them to abduct a certain number of people every year in exchange for some advanced technology. Many people think it was Eisenhower who made this deal, but that isn't the case. During his missing time, President Eisenhower met with "Nordic" extraterrestrials at Edwards Air Force Base in California. In that meeting, the Nordics asked him to sign a "peace agreement" where the US would give up their nuclear weapons, and in exchange they would give us technology which would change the world. Allegedly Eisenhower turned the deal down because he didn't trust that Russia would do the same, and didn't like the idea of being unarmed while the Soviets still had nukes.

This is what William Cooper (Former US Navy and Naval Intelligence, who claimed to have had access to classified information) had to say about the meeting with the Nordics:

> "This alien group warned us against the aliens that were orbiting the Equator (the Greys) and offered to help us with our spiritual development. They demanded that we dismantle and destroy our nuclear weapons as the major condition. They refused to exchange technology citing that we were spiritually unable to handle our own technology at the time. They believed that we would use any new technology to destroy each other."

So there seems to be a contradiction of information where some people say that the Nordics did offer us technology, but others, including William Cooper, say that they refused to offer us technology because we were too spiritually immature. Though all sources seem to be congruent with the rest of the information about Eisenhower meeting with Nordics and turning down their offer under the condition of nuclear disarmament. Even though Eisenhower turned down the deal with the Nordics, that doesn't mean that he is the one that signed the deal with the Greys.

Majestic Twelve, or MJ-12, is a group connected to the Cabal which specifically deals with ETs, UFOs, and advanced technology gained from them, and appears to be the group that actually made the deal with these extraterrestrials without Eisenhower's knowledge and against his will.

This deal is known as the Greada Treaty (or Grenada Treaty). This was an agreement made with the Greys that would allow them to abduct Humans in exchange for advanced technology. They would also agree to not interfere in human affairs, and to cooperate in certain covert projects. The deal was made by MJ-12 (Deep State / Cabal) behind Eisenhower's back, and Eisenhower was used as the "fall guy." Allegedly this treaty gets renewed every ten years (until recently). A complete list of abductees was to be given to our government in an effort to keep tabs on who was being taken.

William Cooper said this:

> "According to this agreement, the US Government would allow people to be abducted on the condition that they would not be harmed, that they would be returned safely and that they would not remember the incident. In exchange, the US Government would get highly evolved technology."

In his book *Beyond Esoteric*, Brad Olsen shares the information that Michael Prince (aka James Casbolt) knew about the Greada Treaty and the plans of the Greys and Reptilians:

> "Michael Prince reported that on April 15, 1964, two U.S.

intelligence personnel met under Project Plato with the Greys in the New Mexico desert to arrange a meeting on April 25 at Holloman Air Force base in New Mexico. This meeting was to renew the Greada Treaty that had started in 1934, and was a psychological bid to buy time in order for the "white hats" to solve the problem of the Greys and Draco reptilians. The upper levels of U.S. intelligence discovered the Greys and Draco had this planet time-tabled for invasion and takeover sometime in the first three decades of the 21st century."

The Greys did not hold up their end of the deal and it was found out that they were abducting way more people than agreed. Also they were not just taking genetics and experimenting on Humans. They also were trafficking people as well, and they were actually working with, or were enslaved by, the Draco Reptilians. Many claim that this was the beginning of the negative ET takeover within our government.

Laura Eisenhower, the great granddaughter of President Eisenhower, has been very outspoken about the truth behind what really happened regarding her great grandfather in this whole situation. In her book *Awakening the Truth Frequency* she states:

"According to this man named 'Anonymous,' at a certain point in the 1950s, U.S. President Eisenhower had been getting reports about UFOs and ETs and wanted to find out the truth. However, after the Roswell crash of 1947, and with the help of Truman signing new secrecy and security laws, a secret cabal (who called themselves MJ-12 or Majestic 12) took over the UFO and ET issue and brought the programs underground. It went black. Certain military agencies, unknown even to the President and other intelligence heads, kept the whole thing top secret, keeping the technology to themselves and even cutting deals with some of the aliens."

Supposedly Eisenhower also met on multiple occasions with the well-known being Valiant Thor. In Laura Eisenhower's book, she shares information that Dan Cooper (Secret Space Program experiencer) gave to her about Eisenhower and Valiant Thor:

> "Dwight D. Eisenhower, when he came into office on January 20, 1953, inherited that Treaty of July 19, 1952. Dwight D. Eisenhower had nothing to do with the unconditional surrender of the U.S. to the NAZIs, which occurred on July 19, 1952. Anyone telling you otherwise is lying to you, or worse, passing on lies.

> First contact with the Nordics was by the NAZIs in, no later than, 1929. That is when the Nordics gave them a city in their domain. It is called New Berlin and it is still there.

> Commander Valiant Thor warned the U.S., in 1952, when Truman was POTUS, about the Nordics. He told the U.S. that the Nordics, then, were in bed with the NAZIs.

> Commander Valiant Thor also warned the U.S., in 1952, about the Greys. In 1952, the Greys had agreements with the NAZIs. The NAZIs, in exchange for people, including a 100,000 U.S. citizens per year, received technology from the Greys. I will specify what technologies at a different time. I know precisely what (the tech) the Greys gave to the NAZIs in exchange for a 100,000 people, U.S. citizens, per year."

> "I know a lot about Commander Valiant Thor (Val) from my sources (White Hats). He did in fact advise Ike for years, specifically on how to defeat the ICC/Nazi/Draco Alliance, and end their dominion over humanity."
> — Dan Cooper

In his book *Stranger at the Pentagon*, Frank Stranges talks about how Eisenhower strongly wanted to accept and implement Val Thor's proposals, but "the Secretary of Defense, the head of the Central Intelligence Agency and the Military Chiefs of Staff were opposed to his suggestion. The President attempted to effect a joint meeting before the General Assembly of the United Nations. But this plan too was rejected."

Eisenhower said what he could to warn the public of the horrible reality he became aware of during his presidency. In his closing address, he warns against the out-of-control power of the Military Industrial Complex:

"In the councils of government, we must guard against the acquisition of unwarranted influence, whether sought or unsought, by the military-industrial complex. The potential for the disastrous rise of misplaced power exists and will persist. We must never let the weight of this combination endanger our liberties or democratic processes. We should take nothing for granted. Only an alert and knowledgeable citizenry can compel the proper meshing of the huge industrial and military machinery of defense with our peaceful methods and goals, so that security and liberty may prosper together."

There are now positive groups working behind the scenes and in various secret programs to free humanity from enslavement. Many refer to them as the "White Hats" or the "Alliance." These groups began forming decades ago in response to the Deep State being a major threat to humanity. They are made up of people within the US military and intelligence agencies, along with militaries around the world, that over at least the past 75 years have been coming together and working towards eliminating the Deep State and their threat to the entire planet and beyond.

"Eisenhower is part of the creation of the Secret Space programs—but without his leadership, many failing organizations had no accountability to their actions and infighting between the organizations spread. This continued lack of transparency and continued deception going on between these World powers spread corruption, greed, mind control and horrific crimes against humanity."
– Lisa Renee, Ascension Glossary

CHAPTER 18

Secret Programs with ETs and
Advanced Technology

"We already have the means to travel among the stars, but
these technologies are locked up in black projects and it would
take an act of God to ever get them out to benefit humanity."
— Ben Rich, CEO Lockheed Skunk Works

For the past century, there have been a vast number of secret projects and programs that have been going on dealing with extraterrestrials, their craft, and advanced technology gained from ET craft. These programs exist within deep black and hidden compartments of militaries, intelligence agencies, and aerospace companies.

These secret groups and programs operate completely independently to the president, any world leader, governments, or any laws, with no accountability whatsoever. Many of these are connected to, or controlled by, a group often referred to as the "Cabal," "Deep State," or "Shadow Government," which has created a massive web of power within the Military Industrial Complex through secret compartmentalized projects and programs. These are called "Unacknowledged Special Access Programs" (USAPs). In

Steven Greer's documentary "Unacknowledged" he gives a fantastic introduction and overview of this topic, covering who these people are, how the control structure operates, and what is going on within it.

Over the past four decades, Steven Greer has disclosed much of what he knows about advanced technology and the fact that our governments, militaries, and aerospace companies have had this technology for a long time.

The 2001 Disclosure Project

In 2001, Greer organized the Disclosure Project, which brought forward military and government witnesses with knowledge of UFOs and advanced technology. Over 20 witnesses, including military personnel, government officials, and aerospace industry insiders, provided testimony about their experiences and knowledge of UFO-related incidents and government secrecy.

Greer has briefed U.S. Presidents, members of Congress, and heads of intelligence agencies, and educated them about UFOs, Extraterrestrials, advanced propulsion systems, zero-point energy, and the need for government transparency on these issues.

In 2017, Greer released the documentary "Unacknowledged," which explores the suppression of information about UFOs and advanced technology by government agencies. The film contains testimony from whistleblowers and explores the implications of this secrecy for humanity.

He has spoken publicly about the existence of advanced propulsion systems developed through reverse engineering of extraterrestrial technology. Greer says that these technologies could revolutionize energy production, transportation, and space travel if made public.

Greer has advocated for the disclosure of information about zero-point energy (ZPE), a form of energy that could provide limitless, clean energy to the planet. He says that this technology has been developed but is being suppressed by powerful interests.

He claims that we mastered anti-gravity in 1954:

> "I'll give you a date. October of 1954 is when we mastered gravity control, where we actually went from experimental craft that were unstable–if you look at some of the early UFO films where they're fluttering like a leaf as they are moving, it's because they didn't have the stability of gravity control worked out from '45 to '54. October 1954, according to the top secret scientist at the Naval research labs who was on my team for 15 years–he was the top scientist there– had been in a vault and saw specifically that date is when we mastered gravity control...If you look at the disclosure material, one of these objects that was at the Norton Air Show in 1988 that we have drawings for and a witness who was there, Brad Sorenson, he stated emphatically that that object had been through the solar system and it was operational late 1950s, early 1960s, and it had mercury component parts inside of it. So the technology of electro-

magnetic gravitic, or anti-gravity, that was pretty much under operational function by 1954-55. By the late 50s, early 60s, they had that capability. And I understand eventually there were assets that we put on the moon that are there now, and I know one Navy Seal who actually went on a two week trip out there, on one of these devices."
From: Interview on *Redacted* with Clayton Morris 7/2/23

Eisenhower Finds Out about UFOs, ETs, and Advanced Craft

President Eisenhower found out about the problem within the Military Industrial Complex of UFOs and advanced technology being kept hidden and developed in secret with no accountability whatsoever. He attempted to gain access to these programs and was outright denied and told that he didn't have any jurisdiction over what they were doing!

In his talk "Revealing the Five Alliance Groups" at Contact in the Desert 2018, David Wilcock talks about what happened when Eisenhower found out about the secret UFO and ET projects and was denied access to it:

"In 1952 the Germans overflew the capital. A secret deal was reached where they agreed to join the German secret space program. And this is all becoming a matter of documented history now. We've gotten it from Pete Peterson, we've gotten it from Corey Goode, we've gotten it from William Tompkins, other insiders as well. So the pieces are now fitting together very nicely. With this in mind, the US starts to go deep black. And by the time Eisenhower got into office, the President of the United States was no longer on a need-to-know basis. And so, one of the people we see at all these events, Richard Dolan, broke this incredible story where in 1958 Eisenhower tasked this man, who is actually a CIA agent–he never gave his name… This man claimed he was a CIA agent who was actually hired by Eisenhower to invade Area 51, to lead up that team. So this is the quote from Eisenhower that we get from this whistleblower in that video. Eisenhower the President said: 'We called the people in from MJ-12, from Area 51 and S-4, but they told us that the government had no jurisdiction over what they were doing.'

Eisenhower says 'I want you and your boss to fly out there. I want you to give them a personal message from me. I want you to tell them, whoever is in charge, I want you to tell them that they have this coming week to get into Washington and to report to me. And if they don't, I'm going to get the First Army from Colorado. We are going to go over and take the base over. I don't care what kind of classified material you've got. We are going to rip this thing apart.'

So what ended up happening was that there was a meeting. These people did meet with Eisenhower. These Majestic 12 people. And they were willing to grant him and his inspectors a visit. Now, our CIA agent guy was not in charge. He had a commanding officer. And the commanding officer and the agent and a few others, got to go on a tour of Area 51 where they saw several large hangars that had big garage-style doors that had flying saucers inside. So they got to see that. The agent's boss got to partially interview a Grey ET that was being held in captivity.

So this is pretty amazing stuff. But at the same time, it was sort of like a slap on the wrist. They got to get away with just showing them a little tease. Nothing really happens. So Eisenhower warned in his closing address, which all of us know that one, 'The rise of unwarranted power and influence by the Military Industrial Complex...This secret combination exists and will persist until we rise to oppose it.'"

Dr. Michael Wolf

The following are excerpts from a 1998 interview Dr. Richard J. Boylan conducted with insider Dr. Michael Wolf:

'Dr. Michael Wolf was an insider who worked as an independent contractor to the CIA, NSA and NSC, and though he never overtly stated this, he insinuated that he was a member of MJ-12 in an interview with Richard J. Boylan in 1998. In the interview, Wolf gives a vast overview of all the information he knew about the UFO and ET situation on the planet:

From 1972-1977 Dr. Wolf engaged in covert governmental research into Star Visitor technology. "I met with extraterrestrial individuals every day in my work, and shared living quarters with them," while doing research at extremely-classified underground government research laboratories. He stated, "Zetas work in underground facilities, as requested by the U.S. Government. The Star Visitors are not breaking the U.S. Government-Zeta treaties, but the Government has broken treaties by mistreating ETs, and trying to fire on UFOs." Yet there are some extraterrestrials being held captive. "Government scientists discovered that the Star Visitors cannot dematerialize and escape if there is an extremely-powerful electromagnetic field surrounding them." [By way of corroboration, I have heard a government contractor describe three-foot thick walls with many wires embedded and running through them at Haystack Air Force Laboratory, Edwards AFB, CA.]

Dr. Wolf commented, "Some in the Government want better diplomatic relations [with the Star Visitors], but others in the military want to shoot them down." This is ironic, Wolf said, "because SDI (Star Wars) technology was given to the Government by the Star Visitors." (Not for war but for scientific advancement.)

Some of the Laboratories where Dr. Wolf worked include: (1), S-4 (Laboratory S-4, secreted inside the Papoose Range 13 miles south of Groom Lake, site of the Area 51 Laboratory near the northeast corner of the Nevada Test Range/National Security Site. Dr. Wolf lived and worked at Area 51 for a while; (2) the Foreign Technology Division laboratories at Wright-Patterson Air Force Base, Dayton, Ohio, and (3) the former Dulce Laboratory (under Archuleta Mesa near the New Mexico-Colorado border). Wolf also was aware that Star Visitors work with government scientists at Haystack Air Force Laboratory, deep under Haystack Butte at Edwards Air Force Base, California.

And when I brought up the subject of the underground government installation beneath Cheech Air Force Base, adjacent to Indian Springs, NV on the Nevada National Security Site, Dr. Wolf quickly responded, "I can't say anything about that." (His handlers only let the reins slip so far.) Since 1979 Wolf has served as a scientific consultant to Presidents and the National Security Council on Star Visitor matters. He is also a member of the NSC's unacknowledged UFO information-management subcommittee [Special Studies Group] and its panel of scientists. "The code names I used there were 'Griffin', and 'Nu Kappa Eta'." The NSC Special Studies Group made Dr. Wolf the Chairman of Alphacom Team, its premier Star Nations matters group, which also includes an Admiral from Naval Intelligence.

Wolf observes that the generals he worked with feel impotent in the face of the overwhelming superiority of

Star Visitor technology and their mental abilities. Because of those feelings of powerlessness, (anathema to military officers), the generals had authorized an intense and extensive disinformation campaign (the UFO cover-up), to discourage any attempts by civilians to acquire even the limited understanding of Star Visitors which the generals have managed to gain.

But a far most disturbing revelation from Dr. Wolf concerns the emergence of a renegade group within the military and intelligence agencies which comprise the UFO Cover-Up. Dr. Wolf has labeled this conspiratorial group of plotters "The Cabal." It is made up of extremist, fundamentalist, xenophobic, racist, and paranoiac heads of multinational corporations, international financiers, government officials, and military and intelligence officers. The Cabal fears and hates the Star Visitors.

And the Cabal, without any Presidential or Congressional authorization, has commandeered Star Wars weaponry to shoot down UFOs, taken surviving Star Visitors prisoner, and has attempted to extract information by force, torture, and threats to Star Visitors' family members.

A high military officer, who is considered a "friendly" by the Cabal, but who secretly dislikes the Cabal, passes on information about Cabal planning and activities to Dr. Wolf.

...

Dr. Wolf confirmed that it was Dr. Edward Teller who recommended physicist [and fellow leaker] Bob Lazar for his position at the secret S-4 government Laboratory south of Area 51, where Lazar helped on back-engineering the propulsion systems of Star Visitor spacecraft for application in U.S. advanced aerospace crafts.

When I asked who was MJ-1, the head of the MJ-12 subcommittee, Dr. Wolf declined to identify that person. He did say, "MJ-1 answers to no one, not even the President!"

When I offered the surmise that Michael Wolf himself was yet another MJ-12 member, he hurriedly pointed out that he "could not disclose such a thing." [Wink.] And when I proposed that a notable scientist with a government background, residing in Arizona, was yet another MJ-12 member, Wolf responded with an uncharacteristic silence, which I took to mean that he did not contradict that identification.

...

Another UFO notable with whom Wolf is familiar is Admiral Bobby Ray Inman, former head of NSA, and currently chairman of SAIC, Science Applications International Corporation. SAIC was identified by USAF Colonel Steve Wilson as the company which makes anti-gravity engines for U.S.-copycat UFOs. When I commented to Dr. Wolf that Air Force Colonel Wilson had identified Inman as also in charge of Decision Science Applications Inc. (DSAI), (made up of the heads of corporations involved in classified military weapons development based on ET technology), Wolf commented that "Inman doesn't know as much as the UFO community thinks he does. He doesn't know everything that DSAI is up to."

Wolf also verified that the former head of the Air Force Special Forces' Project Pounce [UFO retrievals unit], Colonel Steve Wilson, and Air Force Technical Sergeant/NSA analyst Dan Sherman, assigned to an NSA unit conducting telepathic communications with the Star Visitors, are who they say they are!

Dr. Wolf provided a revisionist history about the beginning of the modern UFO era. "The first UFO came down in 1941 into the ocean west of San Diego, [Saipan Island - RB], and was retrieved by the Navy." The Navy has held a leadership position in UFO matters ever since. [One such unit dealing with UFOs is the Space and Naval Warfare Systems Command, headquartered at Naval Base Point Loma, San Diego, CA -RB.] A more famous UFO crash followed in 1947, northwest of

Roswell, New Mexico, and was retrieved by the Army Air Corps, as reported by Colonel Corso in his book, The Day After Roswell. Dr. Wolf confirms the truth of Corso's disclosures, and added that LED (light-emitting diodes) and superconductivity are among the numerous technologies which came from looting the Roswell crashed spacecraft.

The U.S. was in possession of a Zeta (extraterrestrial from star Zeta Reticuli), dubbed "EBE" [Extraterrestrial Biological Entity", from 1948 until he died in 1953. Government scientists first communicated with him using pictographs.

About the tone in Corso's book The Day After Roswell that 'aliens are a threat, Dr. Wolf commented that "it was co-author William Birnes who did the anti-alien-propaganda gloss on Corso's manuscript after it was sent to the printer," and that Colonel Corso did not personally view the Star Visitors as "enemy invaders".

Within months of the 1947 Roswell UFO crash, the Army Air Corps became the Air Force; the National Security Act was passed (partly to deal with the extraordinary secrecy the Administration felt UFOs required); and the CIA was created. Soon followed by the National Security Agency.

Wolf personally pioneered a mental-expansion process he called "the Gateway Treatment", which "allows utilization of a vastly-increased percentage of the brain, in order for humans to mentally engage the extraterrestrials in full telepathic mental exchange." The Treatment involves "a way of opening the brain up, a way to stimulate the neurons. It allows billions of synapses to form." The secret of that process went to the grave with Dr. Wolf.

Another project Wolf was involved in was subatomic-particle physics research [now called quantum physics.]. Discoveries by Wolf were "utilized by my [Ph.D. dissertation-advising] professor to develop the neutral particle-beam weapon for the Star Wars program."

He explained the NSA's tiny amount of harvesting of tissue from so-called "cattle mutilations' [most done secretly by special military-intelligence units] "is to prepare organelles to adapt to human bodies, to filter out particulates that are killing us, as we pollute our planet." He said, "The 'Betweens'(human-Star Visitor hybrids) will help us, and will bring the organelles."

The Star Visitors have other concerns, too. They discussed God and death with Wolf. And they pointed out that all worlds are connected. "One Hiroshima atomic bomb can affect millions of cultures in the galaxy. "And they told him, "Thought is energy. It doesn't stop at a galactic 'barrier', and is received on other worlds."
Because of what he learned, Wolf stated, "We are at a crossroads. The issue is to give a viable future to our children." He notes, "Humans are beginning to change, to evolve, and are looking for spiritual roots. There is more to God than people get in church."

A fourth ultra-secret project, mentioned in Wolf's book, was a Department of Defense project having to do with cloning a human being, in order to create the perfect soldier who would obey orders without question. A General "Bunting" [pseudonym] was in charge of that project. The clone turned out to have been born with ethical thinking, and intuitively knew that life was sacred. When the clone disobeyed a test order to kill an innocent dog, Wolf says that "the project officer ordered the clone 'terminated'. It was my judgment that the clone had a soul. So, instead, I surreptitiously allowed the clone to escape, and blew up the building [containing the clone project]".

Naturally, Dr. Wolf keeps aware of significant individuals and developments within the civilian UFO-investigation community. One such figure is former Army Command

Sergeant-Major Robert O. Dean, who was assigned to NATO Headquarters in the 1960s. There CSM Dean read NATO's secret Assessment of Star Visitors. Wolf states that he "has seen that same Assessment." Dr. Wolf also revealed that "the NSA and CIA regularly provide the members of MJ-12 with tapes of major meetings of civilian UFO groups," for example, MUFON conferences.

Some other notable UFO investigators who have talked with Dr. Wolf include Robert Bletchman, James Courant, Linda Moulton Howe, William Hamilton, Michael Hesemann and Dr. Steven Greer.

Some years ago documents were leaked purporting to constitute a Presidential Briefing for Jimmy Carter on extraterrestrial matters. Dr. Wolf affirmed that the information contained therein "is substantially true, but one page was missing from the leaked set. That page describes an individual of joint ET-human heritage, who emerged 2000 years ago to try to end human violence." When I proposed that the page was referring to Jesus, Wolf confirmed that identification. During my visit to Dr. Wolf's apartment, he showed me the missing page !

Dr. Wolf describes various Star Visitor races. "One race has orange skin, very large heads and large dark eyes with no irises or whites, and six-fingered hands. During dissection their brains have been found to have four brain lobes, different optic orbs and nerves, and a sponge-like digestive system. Star Visitor brains are more developed and connected, and have no corpus callosum." He also described a race dubbed the Semitics, of average height and a generally human-like appearance, except for their very large hooked nose. "This was the race which landed at Holloman Air Force Base, [New Mexico, 1960s], and conversed with some generals there." Wolf also described a very human-appearing race called the Nordics. He said, "The Semitics and Nordics come from Altair 4 and 5 [in the Altair Aquila star system] and from the Pleiades."

He noted, "The Star Visitors eat vegetation and mushrooms, and have different requirements. They absorb energy from the air and [certain] particulates. They don't absorb enough water to need to void; they process thoroughly."
Wolf said that "cattle mutilations" tissue harvesting is not related to cloning, but rather is done to acquire nutrients for the hybrid fetuses which Cabal scientists create. Dr. Wolf noted that embryonic fluid contains an anti-rejection factor. He is aware that hardly any cattle tissue sampling is done by Star Visitors; the vast majority is done by Cabal secret paramilitary contractor teams.

Crop circles "were originated by extraterrestrials, and then badly copied by the military, using Strategic Defense Initiative weapons emitting a laser pulsed beam." Wolf noted that "with crop circles made by Star Visitors, the plants were still alive and grew, [after being bent into pictographic patterns.] With SDI-weapon crop circles, the plants die. These SDI weapons are operated from a secret base in the Himalayas."

Concerning the famous 1947 Roswell UFO crash, Dr. Wolf states that there were two UFO crashes, close together in time. "One contained Orange Star Visitors and the other Zetas." One crash-landed near Corona, northwest of Roswell, NM; the other crashed onto the Plains of San Agustin, over a hundred miles to the west. Army Intelligence units soon secured both sites and removed the craft and their Star Visitor crews, most dead.

Another later Visitor-military encounter recounted by Dr. Wolf was similarly grim. "An extraterrestrial on the ground had traveled from Fort Dix, New Jersey to [adjacent] McGuire Air Force Base, where he died on the tarmac" [He was shot by a trigger-happy Military Policeman.]

Michael Wolf worked in several projects, making discoveries

with which in hindsight he now regrets being involved. He particularly had misgivings after he saw what applications these discoveries were put to. He says he now "has immense qualms about those misapplications", repudiates them and is repentant for them.

When Dr. Wolf engaged in government-sponsored studies for his MD degree at McGill University, he engaged in research on neurotransmitters and their role in mental functioning and control. Among the secret projects Dr. Wolf worked on was Remote Viewing, a military-intelligence term for applied clairvoyance. He said, "Ninety-nine percent of telepathy and remote-viewing research is classified." Wolf went far beyond the crude Army Intelligence psi experiments of General Bert Stubblebine, Col. John Alexander and Major Ed Dames, and developed memory-extraction and memory-"capping" [suppression] techniques. Some of his findings "were later incorporated into the infamous MK-ULTRA mind control projects of the CIA, and used on captured KGB agents [to extract information]." He also worked in research on dolphins, which he called "a highly-intelligent alien life form on this planet." [Seeded here eons ago. - R.B.]

While Dr. Wolf was studying at MIT for his Ph.D. in physics, he "discovered a new theory of wave-particle duality, which led to the development of the neutral particle-beam Star Wars weapon." Because of these classified projects, his NSC bosses forbade him to identify his dissertation advisor professors, and MIT and McGill University are forbidden to acknowledge that he studied there.

...

Dr. Wolf disclosed that famed scientist "Albert Einstein had contact with extraterrestrial intelligence." And that a more recent understanding of Zero-Point energy "has to do with a white hole-black hole scenario." The Star Visitors told Wolf that the Void is filled with energy to be tapped. Wolf further stated that experiments by the U.S. Government using exotic technology "ripped holes in time."

...

Wolf also revealed that the U.S. government is working on prototypes of anti-gravity discs based on Star Visitor technology. He says that the Star Visitors traverse the galaxy by manipulating space and time to pull their destination towards them. "Time is reduced to zero, and acceleration is increased to infinity." And that the military are experimenting on having pilots use their mind to guide an advanced plane. Some government scientists found that "some UFOs are living conveyances, and can divide and re-form." Those "living conveyances" are apparently also responsive to thought commands.'

From: https://drboylan.com/wolfqut2.html

Sgt. Clifford Stone

Sergeant Clifford Stone worked as a UFO crash retrieval expert with the U.S. Army. He claimed to have been part of a unit that was responsible for investigating and retrieving downed UFOs. He is a decorated Vietnam war veteran.

Stone was assigned to an "NBC" Team (nuclear, biological and chemical retrieval and abatement detail), but he says that was used as a cover and that they also were tasked with UFO crash retrievals. He claims to have physically seen and touched ET craft and interacted with extraterrestrials.

Stone possesses one of the largest private collections of authentic government UFO/ET documents in the world, to which he has amassed over the period of about 40 years.

"He maintains that the US government has knowledge that intelligent life is visiting this planet in craft capable

of traveling distances of many light years very quickly; effectively bypassing acceptably known physics. Further, he stresses that our recovery of these ET craft and artifacts has enabled our government to make staggering scientific gains of great potential benefit to the world. He maintains, as do many others, that this information is held in deeply secret programs beyond Constitutional controls and safeguards. Despite the end of the cold war, those controlling these 'black projects' have continued to keep these important discoveries to themselves via government cover-ups, for motives known only to them."
From: Gaia.com

John Lear

John Lear was an airline captain and the son of William P. Lear, the inventor of the Lear Jet. Lear claimed to have gained his information from various sources, including his own research, conversations with insiders, leaked documents, and personal experiences. He said that much of his knowledge came from contacts within the military, intelligence agencies, and government who shared classified information with him.

Lear stated that his father, William P. Lear, had high-level connections in the aviation and defense industries, which gave him access to insiders who disclosed sensitive information about UFOs, extraterrestrial visitations, and government cover-ups. He also claims he received leaked documents and briefings from whistleblowers within the military and intelligence community.

John Lear's most famous claim is that the U.S. government has been in contact with extraterrestrial beings for decades and has been hiding advanced alien technology, including anti-gravity propulsion systems and spacecraft. He alleges that there are secret underground bases, such as Area 51 in Nevada, where these technologies are being studied and reverse-engineered.

Lear also talked about the moon being inhabited by extraterrestrial civilizations and that there are structures and mining operations on its surface. He revealed government involvement in nefarious activities, such as mind control experiments, the suppression of free energy technology, and the deliberate spread of diseases like AIDS.

Phil Schneider

Whistleblower testimony and data points to the fact that there are well over 1,500 Deep Underground Military Bases (DUMBs) worldwide, many of which are jointly operated with extraterrestrials. One of the most prominent of these whistleblowers was American engineer Phil Schneider.

Phil Schneider was involved in the construction of secret underground bases, including the "Dulce base" beneath the Archuleta Mesa near Dulce, New Mexico. He claimed that these bases were operated jointly by the United States government and extraterrestrials. Schneider said that he witnessed and participated in the construction of these bases, which he claimed housed advanced technology and served as research facilities for the government's secret projects.

Schneider described having a violent encounter with extraterrestrial beings during the construction of the Dulce base. He stated that while drilling underground tunnels, his team accidentally breached a cavern inhabited by Grey aliens. Schneider claimed that he was shot by one of these Greys with an energy weapon that left him with severe injuries, including the loss of several fingers and deep scars on his chest.

Schneider was found dead in his apartment on January 17, 1996. Though it was officially ruled a "suicide," it is blatantly apparent that he was murdered after several attempts on his and his family's lives. They wanted to silence him and prevent him from revealing further secrets about government involvement with extraterrestrial beings and advanced technology.

In a presentation from 1995, Phil said, "There are 131 active deep underground military bases in the United States. There's 1,477 of them worldwide. Each one has an average cost of seventeen to nineteen billion dollars. It used to take a year to two years to build each one, and now they're capable of building a couple of them a year with sophisticated methods. Now my colleague Al Bielek has actually been on some of the high-speed railways, the magneto Leviton trains, that connect all the deep underground military bases within the United States."

David Adair

David Adair is an American inventor, engineer, and rocket scientist who built rockets for the U.S. military. David had many extraordinary experiences with advanced technology and extraterrestrial encounters.

His involvement with advanced technology began at a young age. As a teenager , he built a rocket engine that attracted the attention of the U.S. military. He was then recruited by the military to work on highly classified projects.

Adair's most famous claim involves an encounter he says he had in the late 1970s or early 1980s at Area 51, a top secret U.S. Air Force facility in Nevada. Adair says that he was taken to a secret underground facility beneath Area 51, where he was shown a massive, sentient engine created by extraterrestrial beings. He describes the engine as a living entity with advanced consciousness. This consciousness actually communicated with him, and he ended up forming a relationship with the being, which he called "Pitholem."

In an interview with Michael Salla, Adair described his first encounter with the sentient engine:

> "This thing felt like it was alive. It's just like you put your hand on a whale. Or a giant shark. It's like it gives just a little bit and then it stops. And wherever you're touching it, wherever my skin was on its skin was these radiating blue waves, really pretty. Hard to describe...Its skeleton is on the outside. But where you put your hand on it where it's smooth–that's the organs. So I climb up what looks to be vertebrates. Got to the top of it and I thought 'This looks familiar.'...You know what it looks like? A human synaptic firing system. Brains. I thought 'Is this thing alive? Or is it a machine?' So it's an organic inorganic entity...What I'm standing on is not a ship. It's a power plant. This thing, and the ship, and the crew—all three merge together in a symbiotic relationship. What a perfect way to fly through space."

Adair then goes on to describe how the entity started communicating telepathically with him, telling him that his name was "Pitholem," and that through consciousness interaction it had led David to connecting with it.

Adair was tasked with reverse-engineering the alien engine, but he refused to participate in the project due to ethical concerns. He claims that he was later threatened by military personnel and warned not to speak about his experiences.

Secret Space Programs

"The Secret Space Program in a nutshell is: Governments, for almost the last 100 years, have made contact with extraterrestrial species, and acquired technology to go offworld."
— Tony Rodrigues, SSP experiencer

Over the last several decades, many people have been coming out with testimonies of their experiences in these various Secret Space Programs. Multiple insiders and whistleblowers over the past 50 years have disclosed their own knowledge or experience within these programs.

William Tompkins

William Mills Tompkins was an aerospace engineer who claimed to have worked on highly classified government projects involving advanced technology and extraterrestrial intelligence. He gained attention for his assertions about secret space programs and interactions with alien beings.

Tompkins was recruited by the United States Navy during World War II due to his exceptional abilities in naval engineering. He was involved in top-secret projects related to advanced aircraft and spacecraft designs. Tompkins worked closely with scientists, engineers, and military personnel to develop advanced aerospace technologies, some of which were reverse-engineered from extraterrestrial craft.

Tompkins designed and constructed spacecraft that he referred to as "flying saucers" or "alien reproduction vehicles" (ARVs). He said that these craft were based on technology obtained from crashed UFOs and were capable of interstellar travel. Tompkins claimed that the United States government had established secret space programs aimed at exploring and colonizing other planets using these advanced spacecraft.

Tompkins talked about his personal encounters with extraterrestrial beings, whom he described as humanoid and possessing advanced technology and knowledge. He said that these beings had been visiting Earth for thousands of years and had interacted with various human civilizations throughout history.

Gary McKinnon

In 2002, British hacker Gary McKinnon broke into computer systems belonging to various United States government agencies, including NASA and the Pentagon. It was described as the "biggest military computer hack of all time." McKinnon claims he was searching for evidence of UFOs and advanced technology.

What he found was information on "non-terrestrial officers," "fleet-to-fleet transfers" and a program called "Solar Warden."

In an interview he said, "I found a list of officers' names ... under the heading 'Non-Terrestrial Officers'. It doesn't mean little green men. What I think it means is not Earth-based. I found a list of 'fleet-to-fleet transfers', and a list of ship names. I looked them up. They weren't US Navy ships. What I saw made me believe they have some kind of spaceship, off-planet."

During a Project Camelot interview, McKinnon said:

> "What I surmised is that an off-planet Space Marines is being formed. And if you actually look at DARPA, the

Defense Advanced Research Projects Agency, literature at the moment and in the last few years, a lot of government and space command stuff is all about space dominance. It is really, you know, the final frontier. Yeah, so I think it's natural for them to want to control space and to be developing a space-going force in secret. I think [they are] most likely using technology reverse-engineered from ETs."

Admiral Byrd

Admiral Richard E. Byrd was a highly decorated American naval officer and explorer known for his pioneering expeditions to Antarctica. One of the most notable expeditions led by Admiral Byrd was Operation Highjump, a large-scale U.S. Navy expedition to Antarctica that took place from 1946 to 1947. Publicly, the main objectives of Operation Highjump were to establish a research base, conduct scientific studies, and explore the uncharted regions of Antarctica. Secretly, the real reason for the expedition was that after the war, when the US found out the Nazis had created bases in Antarctica, they decided they needed to take them out.

The mission was supposed to last for six months. They came back after only two months when they were brutally defeated as advanced flying craft and technology were used against them, to which they were defenseless against and could not even come close to matching.

When he returned, Byrd urged that it was critical for the United States to initiate immediate defense measures against hostile regions. He said that in case of a new war, the continental United States would be attacked by flying objects which "could fly from pole to pole at incredible speeds."

It became clear at that point that the Nazis had developed

bases in Antarctica where they housed anti-gravity craft and an advanced space fleet.

CHAPTER 19

*Covering Up the Truth - Public
Figures Disclosing the Truth*

T here has been a massive attempt to cover-up and conceal the reality of not just UFOs, but of extraterrestrial life and their technology and spiritual wisdom from humanity by the controllers. They do not want our consciousness and our understanding of reality and spiritual knowledge to be expanded, so they do everything they can to keep humanity away from the knowledge of, connecting with, and learning about our connection to extraterrestrial life. In his book The Secret History of Extraterrestrials, Len Kasten elaborates on this:

> "It is slowly dawning on us that the world we see around us is a cleverly designed illusion and that we have been expertly manipulated to believe it to be reality. And believing in it, as we do, we are thereby led to behave in certain ways.
>
> These behaviors are basically simple, repetitive, and essentially mindless, and primarily geared to economic survival and primitive enjoyment. Underneath the seemingly placid surface, there are continual frustrations and angry rumblings that frequently break through to manifest as violent recriminations against each other. We

blame each other for our predicament, so we go to war.

But new technologies and gadgets continue to keep us entertained and distracted and less likely to challenge the status quo. So we are kept on our treadmill. And always there is the overarching fear of death.

Now, in the age of the Internet and thanks to hundreds of books about conspiracies and UFOs as well as fifty years of science-fiction (sci-fi) movies, our mass consciousness has started to expand, and we have begun to examine our cosmic situation objectively and free from religious bias.

As we begin to awaken, we discover that there are some who know the truth but choose to keep it secret. They are our controllers.

...

Now, at the end of the first decade of the twenty-first century, more and more spiritually aware people are asking that burning question, and it is becoming increasingly urgent to find the answer.

But the controllers are heavily invested in keeping us from learning about our true nature. It is beginning to appear that this may be the reason we are not being told about the extraterrestrial presence on Earth.

If we were to be informed that we are now being visited by advanced aliens and that they have the ability to pull us out of our darkness and to shed light on our origins and our spiritual potential, then we would no longer settle for being gentle grazers in the meadow. We too would travel to the stars. It would be 'goodbye sheep, goodbye wool, goodbye mutton.'"

As more and more ET contactees and experiencers come out with their experiences and share the wisdom and knowledge they gained from it, along with more and more information becomes publicly available and shared, humanity is quickly beginning to wake up from its deep slumber and realize that we are not alone, and there is *way* more to reality than we've been programmed to believe.

Fortunately there have been many people in governments, militaries, and organizations around the world who have been brave enough to tell the world what they know, believe, and have experienced about UFOs and extraterrestrial life.

NASA Astronaut Edgar Mitchell

Edgar Mitchell was a United States Navy officer and aviator, test pilot, aeronautical engineer, ufologist, and NASA astronaut.

Edgar Mitchell has publicly stated that he is "90 percent sure that many of the thousands of unidentified flying objects, or UFOs, recorded since the 1940s, belong to visitors from other planets". For the past few decades, He has been a prominent figure speaking out about the existence of ETs, UFOs being of ET origin, and the reality of ETs being not only here on our planet, but have been assisting humanity.

This is a transcript from an interview he did with *Observer*:

> INTERVIEWER: I'd like to follow up on some of your previous comments regarding extraterrestrial life. Going back to the Roswell incident, many believe the crashing of an alien craft was covered up by the government—which supports your claim made in our previous interview. Is there anything that you know that differs from what the public is aware of?
>
> EM: Well I think it's out there in the public. Circumstances

were of course, that the Roswell incident was a post World War II event. We were doing nuclear testing over in the White Sands proving ground which was right across the mountain from Roswell and the Roswell AirField was a military base supporting that. So it seems that most likely what the aliens were interested in was the fact we had a weapons testing facility at the White Sands Proving Ground and were also interested in what we were doing or what the U.S. military was doing.

INTERVIEWER: What exactly were these crashed aliens doing there?

EM: They were observing our activities at the White Sands proving ground and were monitoring our development.

INTERVIEWER: A story went viral two weeks ago citing you as saying, "My own experience talking to people has made it clear the ETs had been attempting to keep us from going to war and help create peace on Earth." Can you elaborate?

EM: I don't remember speaking to them personally. I don't know where they got that information. I didn't make those statements. Somebody has added to my words. Those weren't my exact words but I don't necessarily disagree with those statements.

INTERVIEWER: But have you been told by individuals who worked at the White Sands nuclear testing facility that there was UFO activity?

EM: Yes I have.

INTERVIEWER: You grew up near the site of the Roswell incident. Did you ever see any UFOs?

EM: No, I have not personally, but I've spoken to individuals who were in the military and worked at the base at the time.

INTERVIEWER: You mentioned in a previous interview that the existence of extraterrestrials was being kept from the public because of the technology they can offer and that may affect the 'moneyed' interest. Who are these people that keep the information secret?

EM: Whoever sets the stage for military or government activity. We'll probably never know the exact reason for why they do what they do but those are the interpretations that seem common.

INTERVIEWER: Switching gears now, I recently interviewed a startup that you sit on the advisory board of, SpaceVR. Do you think their technology will assist consumers in experiencing a similar effect you had during Apollo 14?

EM: They could react to it that way. There's a long history in human civilization where people have these powerful effects and responses to different perspectives. My experience in space is what people call a samadhi experience. I think that back in time people were having these kinds of experiences and being overwhelmed by them. Seeing the big picture. That seems to go back in history. You'll find that those kinds of experiences have been around a long time.

INTERVIEWER: Samadhi—is that a term from Hinduism?

EM: I think that came out of the hindu tradition, yes. In the greek tradition it was metanoia—change of mind, change of heart. I believe in the Buddhist tradition Satori was enlightenment. In other words, these various traditions of the past have added the sub verbiage to these types of expressions of people's reactions to a new experience of some sort. A powerful experience that caused a change of thinking.

INTERVIEWER: Do you subscribe to any one religion?

EM: Let's put it this way, I think most of our religions are early attempts at cosmology. In other words, explaining ourselves. How did we get here? Where are we going? Where did all this come from? How did it happen? People from all times have asked these sorts of questions and they came up with their own answers throughout history. That's perfectly natural. All of our religious experiences are the same thing. Attempts to answer these ancient cosmological questions.

INTERVIEWER: You have been cited many times when discussing the future of quantum physics as a science that could link spirituality and consciousness to everyday science. Can you explain this?

EM: Well let's put it in context. Quantum physics didn't exist until the 20th century. It was the result of the work of Max Planck, Albert Einstein and the greats at the end of the 19th and into the 20th century. When quantum physics was formalized, we recognized the interactions between particles and that's when we started to explain it. The awareness of particles and their interactions down at that level of nature have not been studied or understood before. That's the quantum world as we understand it. We now know that particles interact. That they are aware of each other. We use that term that they are "aware" because they interact with each other. That was only quantified in the early 20th century. In the 1920s, quantum mechanics had a fairly good scientific organization and it's taken us all the 20th century to be able to explain that these particles can show consciousness and awareness.

I think we can have a science for it.

Here is an excerpt from an article in *The Mirror:*

"[Dr. Mitchell] told us military insiders had seen strange crafts flying over missile bases and the famous White Sands facility, where the world's first ever nuclear bomb was detonated in 1945.... "My own experience talking to people has made it clear the ETs had been attempting to keep us from going to war and help create peace on Earth." Mitchell also suggested he had heard similar stories from people who manned missile bases during the most tense parts of the twentieth century. "I have spoken to many Air Force officers who worked at these silos during the Cold War," he continued. "They told me UFOs were frequently seen overhead and often disabled their missiles. Other officers from bases on the Pacific coast told me their [test] missiles were frequently shot down by alien spacecraft."

Dr. Brian O'Leary - NASA astronaut and former Princeton Physics Professor

"There is much evidence that we have been contacted by aliens, and that these civilizations have been visiting us for a very long time, their appearance may be bizarre from any traditional Western materialistic point of view. These visitors use consciousness-influencing technologies – the toroid and use co-rotating magnetic disks for their propulsion systems, which appear to be the common denominator of the UFO phenomenon."
— Dr. Brian O'Leary

Paul Hellyer - Former Minister of National Defence of Canada

Paul Hellyer (August 6, 1923 – August 8, 2021) was a Canadian Defence Minister who was very outspoken about what he knew about extraterrestrials.

In 2007, the Ottawa Citizen reported that Hellyer was demanding that world governments disclose alien technology that could be used to solve many of our problems on the planet. In a 2014 interview with RT, he said that for thousands of years there have been at least four species of aliens visiting Earth, most of them coming from other star systems, although there are some living on Venus, Mars and Saturn's moon.

"From time to time, aliens have interfered with the control systems of nuclear missile launchers on Earth. The aliens conducted an 'inventory' of Earth's events. They have a complete picture of what is happening on the planet. And believe me, they are not amused by what they see. I think they look at us and think the kids are playing with matches."
— Paul Hellyer

The Disclosure Project – National Press Club 2001 Public Hearing

On May 9, 2001, at the National Press Club in Washington DC, Steven Greer assembled more than 20 military, intelligence, government, corporate and scientific witnesses for a public press conference to disclose the reality of UFOs or extraterrestrial vehicles, extraterrestrial life forms, and resulting advanced energy and propulsion technologies. This was and still is to this day, the single largest public disclosure testimonial event ever to have occurred. It was the highest viewed broadcast, and still is to this day, from the National Press Club.

Mikhail Gorbachev, Former President Of The Soviet Union

Gorbachev stated: "The phenomenon of UFOs does exist, and it must be treated seriously."

Haim Eshed, Former Israeli Space Security Chief

In 2020, Former Israeli space security chief Haim Eshed said that governments on Earth have been in contact with extraterrestrials from a "galactic federation."

"The Unidentified Flying Objects have asked not to publish that they are here, humanity is not ready yet."

"There is an agreement between the U.S. government and the aliens. They signed a contract with us to do experiments here," he said.

Eshed also said that President Donald Trump was aware of their existence and was "on the verge of revealing" this information but was asked to not speak about it as to prevent "mass hysteria."

Eshed said "They have been waiting until today for humanity to develop and reach a stage where we will understand, in general, what space and spaceships are."

Buzz Aldrin, Former Apollo 11 Astronaut

On C-SPAN in 2009, Buzz Aldrin stated that there is a monolith on Phobos, a moon of Mars:

"We should go boldly where man has not gone before. Fly by the comets. Visit asteroids. Visit the moon of Mars. There's a monolith there. A very unusual structure on this little potato-shaped object that goes around Mars once in seven hours. When people find out about that they're gonna say 'Who put that there?! Who put that there?!' Well...the universe put it there. If you choose, God put it there."

Avi Loeb, Israeli-American astrophysicist / Harvard professor

Avi Loeb, an astrophysicist and Harvard professor, has been vocal about his theories regarding the interstellar object 'Oumuamua. He proposed the controversial hypothesis that 'Oumuamua could be an artificial object of extraterrestrial origin. He suggests that its unusual properties, such as its elongated shape and unexpected acceleration, could be indicative of technological characteristics.

'Oumuamua is the first confirmed interstellar object to visit our solar system (according to NASA). It's a rocky, cigar-shaped reddish object. It was discovered from a Hawaiian observatory and received the name 'Oumuamua, which means "a messenger from afar arriving first' in Hawaiian.

Avi Loeb has written a book titled "Extraterrestrial: The First Sign of Intelligent Life Beyond Earth," in which he discusses his theory about 'Oumuamua being of artificial origin. He has also published scientific papers exploring the subject and calling for further investigation into the nature of interstellar objects.

John Mack, Pulitzer Prize-winning Harvard psychiatrist

John E. Mack, MD was a highly respected psychiatrist and researcher known for his work in the field of alien abduction experiences and extraterrestrial encounters. He served as the head of the department of psychiatry at Harvard Medical School from 1977 to 2004, and won a Pulitzer Prize in 1977 for his book *A Prince of Our Disorder*.

In the 1990s, John Mack gained international attention for his research into alien abduction experiences. He conducted interviews with people who claimed to have been abducted by extraterrestrial beings, seeking to understand the psychological and existential implications of their experiences.

He published several books on the topic of alien abductions, including *Abduction: Human Encounters with Aliens* (1994) and *Passport to the Cosmos: Human Transformation and Alien Encounters* (1999). In his books, Mack explored themes such as trauma, consciousness, and the spiritual dimensions of alien encounters.

Despite being heavily criticized and attacked from the mainstream scientific and academic communities, he remained committed to his investigation of the alien abduction phenomenon and continued to advocate for a more open-minded and compassionate approach to understanding these experiences.

David Grusch, United States Air Force officer and former intelligence official

Excerpt from an interview Grusch did with NewsNation:

'He told NewsNation he was entrusted with some of the country's most intimate secrets.

The most earth-shattering of those secrets, he claims, were revealed after 2019, when he was invited to join the UAP task force.

"I have, based on my full security clearance and multiple polygraphs (lie detector tests), had the ability to be read into any program that I needed," he said. "At one point in time, I was extremely highly cleared."

During that time, Grusch claims the UAP Task Force was refused access to a broad crash retrieval program.

"These are retrieving non-human origin technical vehicles, call it space-craft if you will. Non-human exotic origin vehicles that have either landed or crashed," he said.

Grusch told NewsNation that the U.S. is in possession of "quite a number" of these "non-human" vehicles.

He says he didn't believe it at first.

"I thought it was totally nuts and I thought at first I was being deceived. People started to confide in me ... approaching me. I had plenty of senior, former intelligence officers that came to me, many of which I knew almost my whole career, that confided in me that they were part of a program," he said. "They named the program ... I'd never heard of it. They told me, based on their oral testimony, and they provided me documents and other proof, that there was in fact a program that the UAP Task Force was not read into."

Grusch, however, is hesitant to use the term "alien life."

"I couch it as somebody who has studied physics, where you know, maybe they're coming from a different physical dimension as described in quantum mechanics. We know there are extra dimensions due to high-energy particle collisions, etc., and there's a theoretical framework to explain that," he said.

In other words, Grusch believes humans are not alone. He says there is "potentially extraterrestrial life" out there.

He's never personally seen non-human intelligence but says he's spoken to enough people directly involved in what he calls "the program," that he's convinced it's real.'

Richard C. Hoagland - Author, former NASA consultant, and former Science Advisor to Walter Cronkite and CBS News

Richard C. Hoagland gained attention in the 1970s when he worked as a science advisor to CBS News during their coverage of the Apollo moon missions. He later became known for his discoveries of anomalous structures on Mars, particularly the "Face on Mars" and other features in the Cydonia region. Hoagland suggested that these structures could be evidence of ancient extraterrestrial civilizations or advanced technology.

Hoagland has claimed that NASA and other space agencies are withholding information about advanced technology, ancient artifacts on other planets, and potential evidence of extraterrestrial life.

He has authored several books, including "The Monuments of Mars: A City on the Edge of Forever," which explores the structures on Mars.

Command Sergeant Major Robert Dean

Robert O. Dean, often referred to as Bob Dean, was a retired Command Sergeant Major in the United States Army who became notable for his claims about extraterrestrial life and government cover-ups regarding UFOs. Dean gained attention in the UFO community after publicly disclosing his experiences and knowledge regarding alleged classified documents and encounters with extraterrestrial beings.

Dean became widely known for his assertions regarding UFOs and extraterrestrial life after he retired from the military. He claimed to have been exposed to classified documents during his time at the Supreme Headquarters Allied Powers Europe (SHAPE) in France during the 1960s, which allegedly detailed UFO sightings and the existence of extraterrestrial civilizations.

One of Dean's most notable claims was his assertion that he saw a classified NATO document known as the "Assessment," which purportedly outlined the reality of extraterrestrial visitation to Earth and the presence of multiple alien species. According to Dean, this document and others he claimed to have seen provided evidence of a government cover-up of UFO information.

Dean said that the ET and UFO subject goes beyond simply their visitation and potential integration into our society. He talked about the existence of portals through which inter-dimensional beings can travel through multiple realities, and said they represent the most advanced civilizations among alien societies. Dean said that these beings may have been seen as gods in ancient times, citing the existence of ancient ruins that defy conventional explanation. He talked about the "godlike technology" that would've been required to construct these ruins and said that the United States government now has access to these capabilities.

While he was sympathetic to the government's nondisclosure policies to a point, Dean said that the only way for humanity to wake up to the truth, move forward, and grow is through Full Disclosure. He communicated that we should not be waiting for anyone to tell us what is or isn't true. It is up to us to BE the disclosure.

CHAPTER 20

Disclosure through Media

Disclosure of Extraterrestrial life, secret programs, secret advanced technology, and hidden truths are replete throughout media and entertainment. Particularly in movies and TV shows, and especially anything in the so-called science "fiction" genre.

Star Wars

Many people claim that Star Wars is actually a portrayal of the ancient "Orion Wars" that happened millions of years ago in our own Milky Way galaxy. Many of the beings shown in Star Wars have been reported by both ET experiencers and insiders as being real, as well as other aspects such as the Force, the Jedi, the Death Star, the Empire, and various types of ships. Many insiders and researchers claim, and there is evidence to suggest that George Lucas was actually given the information for Star Wars and was sworn to secrecy. In *The Ascension Mysteries*, David Wilcock writes:

'I was told by several people in the know that George Lucas was approached, given certain pieces of information, and sworn to secrecy on pain of torture and death, as usual. In this case, the insiders were hoping to fill in more of the details than what we received from Arthur C. Clarke's 2001. When Star Wars opens up with "A long time ago in a galaxy far, far away," only the first half of that sentence is true. The history we are seeing in Star Wars is our own. Two different insiders even confirmed that the Ancient Builder Race, or some other group after them, built robotic androids that look extremely similar to the gold-colored metallic droid C-3PO. There are countless numbers of these robots that have been found on and inside moons in a deactivated, nonfunctional state.

As I was finalizing this book, I asked Corey if the secret space program had explored neighboring star systems and looked for artifacts. Much to my astonishment, he revealed that transparent aluminum Ancient Builder Race artifacts are found on planets and moons throughout our entire Local Cluster. This includes massive, Death Star–type moons. This created a unified protection grid for all intelligent civilizations living in the Local Cluster. We were free to peacefully explore, meet our neighbors, and be protected from any outside conquerors. Our own warlike human nature screwed it all up and knocked the grid down.'

Star Trek

There is much evidence to suggest that Gene Roddenberry based Star Trek off of true information. Many insiders and researchers have pointed out that Star Trek is disclosing the U.S. Navy's Secret Space Program, known as Solar Warden.

In a book called "The Only Planet of Choice: Essential Briefings from Deep Space," it's claimed that beings known as "the Nine" were channeled through Phyllis Schlemmer, as a part of the work done by The Roundtable Foundation. These entities claimed to be the nine principles of the Universe, and that they've been watching over and guiding humanity since our beginning.

Gene Roddenberry actually attended and participated in many of these sessions, and was influenced by it to create the Star Trek series. Scholar, author, and mystic J.J. Hurtak, who was also a part of this group, talked about his experience with Roddenberry:

> "Of all of the famous guests, Gene Roddenberry was one of the most gifted and was a part of our team. Taking notes and scoring information that he felt would eventually be used worldwide. What is exciting is some of what Gene saw there in our work together was produced in some of the episodes of Star Trek."

These sessions are where Roddenberry heard about the "Prime Directive," which became an idea used in the Star Trek series. The Prime Directive is a guiding principle of extraterrestrial civilizations which dictates that they cannot interfere with the internal development of a civilization, especially any less advanced civilization.

In an interview on Jock Doubleday's show "Transition to New Terra," Ken Rohla reveals that he actually met and spent time with Phyllis Schlemmer, who gave him inside information about Gene Roddenberry and the real story behind the makings of Star Trek:

> 'Years ago, I met a lady named Phyllis Schlemmer...And turns out she lived about a half hour north of me, and so I got to know her a little bit. And it turns out, back in the 60s, she lived with Gene Roddenberry and his wife Majel Barrett. They were roommates in Los Angeles. Phyllis was channeling all of this ET stuff from this group that she called "The Council of Nine." With her permission, Roddenberry was taking the channelings and turning them

into Star Trek scripts. So one of the reasons I think that Star Trek resonated with so many people, and especially starseeds, is because that information was coming from some kind of a channeled, probably extraterrestrial source. And Phyllis Schlemmer had a bunch of physical ET contact also, and she had worked with a lot of really interesting people in the government.

Years after Roddenberry died, Majel Barrett, who played counselor Troi's mother in The Next Generation...still had all these recordings of Phyllis Schlemmer's channelings from the 60s. And she wound up taking that and turning it into Deep Space Nine. Which is pretty mind blowing, the reason that it's named Deep Space Nine, and there were nine prophets in this wormhole, is because of Phyllis Schlemmer's Council of Nine. And in Phyllis' channelings the Council of Nine were, what they called "Keepers of the Time" or they were some kind of really advanced extraterrestrials who were non-corporeal and they kind of managed time so that Time Jumpers couldn't just come in and screw with Earth all the time.

There's also stories that Roddenberry was going out into the desert and having ET contact in Southern California. And Leonard Nemoy who wrote the book "I Am Not Spock," in that book he said that there were people several times that came to the Desilu Studios--apparently back then I guess they had open sets where people could just come up--So this group from Roswell, New Mexico came and told Nemoy that they had encountered extraterrestrials, and those extraterrestrials told them that they were giving Nemoy information in the dream state on how to portray the Spock character so that humans would have a positive attitude toward extraterrestrials. So there was a lot of stuff going on with Star Trek and other Science Fiction like that behind the scenes I'm sure.'

Stargate and Stargate SG-1

Many insiders have said that the movie *Stargate*, and its continuation in the show *Stargate SG-1*, are actual disclosures of real programs that have been in operation for a long time.

The premise of Stargate and Stargate SG-1, is that a stargate that was found in Egypt in the 1920s is taken and kept secret by the U.S. military. They eventually figure out how to activate the stargate, and use it to travel to distant planets and civilizations and carry out missions. The team, called SG-1, encounters various alien species, both friendly and hostile, and they work to protect Earth from the threat of negative and hostile beings while simultaneously uncovering the secrets of the universe. Stargate SG-1 also discloses the reality of "ascension" and higher dimensional beings.

Stargates and portals are used by civilizations throughout the universe. Some portals are naturally occurring at certain times and at certain places on the planet. Some of them are artificially made using technology. Some beings are evolved enough to create portals with their own consciousness, and some can actually travel and teleport instantaneously with thought.

Multiple insiders have spoken about an ancient stargate system that exists throughout the universe, and that our planet has two of these ancient stargates. This ancient stargate system utilizes the "cosmic web," which is a web of plasma filaments that exists throughout the galaxy and the universe. These are able to be used as wormholes to travel the cosmos. An extremely ancient race of beings apparently built this ancient stargate system, and all planets with intelligent life have one of these stargates. In his book *The Ascension Mysteries*, David Wilcock talks about what an insider who went by the pseudonym "Daniel" told him:

> 'Daniel also fascinated me by revealing that the television show Stargate SG-1 was chock-full of truthful information he had encountered at his job. There is indeed an ancient stargate network that allows travel from place to place through the "cosmic web," as it has been called. A series of plasma filaments connects each star to its neighbors, and these filaments also serve as traversable wormholes. Proof of these filaments was deliberately presented in The Source Field Investigations after I had heard all this.
>
> A very ancient and highly advanced extraterrestrial race that Daniel called "the Elders" had apparently built this stargate network. Other groups continually maintained it. I was told that each planet with intelligent life is given its own stargate. The network is intended to allow for peaceful exploration and communication with a wide variety of worlds, which is a natural part of the ascension process.'

Insiders have said that the Internet Protocol address (IP address) was actually created based on this stargate network. Each planet has its own address, which reads exactly like an IP address. "Daniel" revealed that the Earth's gate address is

7.5.3.84.70.24.606. The last three digits deal with planets in our local solar system. The three digit number for Mars is 605.

'Our local gate address of 1 is an inhabited asteroid that orbits a pulsar. This unique energetic configuration has made it very stable over long periods of time. The people who live there have visited Earth for thousands of years, and introduced themselves to the Vikings as the Aesir or Asgard. The term Asgard was later misinterpreted by early 1950s telepathic channelers as "Ashtar," and the Aesir became known as the "Ashtar Command." The Aesirian "god" Thor had a devastating "hammer" that was actually a particle-beam weapon, and the mystical land of Valhalla was actually the Aesir homeworld'
— David Wilcock, *The Ascension Mysteries*

CHAPTER 21

*Extraterrestrial Intervention
and the Great Shift*

*"As we approach the Golden Age, the veils shall be
removed and the people of the Earth shall become
aware of the people of the Universe."*
— Edgar Cayce

There are a wide variety of ETs that have been on our planet, or have been visiting our planet for a very long time. If any one race of beings wanted to take us out or overtly take us over, it would've happened a long time ago. The more positive and benevolent ETs operate with a "Prime Directive." The more malevolent or "service-to-self" beings often seem to prefer to take over civilizations through shadowy manipulation and coercion. They keep the general population completely ignorant to their presence while keeping them suppressed and enslaved, often using them as food, resources and slave labor. They seem to only be able to get away with so much though, as there are federations and councils of ETs that oversee and manage different regions of space, and will intervene if a hostile species violates cosmic law or is a threat to other civilizations. The malevolent beings on Earth have seemed to sneak past this by making dishonest agreements with governments, and through covert manipulation and influence of key people in positions of power. This has been their game on Earth for thousands of years, potentially going back into the times of Atlantis.

I've already spoken about the negative or "service-to-self" ET manipulation of humanity, but there are also many more benevolent or "service-to-others" oriented ETs who have been helping, guiding, and protecting planet Earth and humanity for thousands of years. Especially in the last century, the ETs have been working to help humanity awaken from its deep sleep, and to the fact that it's not just us here. For a long time they've been guiding and helping humanity, and have been assisting in the raising of our consciousness.

In Dolores Cannon's book *Keepers of the Garden*, she recounts the experiences of a client named Phil, who undergoes past life regression sessions with her. Through these sessions, Phil reveals memories of his interactions with extraterrestrial beings and his role as a "Keeper of the Garden."

Phil was a being from another planet who volunteered to incarnate on Earth to assist humanity during a crucial period of transition and awakening. He describes his experiences of being part of a group of beings who monitor and guide human evolution from behind the scenes, acting as custodians or "Keepers" of Earth's development.

He talks about other planets that are much different than Earth, including one containing a fourth-dimensional city with beings who are pure energy. Phil constantly reverts to a scene where he sees three spires, which causes him to become emotional because he knows this place is his true home.

Information is revealed through Phil on the topics of the origins of human life, the existence of extraterrestrial civilizations, and the interconnectedness of all beings in the universe. Information is imparted on the concepts of higher consciousness, spiritual growth, and the purpose of existence from a cosmic perspective.

Right now the planet is at the end of a cycle. Many people actually say we're at the end of multiple cycles which are all converging right now. Many have termed this as the "Ascension," or "The Shift." The vibration and frequency of the planet is currently rising and there is an "awakening" happening with much of humanity. Right now the overall level of consciousness in humanity is rising and shifting.

The controllers have been well aware of this Shift for a long time. They are absolutely *terrified* of humanity waking up to who we really are and tapping into our true potential. So they have been doing everything they can to stop, or at least slow down humanity's awakening and raising of our consciousness. Jason Quitt talks about this in an interview:

> "I think they're much more aware than what we think they know, and because of that they're 10 steps ahead and they foresaw this for a very long time. I would say probably since the first World War they knew about this time, and they took a lot of steps to kind of contain the situation if you know what I mean. Different educational things, propaganda programming, television programming, what's being taught in the educational system, what's being taught in religions... It's almost like that part of us, that Awakening part of us, is so dangerous to the establishment that it's almost like they're trying to stamp it out with different programs. I would even say pharmaceuticals or different toxins that are being put in our air and our food. It's changing us at a very deep level which is making it very difficult for us to transition because you know...I'll give you a definition for awakening or transitioning. Awakening is: you have to deal with your stuff. That's what Awakening is. You're holding on to all these things and you need a strong spiritual,

mental, emotional or energetic spiritual body to process this information because that's what it is. It's processing. So you have things within you and around you or even multi-dimensionally that need to be processed. And if your body and mind and emotions are plagued with toxins, work, fear, basically all those systems shut down and then you stop processing. So if we say okay I'm going to heal now, that means healing is: I'm now taking responsibility for the energy I carry and I'm going to process it."
From: Ep. 580 FADE to BLACK w/ Jimmy Church

The Awakening and the Shift are inevitable. It's happening whether they like it or not. All they can really do is delay it slightly, but they can only do that so much. They absolutely *cannot* stop it. *Nothing* can stop it. That won't stop them from trying though and throwing everything they can at us in order to keep us suppressed, asleep and in a state of fear.

"The only war going on on this planet is a war against the expansion of consciousness, and every other thing that we see is a symptom of that."
— Niara Isley

Fortunately, we have much help and support through guides, higher dimensional beings, and our ET star families. There are many extraterrestrials that are here right now to ensure that both humanity and the Earth make it through this shift safely and smoothly.

ET contactee Barry Littleton talks about his knowledge of this in the documentary *The Cosmic Secret*:

"I believe what is happening on the planet right now is a shift in consciousness. I've heard it called other things such as Ascension, we're going to go to another dimension. I've heard all these things, but I think in reality it's a shift of consciousness. Because at least in my opinion, 85 to 90 percent of our population has had extreme contact but they can't remember it. They're unaware of it due to the fact our perception is so molded...And like I said it was the indoctrination of religion that kind of stopped that to a degree. But right now I think that the fact that certain people are coming forward and taking a few darts is making it more accessible to others, and others more comfortable about it. I believe they are reaching out because they're wanting right now to help us with this shift in consciousness. And what has been shown to me is Humanity does have a type of free will, but we're not going to be allowed to destroy the Earth anymore."

Intervention with Nuclear Missiles

"The extraterrestrials' directive to the inhabitants of planet Earth was not to use nuclear weapons in space. They essentially told the U.S. and the Russians that they would not put up with it. However, much later, in 1995, France tested its own nuclear weapons in the South Pacific near Tahiti and blew a hole in the Earth's mantle. In their ignorance, they precipitated profound changes in the world climate and created a hole in the ozone layer over the Antarctic. The extraterrestrials apparently know how humans think and had thus warned us years earlier so we would avoid such unintended consequences.

The extraterrestrials finally convinced the U.S. to stop using nuclear weapons in space, but where do you think our spare nuclear weapons went? The U.S. and Russia parked them in space as a first line of defense! Those nuclear weapons are still up there today. World leaders wonder why the extraterrestrials come here and what they want; they are suspicious of their motives. In the face of those fears,

our response has been to weaponize space. Military minds figured that if the extraterrestrials became aggressive, the military would blow them up, but the ETs have proven that they can render our weapons harmless."
— Daniel Salter, *Life with a Cosmos Clearance*

It appears that when we started setting off nuclear explosions, it alerted ETs throughout the galaxy, and the ones that were already here, that humans were playing with dangerous toys that were not only an extreme threat to ourselves and the planet we live on, but to many other beings and civilizations as well.

When a nuclear explosion happens, it doesn't just affect our planet and the third dimension. It also affects other dimensions and the beings and civilizations in those dimensions. It sends a pulse through the cosmic web that affects life outside of our planet. For the past almost 80 years, ETs have been disarming nuclear missile sites and disabling nuclear missiles. They understand the importance of our planet and of our own species more than most of humanity currently does, and they are not going to allow us to blow ourselves up, nor destroy the planet we live on.

They have made that abundantly clear. It will not be allowed. Period.

There have been many documented cases of nuclear missile systems being shut down, which all clearly indicate ET and UFO involvement. The most famous of these being the Malmstrom Air Force Base incident. Ex-US Air Force Captain Robert Salas testified that in 1967, a UFO completely shut down the weapons system at Malmstrom Air Force Base in Montana, the nuclear missile base he was working on at the time. The incident was covered up and concealed from the public.

Salas says that despite a significant portion of the US nuclear arsenal potentially being compromised, they didn't conduct an investigation. He said that he, and everyone working the base during the incident, were forced to sign NDA documents that swore them to secrecy.

Dolores Cannon was made aware of the ET intervention with nuclear bombs through many of her hypnosis sessions:

"These higher beings continued to observe our evolution from afar, but something happened in 1945 that really caught their attention: the explosion of the atomic bomb at the end of World War II. We were not supposed to have atomic power at that stage in our evolution. They knew we would not be able to control it, that we would use it for destruction.

When atomic power was supposed to be introduced into our timeline, it was intended to be used for good. I said that we were using it for good, electricity and such as that. They explained that because it was first created as a weapon it would always carry that negative aura, and never have the great benefit it was supposed to have. We had just come through the horrible World War II, so they knew we would never be able to control something as powerful as atomic power. It was just human nature, and they were extremely worried that this could lead to destruction.

...

They were told that they could conceivably ignite all of the hydrogen atoms in the atmosphere and cause a massive explosion that could destroy our world. But the scientists ignored this advice and their curiosity kept them experimenting.

...

It was during this time, at the end of the 1940s and beginning of the 1950s, that UFO sightings began to be publicized. The higher beings went back to the Council and asked what to do since they are not allowed to interfere with mankind's free will. That is when the Council came up with what I think is a brilliant plan. They said, 'We cannot interfere from the outside, but what about if we help from the inside?' It is not interfering when you ask for volunteers to come in and help. This is how the call was given throughout the universe for souls to come to help the Earth."

Starseeds

Many ET races and higher dimensional beings have been helping and guiding humanity in the ways that they could for a long time. We are currently in the time of a great ending to a cycle, or multiple cycles, and of a massive Shift on our planet, and because of the great suppression and manipulation, humanity was mostly sound asleep. We needed a lot of help waking up, raising our consciousness, anchoring the energies coming into the planet, and making it through this great Shift. They are also helping to protect the Earth during this time, as the planet itself, often referred to as Gaia or Terra, is a living conscious being and is ascending right now. If we're going to go with the planet, we have to be at a high enough frequency to match the planet's frequency. Those who are not at a high enough frequency will be going elsewhere.

Dolores Cannon often talked about "Starseeds," or extraterrestrial or higher dimensional beings (more advanced souls), coming to Earth at this time to incarnate as human beings in order to help both humanity and the planet in this great time of need. Much information would come through her sessions about her clients being a "Starseed" who incarnated on Earth at this time because they heard "the call" and wanted to help the planet and be a part of this great Shift.

> "You have lived on other planets and in other dimensions. You have done many, many things you cannot even imagine. Many of the people I have worked with in the last few years have regressed to lifetimes where they were light beings living in a state of bliss. They had no reason to come into the Earth's density and negativity. They volunteered to come to help mankind and the Earth at this time. I have encountered what I consider to be three waves of these new souls who are living on Earth. They have come at this time because most of those people who have been here for lifetime after lifetime have become bogged down in karma and are not advancing. They have lost sight of their purpose of living on the Earth."
> — Dolores Cannon, *The Three Waves of Volunteers and the New Earth*

The controllers know about the Starseeds, and they are not allowed to just kill or take them out, but they are doing everything in their power to thwart their effectiveness and to keep humanity from waking up and rising in consciousness. They know how powerful humanity really is, and they are terrified of us waking up and tapping into our true power and potential. Once a certain threshold of awakening happens on the planet it's Game Over for the controllers and their slave system. The Starseeds are essentially the "ground crew" of extraterrestrial help at this time on the planet.

During a Michael Salla interview, Alex Collier summed it up well:

> "It doesn't matter how many we are. If we have no idea who we are, we're going to be controllable. We're going to be slaves. But if you know who you are, even a small group of people who know who they are are a force to reckon with. But when you have a population of billions and they

know who they are, we can change and do anything, with a vision, with clear goals of what it is that we want. They wanted to make sure we never got there. And if it weren't for the fact that we had all these amazing soul groups coming in here from different dimensions wanting to attach to this royal physicality and seeing the potential of shifting and changing the frequency of our galaxy, I don't know what would have happened to us. But thank God they did, we did. We saw the potential and the possibility of making this type of change and then this is where we are. This is the piece of information that's coming to humanity."

"We are in the middle of the greatest shift that humanity has ever witnessed. You are not here by accident. You are here by design."
— Kryon

"As we approach the Golden Age, the veils shall be removed and the people of the Earth shall become aware of the people of the Universe."
— Edgar Cayce

There is a massive Shift happening on the planet right now, where the old energy and systems are on their way out, and the new energy and consciousness is rising on the planet. Much came through the hypnosis sessions of Dolores Cannon about this. It was always described as a "split" between the "Old Earth" and the "New Earth." The planet is moving into a higher frequency and vibration. We will only be able to stay on the planet if we are a match to that frequency.

ET contactee Sherry Wilde was told many times about this Shift from her Star Family:

"They taught me how to be a light reader. And I thought,

'Why would they teach me to be a light reader?' That is to read the vibration of people. Because they told me that the Earth was going to be going through some changes, and that Gaia was going to be moving into the higher vibrations, the higher frequencies. And only those on her who resonated with that frequency would be going with her. Those who did not would be taken to another planet, another three dimensional planet to continue on their journey. And he said there's no judgement in this Sherry. All will get there eventually. There's no judgement. They talked about the Creator all the time. They taught me the three important things to know, the number one of which is: We are all One with our Creator. There are times when I would sense that he was somewhat frustrated with humanity that we couldn't just *get that*. That we are all One with our Creator."
— Sherry Wilde, from her presentation at the 2014 Ozark Mountain Transformation Conference

Teri Wade beautifully describes in a Facebook post what is happening on the planet right now and what the Ascension/Shift really is:

"Many people are attempting to describe Ascension as in the Mayan calendar, the 2012 timeline, a quantum leap etc. What Ascension means is there are mechanics behind creation of which consciousness moves and evolves through dimensional space. Meaning, evolution progresses through the rising of frequency which brings forth a higher reality which consists of higher awareness, knowledge, wisdom, insight etc. We are transitioning into a broader spectrum of reality which is brought on by experience. We evolve through experience. We are skipping through time which is a change in the focus of our consciousness, an elevation of our awareness. This is why many of you are currently experiencing this Ascension process. It's no coincidence this is happening to so many people. We're experiencing a timeline split.

The ones who have chosen the Ascension timeline are still the minority but we are growing more and more everyday. Every one of us are experiencing and doing this process at our own pace which was planned out before this incarnation. For those of you who are waking up to this Ascension process are transitioning due to DNA activation. You are having non-human memory brought forward into your human experience. We are here to lay the groundwork into this new reality. You need to ask yourself why are you resonating to this particular material and so many around you have no interest? Well, it's quite simple. It's all about where you're at in frequency. You are an energetic leader in this particular process. Ascension is the spiritual science behind consciousness. Again, there are mechanics behind creation. We are becoming more aware of how this framework works.

At the beginning of this Ascension process many people go through what they call the 'Dark night of the Soul' which is the dismantling of your 3D identity. It can be tough for many. Some will fragment and some skate right through it. When you realize there's a reason for this happening to you it makes it much easier and the dots begin to connect. What's happening is you're being downloaded with tremendous amounts of data and information and it will take time for our human minds to comprehend it all. Down here in these lower, denser realms we experience a lag and that's what makes it tough. We are going through a consciousness revolution. We are reaching levels of consciousness integration that this human form currently cannot even imagine, let alone comprehend. We are in a learn-as-you-go period. As I see it there are two levels of Awake so to speak that's going on.

There are those that are awakening to the horrors on our planet, meaning the elite pedophile network, the satanic ritual abuse that goes on with the children, the negative off-world, anti-life presence that's been ruling our existence for thousands of years, etc. Then there are those that are Awake that see beyond that in the way of levels of dimensional frequency, the levels of consciousness awareness which is bringing in this higher reality of insight, knowledge and wisdom etc. This higher knowledge is in each and every one of us. We just need to get past the mental limitations and programming that keeps us suppressed. We are going through the un-layering process. We are preparing ourselves to embody this higher frequency which is like being plugged into voltage that our minds can't even comprehend. We need to understand that our bodies are transitioning from a carbon-based to a crystalline-based embodiment.

We're transforming to a less dense state of matter. If we didn't do this by slow process our physical bodies would combust. We would burn out our Central Nervous System etc. Remember, Ascension has never happened before to a being in such a physical, dense state. Our goal as the human being is 'Biological Ascension.' This is why we are the greatest show on Earth or the Universe for that matter. We are literally drawing in a higher intelligence. You must surrender to this process. It's like opening the floodgates to get access to this higher intelligence. This is what's happening to many of you. Like I've said many times the people that are fighting this, the resistors, are just making it harder on themselves. Because, eventually it's going to happen to everybody no doubt about it. There's no other option.

We are all Galactically based and we all have different

roles in this Ascension process. But, generally those who are currently interested in this particular information are being recruited for leadership, are part of the planetary grid work which means particular people are being sent to different locations on Earth to transmit their codes. I'm an example of being transferred to a different location. I grew up in Minnesota most of my life, never went to church nor believed in what the church taught. I found myself moving to North Carolina 10 years ago coincidentally experiencing an incredible spontaneous awakening as I call it (My grocery store incident) in the middle of the Bible belt! Meaning, there is no coincidence.

We need to understand that the physical body is the Holy Grail. Many in the spiritual field concentrate on spirituality of the mind and higher realms but we need to understand what our biological structure is going through and it's extremely monumental and profound. Biological Ascension is the resurrection, so to speak, dissolving the anti-life force of this 3D structure. Our bodies have been born into an anti-life force which is the third dimensional structure that unfortunately has genetically altered our physical form. We are being ushered into unknown territory physically, spiritually and mentally. It is absolutely amazing what is happening to the human being. We are being monitored, communicated with and contacted. This is why we're seeing an incredible amount of Galactic activity going on above our heads. Earth is going through a monumental transformation and we all feel like we're traveling blindly through space trying to figure it all out. But, remember every one of us are exactly where we're supposed to be so be easy on yourselves."

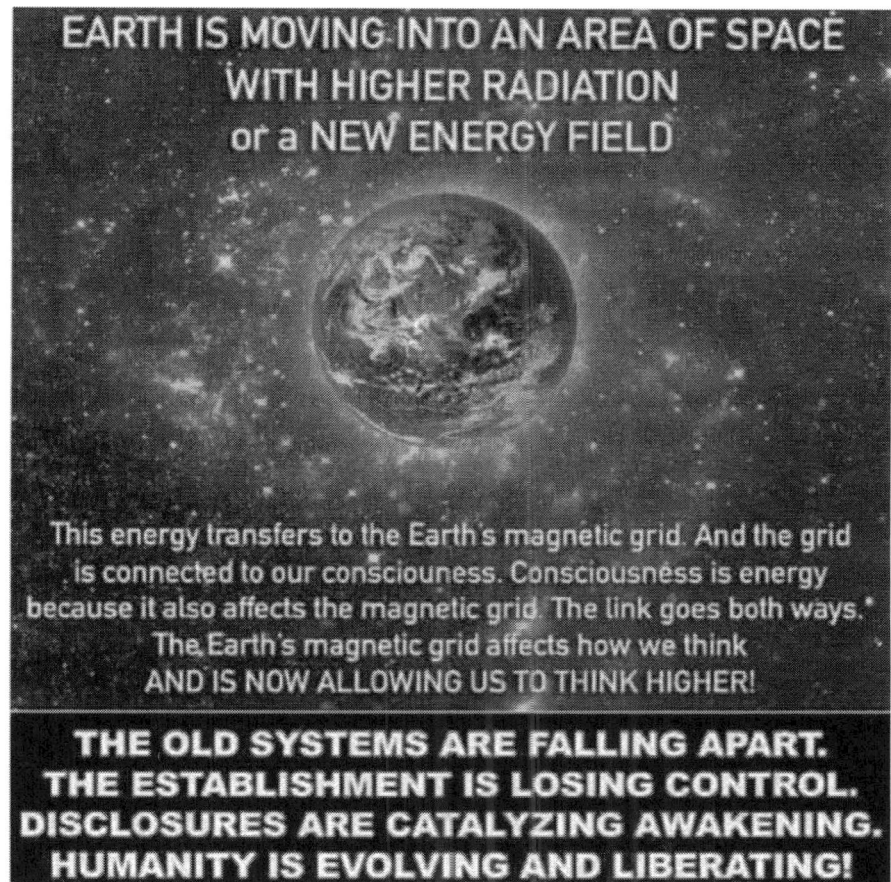

CHAPTER 22

*Contact with Extraterrestrials
and Non-Human Intelligence*

Many people claim that there are no extraterrestrials. Many say they believe extraterrestrial life likely does exist throughout the universe, but there is "no evidence" that they've ever been to our planet or interacted with humanity. This is of course with an extremely narrow and skewed belief about what constitutes evidence or proof.

SETI (Search for Extraterrestrial Intelligence) is a research institute that is supposedly searching for extraterrestrial life by trying to detect radio signals and frequencies. The consciousness of materialist reductionist scientism believes that the best way to search for extraterrestrial life is by searching for...radio signals. They are coming at it from an extremely narrow and limited programmed perspective, and with that they'll never find what they're looking for. Your level of consciousness dictates what kind of contact you have, or if you have contact at all. So there are well intentioned people coming at this from a very narrow and programmed mindset, and truly believing that "there is no evidence." Meanwhile *mountains* of evidence have been sitting right here the entire time. Anyone can simply go to any one of the many different UFO hot-spots on the planet and see the ships for themselves. They can do a CE5 and make contact themselves. They can do some actual research and investigation and find out that ETs have *always* been here. People have been being contacted by them for thousands of years, and many are in contact with them today.

When you investigate and research the voluminous information out there concerning ET life and contact with humanity, listen to the experiences of actual ET contactees, and even have your own ET contact, it becomes *abundantly* clear that (in the line from Ancient Aliens) "We are not alone. We've never been alone."

Just as there are different levels of consciousness and spiritual maturity throughout humans on Earth, the universe consists of many different types of beings with various levels of consciousness and spiritual and technological advancement. Also, these beings seem to reside in various different dimensions or densities, beyond just the third dimension that we exist in.

There are three general categories of consciousness that ETs can be classified: Service-to-self / malevolent, Neutral, and Service-to-others / benevolent. All three of these categories of extraterrestrials have lived on (or in) or have been visiting Earth throughout the planet's history. Many of the more benevolent or service-to-others oriented ETs have been guiding humanity in raising its consciousness and spiritual maturity, and protecting humanity for thousands of years. Many of these ET races have seeded their genetics in humanity and are therefore our cosmic Star Family.

Throughout time, these beings have communicated the same themes and messages to humanity and to the people they've been in contact with. These general messages are as follows:

1. They have great love for us, are connected to us, and do not wish for us to destroy ourselves or the planet

we live on. They are attempting to help us awaken, raise our consciousness, and thrive.

2. Our technological development has far outpaced our spiritual development, which has put our species and our planet in great danger of being destroyed.

3. We will not be allowed to continue using nuclear weapons because it could not only destroy ourselves and our planet, but the nuclear explosions actually impact other dimensions and other beings and civilizations as well, far beyond our own planet.

4. It's absolutely imperative that we stop fighting and killing each other, stop polluting and killing the planet we live on, and wake up and stop allowing ourselves to be controlled and enslaved by the beings who have been doing so for a long time.

We can contact ETs and higher dimensional beings ourselves (while using discernment and protection) through meditation, and through asking and using our intent. This is often done through CE5 meditations.

CE5 meditation (Close Encounters of the Fifth Kind meditation) is a practice where a group of people get together to contact and communicate with extraterrestrial beings through meditation and mental techniques. The name "CE5" comes from a system used to classify close encounters with UFOs. A "Close Encounter of the Fifth Kind" means direct communication between humans and aliens. During CE5 meditation, participants focus on raising their awareness and sending out loving thoughts with the intent to connect with extraterrestrial civilizations through telepathic communication.

We also can and should be listening to the testimonies and

experiences of people who have had actual contact with extraterrestrial beings, or non-human intelligence (NHI).

There are WAY too many ET and NHI contactees and experiencers for me to cover them all here, and that's only considering the people who have publicly told of their experiences. I'll go over, in my personal opinion, some of the most compelling contactees and experiencers. Each person's story and information is unique, and gives valuable insight into the nature of our reality. They each add their own piece to the puzzle. I'm starting out with the more well-known and classic contactees, and then going from there.

George Adamski

George Adamski claimed to have had multiple encounters with extraterrestrial beings and to have traveled to other planets in our solar system. His most famous encounter was with a Nordic alien named Orthon in the California desert in 1952, which he documented in his book "Flying Saucers Have Landed," co-authored with Desmond Leslie. Adamski also met with two other beings named Firkon & Ramu who invited him onto their ships and discussed Universal Law and our planetary problems and dangers with him. The beings took Adamski on trips to other planets and bodies within our solar system including Venus, Mars, and the Moon. He observed and interacted with the inhabitants of these planets, describing them as humanoid beings with advanced technology and peaceful civilizations.

After being gifted a telescope in his forties, Adamski felt the strong urge to start observing the night sky. While doing so, he spotted a UFO during a meteor shower. This further cemented his belief in extraterrestrial life and he began photographing and documenting his sightings.

On November 18, 1952, Adamski and a group of people traveled to Blythe, California, where they stopped and began observing the skies. They spotted a large cigar-shaped craft, and Adamski felt a strong sense that the beings on the craft wanted him to capture photos, but not from their current location. They drove further and noticed the spacecraft was following them overhead. Eventually they stopped at a spot where Adamski set up his telescope and camera. As the spacecraft left, another one appeared, and Adamski managed to capture a few photos before it disappeared. Shortly after this, Adamski came in contact with a man who spoke to him telepathically and claimed to be from Venus. He told Adamski about his home planet, their concerns about nuclear radiation, and their craft's capabilities. Reports from an Air Force pilot in the area corroborated aspects of Adamski's encounter, which further validated his claims.

George Van Tassel

George Van Tassel became well known in the mid-20th century for his claims of extraterrestrial contact and his involvement in the construction of the Integratron, a dome-shaped structure located in Landers, California.

Van Tassel claimed that in 1953, he had a telepathic encounter with extraterrestrial beings from Venus during a meditation session in the Mojave Desert. The beings provided him with instructions for constructing the Integratron, a machine designed to heal, rejuvenate, and extend human life, and while also operating as a time traveling device.

The Integratron was intended to be a device for time travel, anti-gravity, and energy healing, based on principles Van Tassel claimed to have received from the extraterrestrial beings. Van Tassel held annual gatherings at the Integratron known as the Giant Rock Spacecraft Conventions, where UFO enthusiasts and seekers of alternative knowledge would gather to discuss topics related to UFOs, spirituality, and consciousness. Van Tassel died in 1978 before the construction of the Integratron could be finished. The timing and circumstances of his death seemed very suspect.

The following excerpt is from an article in the Ashtabula, Ohio "Star Beacon," June 20, 1998:

> 'His death came as a surprise to all, because Van Tassel was a healthy individual and he suffered no warning signs of an attack.
>
> Davidson said some people believe Van Tassel was getting too close to proving ground-breaking science and he had to be silenced. "He suddenly and mysteriously died when he should have been at his zenith," Davidson said. Manyo is suspicious of his second wife and Davidson believes she may have been working for a group determined to silence him.
>
> "We think he was done away with," Manyo said. "She had him cremated even before the daughters had been notified that he had died." Manyo said Van Tassel's second wife was a chiropractor and would have had access to medical means of inducing death. She said the woman had been married twice before and both of those husbands died in strange circumstances. "After George died, she went completely out of her mind," Manyo said. "She barricaded herself in a trailer and put a big, high fence around it."
>
> The core and other critical components of the Integratron disappeared shortly after Van Tassel's death, giving weight to a conspiracy theory. Further, another scientist who had worked on a similar project in the 1940s and

`50s, also had suffered a sudden heart attack under unusual circumstances. Wilhelm Reich, whose Orgone Accumulator had come under attack by the Food and Drug Administration, had been imprisoned as an imperious tyrant. Reich died Nov. 1, 1957, just three days before he was to be released from prison. Davidson believes controlling interests saw both Reich and Van Tassel as too powerful, creative and threatening for the science of the times.'

Betty and Barney Hill

In September of 1961, Betty and Barney Hill were driving home to Portsmouth, New Hampshire, after a vacation in Canada on the night of September 19, 1961. As they traveled through rural New Hampshire, they noticed a strange object in the sky that seemed to follow their car. Betty and Barney both experienced a period of missing time. They arrived home later than expected and couldn't account for several hours of their trip. They also noticed unusual physical sensations and odd marks on their car.

Disturbed by their experience, Betty and Barney sought help from psychiatrist Dr. Benjamin Simon. Through a series of hypnosis sessions, they each recalled fragmented memories of their encounter with the UFO and its occupants. Under hypnosis, Betty and Barney recounted being taken aboard the UFO by humanoid beings with large, wraparound eyes and gray skin. They described medical examinations and communication with the beings, who spoke to them telepathically. Once inside the craft, they were medically examined by the beings and their memories were erased.

Later, under hypnosis, Betty recreated the star map the beings had shown to her. The map was later shown to be the binary star system Zeta Reticuli 1 and Zeta Reticuli 2. There was no public data available to make such a map in 1961 when Betty saw it, nor in 1964 when she drew it. This fact alone proves that it could not possibly have been a hoax. There were also magnetic anomalies found on their car, and a strange unknown substance was left on Betty's dress.

Travis Walton

Travis Walton was part of a logging crew working in the Apache-Sitgreaves National Forest near Snowflake, Arizona, on November 5, 1975. After a long day of work, the crew headed home in their truck. While driving through the forest, the crew spotted a glowing disc-shaped object hovering above the trees. Travis, intrigued, jumped out of the truck and approached the object, against the warnings of his crewmates.

As Travis got closer to the object, a beam of light shot out from the UFO, hitting him and knocking him unconscious. Terrified, the crew fled the scene, leaving Travis behind. When they returned minutes later, both Travis and the UFO were gone. After being struck by a beam of light from the UFO and losing consciousness, Travis found himself aboard the alien craft. He described feeling disoriented and confused, unsure of where he was or what was happening to him.

Upon regaining awareness, Travis found himself in a brightly lit, sterile-looking environment. He then encountered several small, humanoid beings that looked very much like the typical image of "grey" aliens. These beings appeared to be conducting medical examinations on him. Travis says the beings conducted various medical examinations and procedures on him, including examinations of his eyes, skin, and other bodily functions. He described feeling immobilized and unable to move during these examinations. He was in intense fear and emotional distress while aboard the alien craft. He described feeling helpless and terrified by the unfamiliar surroundings and the presence of the alien beings. While there were gaps in his memory of the experience, he was 100% certain that the experience was absolutely real and happened.

After what seemed like several hours aboard the craft, Travis claimed to have been returned to Earth and found himself lying on the side of the road near a gas station in Heber, Arizona. He was disoriented and traumatized but physically unharmed. Travis' crewmates hesitated at first to report the incident, fearing ridicule and disbelief. They eventually contacted authorities and a massive search was launched to find Travis, who was missing for five days.

Five days after his disappearance, Travis reappeared, disoriented and traumatized, near a gas station in Heber, Arizona. He claimed to have been abducted by the occupants of the UFO and subjected to medical examinations aboard their craft. The crew underwent extensive polygraph testing, which indicated they were telling the truth about witnessing Travis' abduction.

A book about Travis' story called "Fire in the Sky" was published in 1979. The movie about it with the same name came out in 1993. Though Travis says that many things depicted in the movie are inaccurate.

Alex Collier

Alex Collier has been in contact with extraterrestrial beings from Andromeda for almost his entire life. They have taken him aboard their craft, taught him many things, and given him detailed information about the nature of the universe, Galactic information, the history of Earth, and the future of humanity.

He says that he is a part of their soul group, and was an Andromedan being like them before he incarnated on Earth many lifetimes ago. Collier says that when the beings first contacted him, he felt an instant love for them and had a soul-level recognition of them. The main two beings he has been in contact with are named Vissaeus and Morenae.

From his book *Defending Sacred Ground*:

"The Andromedans are a very, very old race. Apparently, all of the human race comes from Lyrae. There is a lot of information about this. Billy Meier also talks about it. The human race did not originally exist in Lyrae - it came from some other galaxy but first began to evolve in our galaxy in the Lyran system. According to the Andromedans, there are over 135 billion human beings in the 8 galaxies closest to ours. Now, there are also other races out there. Some of these races have had a lot of conflicts with the human race, and that conflict continues. But, there are things that are happening that will hopefully alleviate that problem. It comes down to philosophies, more than anything else. The Andromedans are a telepathic race. Morenae, over the last ten years, has learned to use his vocal chords...The Andromedans care really deeply about what is going on, and a lot of it apparently has to do with who we are as souls, who we are genetically, and it also has to do with the future - a future in which we will probably be in other physical forms. We're talking about the future between now and 357 years from now...Everything in our universe, including us, came from a black hole. The Andromedans say there is no age to us. We truly are infinite."

Alex tells his story and gives his knowledge in his book *Defending Sacred Ground*.

Charles Hall

Charles Hall is an American author who claims to have had direct contact with extraterrestrial beings during his time as a weather observer at Nellis Air Force Base in Nevada in the 1960s. He is best known for his series of books known as the "Millennial Hospitality" series, in which he recounts his experiences with a group of tall blonde humanoid extraterrestrial beings he calls the "Tall Whites."

Hall encountered the Tall Whites while stationed at Nellis Air Force Base, where they lived in a secluded area of the nearby desert. They formed a treaty with the Air Force allowing them to have a base there. He describes the Tall Whites as being around 8 to 9 feet tall, with chalk-white skin, elongated features, and large, wraparound eyes. He claims to have interacted with them over a period of several years, during which time they communicated with him telepathically and allowed him to observe their activities.

Hall witnessed their advanced technology, including their spacecraft and energy weapons, and also observed their social interactions and customs. He also describes instances of both friendly and tense interactions with the beings, as well as moments of fear and intimidation.

In Hall's "Millennial Hospitality" series of books he details his experiences with the Tall Whites and gives his perspective on the implications of extraterrestrial contact for humanity.

Steven Greer

In 1973, after having a Near Death Experience at age 17 and being profoundly changed by it, Steven Greer was meditating on top of a mountain outside Boone, North Carolina when he claims he was contacted by an extraterrestrial being. He said at first he thought it was a deer standing on its hind legs looking at him. He soon realized it was an ET as it walked up and touched him on his right shoulder, and an electromagnetic field then surrounded him making all of his hair stand up. He described it as an incredibly beautiful and blissful experience and said he was not at all frightened.

"One crystal clear afternoon, I decided to go to see the sunset from atop this mountain. I reached the top in time to sit in meditation at sunset.

Before starting, I glanced towards the southwest and saw an extraterrestrial vehicle. It was some distance away, but was just like the one I had seen as a nine year old. For some reason, my reaction at that moment was, 'It's them again' - and I didn't really think much more about it - I simply accepted the fact that they were here. Then the ship winked out, just like the one I'd seen years before.

I then began meditating and had a beautiful, deep experience in unbounded Mind. Afterward, I opened my eyes and it was pitch dark, with the stars all visible. Imagine being at that altitude in the crystal clear dry air, viewing the Milky Way and countless stars! Standing there, suddenly a thought not my own came to mind: 'Behold what a beautiful universe God has made.'

With that, I went into the exact state of consciousness I

had when I died, that God consciousness where I was fully awake, at one with the entire creation, and yet present standing on the mountain. It was magnificent.

When I began the walk down, I noticed a glow off the edge of the mountain and sensed someone was there. Suddenly, on my right, an extraterrestrial biological life form appeared and touched my shoulder so firmly that it was like a strong finger touching me. I looked down and saw the imprint on my jacket: every hair on my head stood on end!

Somewhat childishly, my first thought was, 'What does this creature want with me?' I got down close to the ground (I hate to admit this!) in a fetal position, looking up – and he was looking back. Its gender was male. He was quite peaceful and non-threatening, with beautiful, deer-like eyes.

Then I suddenly found myself transported onto the craft. We were just out in space, sitting. I recall that the craft became completely translucent. It felt like I was floating in space with nothing around, as if the whole craft was made of fiber optics, and its shell could disappear. Space was visible all around us.

So I stayed there with these ETs, who were three or four feet tall, all with those appealing eyes. It appeared that we were there for one purpose; meditating together. They were interested in me because they wanted contact with a human being experiencing cosmic consciousness as we do, participating with them. At this point I taught them what that state is like for us. We shared it together - an incredible encounter, entirely different from stories usually circulated about extraterrestrial contact.

It was a very non-local experience, with time, space, and

relativity in a realm unlike what's normal for us. In that state of consciousness seconds, hours, or years no longer matter, because time and space have been transcended. This infinite eternity is the true nature of the mind, the awake self within all of us.

While with these beings, we co-created a code for humans communicating with them. This was actually the birth of the CE-5 - Close Encounters of the Fifth Kind – initiative. We utilized not only sounds and light but also non-local consciousness and directed, coherent thought to communicate with extraterrestrial beings and their electronic devices. This was October of 1973, during the time of the Yom Kippur war.

It was clear to me that the ETs wanted humans to move beyond mutually assured destruction and into a peaceful civilization that could co-exist with space in harmony."
— Steven Greer, *Hidden Truth, Forbidden Knowledge*

Greer has dedicated his life to the disclosure of the truth of ETs and hidden technology, helping humanity connect with their cosmic family, and working towards helping to end the slavery system on Earth.

Greer has organized many CE5 (Close Encounters of the 5th Kind) gatherings where they do meditations and use light signals or other methods to invite ET craft to appear, and has had many UFO and ET encounters at these events. He says he has communicated telepathically with the beings onboard the craft, who have given him messages of peace, unity, and the potential for humanity to join an interstellar community.

Dorothy Izatt

In the early 1970s, Dorothy Izatt began witnessing strange lights in the sky near her home in Vancouver, British Columbia. She started filming these lights using a Super 8 camera, capturing images of UFOs and orbs of light.

Over the years, Izatt continued to film her sightings, amassing a large collection of footage documenting her encounters. She claimed that the UFOs she observed exhibited unusual movements and behaviors, including rapid acceleration, sudden stops, and changes in direction.

In addition to her UFO sightings, Izatt claimed to have had telepathic communications with the beings aboard the craft she observed. She describes feeling a sense of tremendous peace and love from the beings she encountered, along with a strong feeling of connection to them.

Dorothy Izatt has over 30,000 feet of film footage of her UFO sightings. Over the years her footage has been analyzed by various experts and researchers and has been determined to depict genuine "unidentified phenomena."

Sherry Wilde

Sherry Wilde is a contactee whose experiences began in 1987 when she witnessed a UFO hovering near her home in Wisconsin. After this event she would go on to have many strange and frightening experiences where she would have missing time, unexplained marks on her and her daughter's body, and eventually remember her encounters with extraterrestrial beings.

At first these experiences terrified her and she thought she might be going insane. Eventually she came to realize that these beings were her "Star Family" and that they were there to help and protect her and her family. She claims that she and her family were frequently visited by beings she describes as "Tall Whites," who communicated with her telepathically and imparted messages of peace, love, and spiritual awakening.

Over time, Sherry's encounters became more frequent and profound. She was taken aboard their craft, where she underwent various physical and mental examinations. Despite the initially frightening nature of these experiences, she ultimately came to view the extraterrestrial beings as benevolent loving beings with a mission to help humanity evolve spiritually.

One of the most profound things they told her was that the Earth is ascending, and that only beings who are of a high enough frequency and vibration will be ascending with Her. Beings who are not at a high enough frequency will be going elsewhere. They said that this will be happening very soon. This information lines up with much information that came through many QHHT sessions of Dolores Cannon about the coming ascension to "New Earth" and the splitting between the "Old" and "New" Earth.

She details her entire story in her book *The Forgotten Promise: Rejoining Our Cosmic Family*

Margie Kay

Margie Kay is an acclaimed paranormal and UFO investigator, psychic medium, contactee, remote viewer, and author of 12 books and counting. She is a veteran paranormal investigator of over 40 years and has conducted numerous investigations across the country. She had helped solve over sixty homicides, theft, and missing person cases while working with multiple three-letter agencies, police, and private investigators.

Margie has had contact with various extraterrestrials, and she has been in contact with the well-known being Valiant Thor for much of her life. Valiant Thor is an extraterrestrial being who visited Earth in the 1950s and has had interactions with various individuals, including government officials.

Margie Kay has had personal encounters with and has been in telepathic communication with Valiant Thor her entire life. He gave her information about his origins, mission on Earth, and perspectives on humanity and its future. Margie says that Valiant Thor gave her the ability of X-ray vision, has saved her life on at least one occasion, and has helped her in various ways throughout her life.

"And then the therapist says, 'Now what do you see?' And I look up, and I see a skeleton standing there, and only a skeleton standing there where he was. And I just had the thought, 'What the heck is going on?' when this other voice comes from the side on the wall, and I look over. Well I recognize the voice, so I wasn't afraid of it. And this head appeared on the wall. He had an M-shaped helmet on, and he said 'I am Thor and now you have X-ray vision.' I didn't know what that meant. And he said 'I'll be in contact with you in the future, and we will be working together.' This was like an order. It wasn't a request...Then I turned to everybody and I said 'Did you guys see that?' and they're like 'See what?'"

"I found out later that I've been involved with a Mantis being and he took me to his crystal planet, and they implanted seeds in my light bodies. So when you're not using this body anymore you leave it, but all of your light bodies go with you. And I saw these implants in each one, and something will activate them at a certain time. So they can follow you through multiple lifetimes as this is being done."

— Margie Kay, from her presentation at Journey to Truth Conference 2023

From Margie's Bio:

"Kay has spoken at over two hundred conferences and meetings nationwide including the Psychical Research Society, the Psychic Studies Institute, Missouri MUFON, Midwest Conference on the Unknown, Arkansas MUFON, PARACON, Nebraska MUFON, Mysteries of the Universe Conferences, Phenomecon and others. She has hosted annual conferences in Kansas City since 2007. Kay also does presentations and demonstrates remote viewing for audience participants. Her specialty is medical diagnostic reading, in which she remote views the interior of the human body or vehicles. She always amazes audiences with extremely accurate readings."

Peter Maxwell Slattery

Peter Maxwell Slattery has been experiencing UFO sightings and contact with extraterrestrials for most of his life. He has an enormous amount of some of the most incredible UFO footage on the planet, and he is still to this day having constant UFO and ET contact.

He has been in contact with a higher dimensional Pleiadian being named Shi-Ji for many years now, and has written four books (*The Book of Shi-Ji 1-4*) detailing the information given to him by this being. He says that he eventually learned Shi-Ji is actually an Elohim Being who has many different facets, and that he himself is a facet of this being.

Books by Peter Slattery:
The Book of Shi-Ji (Books 1-4)
My Awakening: A Paranormal UFO Story
Connect to your Spirit and ET Guides
AWAKENING: UFOs and Other Strange Happenings
CE-5: Initiating Contact with Extraterrestrials
Operation Starseed: A Temporal War
Self Mastery: The Path to Ascension
Extraterrestrials: Their Messages for Humanity
Light Body Activation: Breaking Free from the Illusion

Michele Desmarquet

Michele Desmarquet became known for his book *Thiaoouba Prophecy* where he shares his story of being taken by extraterrestrial beings to their planet, Thiaoouba. He was visited by an alien named Thao, who took him on a journey through space to Thiaoouba.

During his time on Thiaoouba, Desmarquet learned about advanced spiritual and technological concepts from the inhabitants of the planet. He describes the Thiaooubans as highly evolved beings who live in harmony with nature and possess advanced knowledge of science and spirituality. While there Desmarquet witnessed advanced technologies, participated in spiritual ceremonies, and received teachings about the nature of the universe and humanity's place within it. He learned that the Thiaooubans are a level 9 civilization, while Earth in its current state is a level 1. To put it in perspective, they would be like college professors while Earth would be like kindergarteners.

After returning to Earth, Desmarquet wrote "Thiaoouba Prophecy" to share his experiences and the teachings he received on Thiaoouba with the world.

Since Desmarquet's death in 2018, Samuel Chong has been carrying on his story and message to the world.

Dannion Brinkley

Dannion Brinkley is an author, speaker, and near-death experiencer (NDE). He was struck by lightning *twice*, and has had three separate near-death experiences, each profoundly impacting his life and beliefs.

On September 17, 1975, Dannion Brinkley was struck by lightning and died. After about half an hour, he miraculously came back to life in a morgue. While he was "dead" he says he went through a dark tunnel, and came to a beautiful crystal city and a "cathedral of knowledge", where there were thirteen angels who showed him events that would happen in the future, most of which have already occurred. After this experience he gained psychic abilities, including being able to read minds.

Later on he was struck by lightning *again* and had another near-death experience where the angels told him he should use his new abilities to help sick people. Since then, he has dedicated his life to caring for the sick and elderly, and sharing his incredible story with others. In 1994, he wrote his first book *Saved By the Light* detailing his experiences and the knowledge and transformation that occurred from them.

Jason Quitt

Jason Quitt began having contact as a small child where he would see an ethereal being in his room at night. Eventually multiple beings started taking him on astral out of body experiences where the beings would show him things in other timelines, Jason's own past lives, other planets, and potential future timelines on Earth. At one point the beings took him to Ancient Egypt where they taught him what he calls "postures of power," where he is able to harness universal energy for various purposes.

Jason says that he not only remembers his past lives, but he remembers his experience in the "between life" realm before his current incarnation. He says while he was in that space, he remembers choosing his parents and his current life.

Jason has also had experiences with various ETs, including a Grey ET who appeared in his room one night attempting to mind controlling him into thinking he was a short old man. He said he heard the words in his mind "I am a short, old man." Jason telepathically told the being "No you're not. You're a Grey extraterrestrial." And the being then immediately left.

Jason tells his story and gives his insights in his book *Forbidden Knowledge*.

Other books by Jason: *Egyptian Postures of Power*, *Astral Genesis*, *Gates of the Anunnaki*, and *The Yosef Codes*.

Darryl Anka / Bashar

Bashar is an extraterrestrial consciousness channeled by Darryl Anka, an American channeler and author. Anka claims to have started receiving communications from Bashar in 1983 during a UFO sighting, and he has been channeling Bashar's messages ever since.

According to Bashar's teachings, he is a being from the future, specifically from a civilization on a planet called Essassani, which is said to exist in what we perceive as the future of our timeline. Bashar's messages often focus on personal empowerment, spiritual growth, and the nature of reality. He shares insights on topics such as manifestation, belief systems, and the importance of following one's passions and excitement.

Anka's first contact with Bashar occurred in 1973 when he and his wife were camping in the California desert near the town of Borrego Springs. At night, they witnessed a glowing, triangular-shaped craft hovering silently in the sky. The sighting had a profound impact on Anka and sparked his curiosity about the nature of extraterrestrial life and the mysteries of the universe.

However, it wasn't until 1983 that Anka began receiving communications from Bashar. He says the initial encounter occurred while he was experimenting with meditation and exploring altered states of consciousness. During one of these sessions, he experienced a sudden and unexpected telepathic communication from an extraterrestrial entity who identified himself as Bashar.

Anka says that Bashar's messages began as personal guidance and insights but eventually evolved into broader teachings about the nature of reality, human potential, and the interconnectedness of all things. He claims to have undergone a period of adjustment and skepticism before fully accepting his role as a channel for Bashar's communications.

Viviane Chauvet

Viviane Chauvet is an Arcturian hybrid avatar. She is an incarnated Arcturian Starseed who is also physically half-

Arcturian. She is here on Earth at this time to be an ambassador, teacher, healer, and conduit for higher energies to be channeled into the planet. She says she is continually in contact with her Arcturian Star Family.

From her website *Infinite Healing from the Stars*:

> "Viviane Chauvet is an interstellar Arcturian being who ascended thousands of years ago. Her Soul Avatar Essence has returned in a projected holographic form that contains biofeedback.
>
> She is an Arcturian Ambassador and clear conduit for a delegation of enlightened and spiritually advanced intergalactic civilizations."
> https://www.infinitehealingfromthestars.com/

Tony Rodrigues

Tony Rodrigues is a Remote Viewer and Secret Space Program experiencer. He was involved in a covert program known as the "20 and Back" program, in which he was taken into service for a period of 20 years, then age-regressed and returned to his original timeline with his memories erased. Tony was taken as a child and forced into the program where he underwent training and missions in space. Before he was taken off-planet, for years he was abused and exploited as a child, and was moved around to various locations on the planet. He has since gone to many of these locations and further verified his experiences there. My podcast partner Tyler Kiwala went with him to the Inyokern, California location and documented the experience on video.

Tony talks about his experiences aboard spacecraft, interactions with extraterrestrial beings, and involvement in various missions and operations. He claims to have been subjected to mind control techniques and traumatic experiences during his time in the program.

For the past nine years, Tony has been publicly telling his story and working to expose the truth of these programs to humanity.

> "The Secret Space Program in a nutshell is: Governments, for almost the last 100 years, have made contact with extraterrestrial species, and acquired technology to go offworld."
> — Tony Rodrigues

Tony details his story and experiences in his books *Ceres Colony Cavalier* and *Project Starmaker*.

His new book is *Beyond Sight: The Hidden History of Remote Viewing and Psycho Energetics*

Niara Isley

Niara Isley is a MILAB and ET experiencer who served in the United States Air Force (USAF) and was stationed at Nellis Air Force Base in Nevada in the 1980s. During her time there, she was subjected to mind control experiments, was sexually abused, and was taken aboard an advanced spacecraft to a base on the moon as part of a covert operation.

Ever since she was a child, Niara had some of her memories come through as strange dreams, or she would be triggered by certain experiences seemingly for no reason. In 1994, she had a regression hypnosis session with the famous UFO abduction researcher Budd Hopkins, in which many of her repressed and erased memories came back to her. Niara recalled being abducted by Grey ETs for their hybrid program in which they sexually abused her and used her to create human/ET hybrids.

She also remembered having a MILAB (Military Abduction) experience which took place during a 3 to 4 month period of time while she was stationed at Tonopah Test Range in Nevada. These few months were at first completely missing from her memory. This terrified her since she claims she has an excellent memory, and there is no possible way that she wouldn't remember anything from such a large period of time. When her memories came back, she remembered being abducted by the military and taken into a secret underground base where they would sexually abuse her and experiment on her. They injected her with a mysterious substance which she says was excruciating and felt like the atoms of her body were coming apart. She remembers a Grey ET standing close by and watching. She also remembers being taken in an advanced spacecraft to a base on the moon.

Niara recounts the beginning of her MILAB experiences in an interview with Richard Dolan:

> "I was taken out in the middle of the night to test the radar that I worked on…at gunpoint. In no uncertain terms were we to speak to each other. We had about 3 people on the crew, and we were taken out there at gunpoint. We were given fatigues to wear with no rank insignia and no name tags. We were forbidden to speak to each other beyond what was necessary to run the radar and do the tests of the aircraft. Then when it was over we were told to stand out on the deck of the radar van and be quiet. When we were standing out there we looked up in the sky and saw the special aircraft that we had been tracking or saucers and other extraterrestrial and/or back-engineered craft.
>
> …
>
> They were pretty unpleasant, laughing in a very unpleasant

way because they had us under control with guns and intimidation and things like that. So when they were done at the radar they put us on a bus with painted over windows and took us to what I believe was either Area 51 or possibly an underground facility mentioned by William Pollock at Tonopah. I'm not sure either place because the windows were painted over. I was taken into a medical facility. All of the people that were out there that night were put in this medical facility. We were sat down in a waiting room. The lights were turned off in the waiting room, I imagined to help with lack of memory retrieval. And one by one they called us into this little side room, and when it was my turn to go in there I was told to lay down fully clothed on a stainless steel examining table. There was a security guard in the room with me with a sidearm standing at parade rest. And then this guy comes in and says "stay calm" three times in a real monotone voice, and when he walks up beside the right side of my head he injected me in the side of the neck with one smooth move like he'd done it a hundred times and the chemical went straight to the brain and my whole body just went into shock.

Then from there two security guards appeared on either side of me, on either side of the table lifting me up by the arms, getting me off the table and taking me down this staircase. At the bottom of the staircase I was thrown in a little room while people watched while I went through the effects of the injection...I'm guessing that they put me in that room and isolated me from everybody else because whatever was in that injection might have had an effect that would spill over onto other people...There's this all this talk about ascension in the world right now. There's going to be a spiritual ascension and everything else like that. I'm sure on the surface the government really poo-poos that, but the people in the deep covert op programs are probably thinking 'Okay what's going on here, is there going to be some kind of dimensional shift?' I really have a pretty strong intuitive hit now that the injection they gave me was to try to chemically create an ascension dimensional shift rather than doing it through a natural spiritual evolutionary process."

Later on, Niara regained her memories of her past lives as a Lyran being, and she began receiving telepathic contact with her Star Family:

"I would get these messages and it would be like words, and I would think 'What is this? Where is this coming from?' And then if it really wanted to get my attention it would keep putting the same idea in there over and over. Finally I went down and I just kind of confronted this whole thing at the American River Confluence near Auburn. I sat down there by the rushing water and I said 'Okay, are you guys really there? Are you really talking to me?' 'Yes, we're really talking to you.' It came that clear, and it's so fast that I barely get the question formed and I barely get the first word of the question out of my mouth before the answer is coming back, and it's been very powerful. I remember thinking 'Wow so I could just check in with you guys and I don't have to make any more stupid human mistakes in my life right?' And they said 'No that's not why you're here. You have to live your own life and bungle through, but we are here to teach you and to try to get you to look at what's important.' And they have been true to that all this time. They are not the Greys. They are beings that look very human but they have bluish skin. They're very loving people, very connected to the earth in the same way that Native Americans are. And I know people are going to say 'Oh she's talking about the movie Avatar.' But James Cameron who made the movie, made it from a dream that he had 20 years before about a planet and blue people and so on and so forth. So did he make a movie? Or did he have a memory of this same place?"

Niara gives her testimony and all of her insights in her book *Facing the Shadow, Embracing the Light*.

Lowell Johnson

Lowell Johnson is an Inner Earth being contactee who was actually invited and physically taken into Telos, the ancient Lemurian city beneath Mt. Shasta.

During his hike on Mount Shasta, Lowell Johnson was meditating when suddenly an opening formed in the rock behind him. There stood a white-robed being who telepathically asked Lowell if he wanted to see Telos. He accepted the invitation and was taken on a guided tour of the Inner Earth city of Telos, which he describes in detail in his testimony.

Lowell describes the city and civilization as being highly advanced, spiritual, telepathic, and existing in a higher dimension. They had to raise his frequency in order for him to experience the city.

> "It's circular in orientation. There are crystal buildings everywhere, and in the center of this city is a white pyramid with a capstone on the top, which was also white that day. I'll learn a year later when I got to know who Diane Robbins was, she said, 'You know, there's correlation between that and the day of the week. You were there on a Sunday. The capstone was white. That's why everyone was wearing white.'"
> — Lowell Johnson, Journey to Truth Podcast Ep. 204

Lowell's Bio:

"Lowell spent the majority of his professional career as a Hospitality Executive - willing to assume leadership roles that were industry and/or community related in every area of the country he lived. He has spoken publicly countless times at events over the course of his career as though he was being prepared to present something bigger down the road. Chasing the same things in this life that we are all conditioned to do, he was quite successful at earning responsibility, recognition and rewards. But he sensed a yearning to know more about spirituality from the time he was young. It's believed his particular wake up call came in the form of a TIA (mini stroke) in late 2015, and has led him down many multidimensional rabbit holes seeking truth. His personal passion for nature, travel and others seemed to lend itself to the life that was being revealed to him. After more than six decades of trips around the sun - he has a clear perspective of who he is, what he's doing here and the truth of the 3rd dimensional world experiment.

One day when seeking solace in the forests of Mount Shasta, he was intentionally seeking an audience with Ascended Masters out in Nature. Largely unaware of Telos and the Lemurians - this was the beginning of a rapidly accelerated learning curve. He certainly didn't expect for the mountain to open up and invite him in. From that experience triggered an awakening that was meant to be shared with all of humanity with wisdom that came from Higher places. It is one thing to think of communicating with Extraterrestrials as seems to be the fever in the world now, but his contact wasn't about beings from other places in the Universe, it's about beings that have been here on Earth long before our current memories would suggest.

Since then, the process of DNA awakening and recall have set the stage for countless experiences multidimensionally beyond just Telos - to a greater comprehension of enhanced

Photon Light we are receiving and what to do with it. The time to share these multidimensional experiences and emphasize to those who've been triggered by this story - that these same abilities are waiting dormant inside you as well, waiting to be brought back into your awareness. If ever there was a time to realize how to maintain high vibrations - the time is in this moment."

Barry Littleton

Barry Littleton has had many paranormal encounters and contact with extraterrestrial beings since his childhood. One of these ETs became Barry's friend as a child. It was later on that he realized this "boy" was actually an extraterrestrial disguising itself as a human child through manipulating his mind's perception. He encountered other ETs throughout his childhood who contacted him and helped him in various ways. Barry has been taken aboard their craft, which he has described in detail both the craft and his experiences on them.

> "It started off with childhood experiences, but then I went into what I call adult onset experiences, which included missing time. So we're looking at almost 20 hours of my life was missing being on board these ships. When I talk about it now it sounds very uniform but it took a lifetime to put the pieces together. Instead I was more into hiding it to a degree and trying to just be normal and whatever it took to try to blend in instead of talk about these experiences. I always heard it is termed as 'demonic' and dealing with demons, and that label somebody as demons and crazy and puts the most negative connotation on it possible. So that's one problem I think there is, and that's a real way to block people from talking about this and ever coming forward.

These beings, they never would give me any revelations about the future but they only gave me information concerning the Earth and always the technologies, and there was a lot of love energy that came off them. Enough to where being in the presence of a non-human, it would somewhat chill you out. Because it's not just a normal thing and it's a great risk of panic there, but the type of vibration coming off them—coming off their biofields—was very calming. It started off with a being that was insectoid, and when he would come and interact with me in my daily life he was doing something with the optic nerves to make him appear even more human, but when I saw him on board craft he was definitely insectoid and ancient. Smaller. That'd be the first being to step forward to me. There was another one to step forward that looks like Earth's brain coral, is the way this being's head looks. Taller, but very peaceful and also very scientific to a degree. I've also seen small blue beings that claim to be from Andromeda. Maybe two and a half feet tall I would say.

Then there's the other portion that I had a hard time dealing with because there's no frame of reference for this. It's the beings onboard these crafts that are non-corporeal, non-physical. They have different containers for their consciousness like plasma or light configurations. The inside of the crafts themselves that I've seen look like a type of a fungus, a type of a hard mushroom that's slightly different. So that told me that these crafts were actually organic. If we're going to become a type one civilization we need to start not just incorporating the spiritual but also the organic components into our space travel."
— Barry Littleton, from *The Cosmic Secret* documentary

Barry's Bio from the DisclosureFest website *disclosurefest.org*:

"Barry Littleton was born awake with fragmented past life memories, & began having paranormal experiences at a very young age. These experiences included telepathic awareness, perceiving ghosts, & various inorganic beings. These encounters, & some of the entities themselves, had a distinct extraterrestrial origin. That led him into a lifetime of research & exploration into both the metaphysical and paranormal fields.

Mr. Littleton majored in psychology, sociology and ethnic studies from Wichita State University. For the 22 years he's worked with at risk youth, & juvenile offenders by utilizing the Cognitive Behavioral approach.

In 2010, Mr. Littleton had a tragic car accident resulting in four Catastrophic Traumatic Brain Injuries (TBI), along with a Near Death Experience (NDE). The event was life changing; it was predicted that his condition would remain in a near vegetable state. Surviving this catastrophic event, with mental faculties intact, spurred him to come forward about contact & paranormal experiences, including Psychic abilities & Mediumship.

Mr. Littleton aims to illustrate how the NDE's & Contact Experiences are not seperate classifications."

Jerry Wills

Jerry Wills is not native to Earth. He was actually brought to this planet as a baby and left in an old, deserted farmhouse. He was intended to be found and raised by a specialized faction within the United States Military, ultimately adopted by a military family. This family knew that Jerry was an extraterrestrial, which allowed them to support him as his unique abilities began to emerge. When Jerry was in his youth, he displayed many psychic and healing abilities, and was considered to be a child prodigy. As Jerry grew up, he encountered beings from his home world from the Tau Ceti star system, who taught him how to harness and control his abilities. The beings didn't tell Jerry that he was an extraterrestrial, nor that they were, but he eventually learned of that later on. Many of these beings became Jerry's friends.

One of these beings Jerry met while on a group trip to Peru. The man said his name was Rich and told him that he was a Pleiadian. Jerry said this man already knew his name and many details about him. He told Jerry that he was an anthropologist and that he was studying humans. The being further proved to Jerry that he was who he claimed by doing various things, one of which was actually flying in a UFO craft and landing it on top of Huayna Picchu, a mountain in Peru.

In an interview, Jerry recounts first meeting Rich:

> "Here's this guy Rich, climbs up on top of the bus with me on the way up to Machu Picchu...and he seems to know my name, and know a little bit about me. Well I'd never seen this guy before. So I ask him some questions, and he very casually says 'Well I'm from the Pleiades.' I'm like 'Ooookaaay...Uh huh.' I said 'You've probably read that book by Barbara Marciniak haven't you?' He says 'Well we know about it, but no we haven't read it.' Next thing we know we're in Machu Picchu. We continue talking. He's a very unusual man. Very, very bright. He's an anthropologist. He'd been up to Venice Beach. He'd been studying the culture at Venice Beach for the past three months, and he decided to get back to something that feels more like home, which was on top of mountains in the Andes.
>
> So I said goodbye to him. He was going to go up to the top of

Huayna Picchu...There's a fellow with me, and he has these great big binoculars...And he's looking around, looking around...He had seen me talking to this guy...And he asked me a little bit about the guy. And I said 'I don't know. He says he's a Pleiadian.' Within 2 minutes...he goes 'Hey, there's that guy you were talking to.' And I said 'No that couldn't be him because he can't get up there that fast.' It had only been like 10, 15 minutes...And he goes 'No I think that's him.' So I said 'Let me see.' I took the binoculars, looked up there, and sure as hell, there's this guy Rich sitting there staring right at me, waving, with a big smile on his face.

So the friendship continued past that point for several years. He introduced me to the others he was there with. Because they were sociologists and anthropologists, they wanted to have permission to talk to the people who were with me in Peru on these trips. He thought that I was bringing some very interesting people with diverse backgrounds with similar interests. And he wanted to have permission so that he could talk to them and kinda pick their brains and find out a little bit about them. I said 'Yeah that's fine.' He said 'Just don't tell them we're Pleiadians, ok' I said 'No I won't do that.' So I never did."
— Jerry Wills, From: Supernatural Girlz - Through the Amanu Maru Portal

Jerry's Bio:

"In September 1953, while still an infant, Jerry Wills was found at an abandoned farm in rural Kentucky near Fort Knox under very unusual circumstances after authorities were notified. He was suffering from frostbite and was taken to a U.S. Army base, where he recovered and was adopted by an Army Officer and his infertile wife. Wills was raised as the couple's son, along with their two adopted daughters. During his youth, Wills displayed unusual psychic abilities such as seeing inside people's bodies, healing illnesses and injuries, telepathic communications, and even seeing into the future.

During his teens, Wills had contact experiences with human-looking extraterrestrials from the Tau Ceti star system. He eventually learned from the Tau Cetians and an unknown "old man" that he was brought to Earth as an infant by virtue of an agreement reached by President Eisenhower and visiting extraterrestrials. The Tau Cetians believed that historical efforts to directly help human evolution were flawed, and so it was decided to indirectly help humanity by dropping off extraterrestrial babies to be raised as ordinary humans, but whose intrinsic gifts would help humanity evolve.

Wills' incredible testimony is supported by a leaked 1989 Defense Intelligence Agency Document that describes the famed 1949 Aztec UFO crash incident where a human-looking extraterrestrial survived along with three infants. Diplomatic negotiations began with the Truman administration and high-level military officials such as General Eisenhower, and the infants were left behind as a gift for the US. With Eisenhower's election in 1952, further agreements were reached, making possible the scenario described by Wills.

After graduating from High School, Wills trained as an electrical engineer at several companies by Ph.D. level scientists and invented advanced healing and technical devices for that time period. What was most unusual was that he was equipped with a full laboratory to build advanced devices valuable to his corporate employers but who gave no credit to him for his accomplishments. Wills subsequently left the corporate sector, traveled extensively searching for ancient cities, and worked as a psychic healer. His remarkable psychic healing abilities were recognized by a Fox News affiliate in Arizona that, over an eleven-year span, did two stories a year on the many individuals Wills had healed."

Miriam Delicado

Miriam Delicado had an encounter with extraterrestrials in 1988 when she was taken aboard a spacecraft in British Columbia, Canada. She met tall, blonde extraterrestrials who gave her vast amounts of information in the form of mental "downloads."

Following this encounter, she began scouring New Age bookstores looking for information. While reading a book by Ruth Montgomery, she started crying when she read, "You are the chosen, to be here at this time," because those exact words were said to her by the ETs. She was taken to an abnormally shaped mountain and the beings told her, "One day you will find this mountain and you will go there." A year later she saw a picture of Ship Rock in northwestern New Mexico and realized it was the mountain they had shown her. She instantly had an inner knowing that she needed to go there, but not until later when the time was right.

Years later, in 2003, Delicado took a trip with a friend to visit Ship Rock. There, she encountered the Hopi Reservation and was struck by the similarities between the Hopi prophecies and the information given to her by the extraterrestrials. This realization led her to believe that her life was intertwined with the Hopi and that she had a role to play in the unfolding events.

When she returned home, Delicado researched the Hopi prophecies and discovered stunning parallels to the information she had received from the extraterrestrials. She later visited the Hopi Reservation again and shared her experiences with one of the Hopi elders, who was amazed by her knowledge and told her he saw her surrounded by tall, blonde aliens.

Delicado believes that she was guided to go to the Four Corners area in 2003 because of the approaching end times.

CHAPTER 23

*Space Photography, ET
Contact & A Great Awakening
- Contribution by Lily Nova*

The following chapter is written by Lily Nova:

E ver since I can remember I was a very intuitive individual. I seemed to understand things at a deeper level and viewed things through a different lens than most of my peers. I always felt drawn to space and the mysteries of our history and the universe.

Where did we come from?

What happens after death?

What else is out there waiting to be discovered in the vast universe?

What is the nature of reality?

These are the types of questions I often pondered. That being said, nothing could have prepared me for what I would come to experience and discover during COVID.

My 'BIG awakening' as I call it would begin in the year 2020, in the middle of the COVID pandemic. I was a nutritionist at the time and taught nutrition and cooking classes around the St. Louis community for Mizzou University Extension. After an abrupt series of unfortunate conflicts with my boss in September 2020, I quit the 'dream job' that I worked so hard to get. I was heartbroken and felt lost.

In the midst of pandemic lockdowns and freshly unemployed, I turned to the stars. Space photography was a hobby I picked up during the lockdowns, and now with more time on my hands, I began spending every single night out under the stars. It was the only place that felt like home and gave me comfort in uncertain times. I focused all of my attention looking up and became very good at photographing the milky way, the moon, and deep space objects. I fell madly in love with the night sky.

My photo of the Andromeda Galaxy

My photo of The Pleiades Star Cluster

After months of nonstop stargazing and photographing the night sky, on the evening of November 17th, 2020, I stepped outside for some fresh air before bed and my life was forever changed. Little did I know, what I thought was preparation for bed turned into first contact with something not of this world.

At 1:50 a.m., I felt called to step out on my front porch one last time before retiring. I was immediately surrounded by the brisk, autumn cold and looked up at the night sky like I always do. This time I instantly locked eyes on a strange, bright light. I began examining what it could be.

Could it be a bright star or a planet? No. It was brighter and larger than any star or planet.

Was it moving, or were my eyes playing tricks on me? No. It was definitely moving.

Could it be a plane or helicopter? No. There were no

flashing lights, and this object was moving back and forth in a circular motion. It was hovering in the same spot above the neighborhood.

Wait, it was hovering!

My eyes widened as I began to question if this was some sort of UFO. In the months that I had been stargazing nearly every night, I never saw anything like this. It was not moving like one of our aircraft. This was different.

I immediately grabbed my phone and began recording the hovering light. It was so dark, my phone camera was going in and out of focus. While trying to focus my camera, a strange blood-orange light suddenly appeared down the street that drew my attention. I looked over to investigate it and found it to be the street light a few houses down, but it looked different. I had never seen the light that vivid blood-orange color before. It was very odd. Time stood still and I became hyper-aware of how bone-chillingly silent and eerie it was outside. I looked around at my surroundings. My neighborhood was like a ghost town. Leafless trees stood perfectly still and silent as dark silhouettes against a clear starry sky, with no wind and no one else around. It was so quiet, you could hear a pin drop.

Suddenly, the silence broke and the wind began to rustle. I looked back over, only to discover a second UFO had appeared, seemingly out of thin air! This one was much closer and larger! It was a strange diamond-shape, and dark gray with a row of red and blue-green lights that went across the middle. The craft was incredibly close, maybe a few houses down. I stood there in shock and awe, bending my neck looking up at it. My mind was having a hard time registering what I was seeing. I was the only one around and I knew this craft was looking right at me.

The diamond UFO seemed to respond to my thoughts and darted to the left, then to the right, shot up and then back down at insane speed, as if to prove to me that it was not a normal aircraft. It seemed to be saying "Yes, I am real." Then the craft slowly started coming straight towards me. I began to tremble in shock, not sure what to do. As the craft grew closer, I decided to step back under my porch and hide under the roof. I lost sight of it as it went right above my head. After a few short seconds went by and I realized it wasn't going to drop a beam of light and pick me up, I jumped out from under my porch to see where it went. It was gone, completely vanished!

I intuitively knew that the UFO must have either flown straight up at ridiculous speed, or it popped into another dimension where I could not see it. I was shaken up and didn't know what to think or do. "They" made it very obvious that they saw me. They literally honed in on me. My whole paradigm instantly shifted and my life forever changed. I could not sleep that night. Little did I know, this would be the first encounter of many.

So, UFOs are real. I thought.

Extraterrestrials are real, and they are here.

The UFO's gave me a couple of months to integrate my first encounter. In January, 2021, I would have my second encounter while alone at a local astronomy park. At around 1:50 a.m. again, while sitting in my car, I suddenly became surrounded by strange lights in every direction. There was a strange hovering light above the treeline to my right as well as to my left, two hovering lights in the treeline behind me, and there were hovering lights about 50 yards in front of me behind a thin layer of trees. I became very curious, unsure if the UFO's knew I was there since my car was off and I was the only one around surrounded by corn fields. I would later discover that they knew I was there and they were there for me.

I began filming the lights with my Nikon D5300 DSLR camera. I did not want to start my car and draw attention to myself, so I decided to record them and wait them out. I was excited to capture evidence of the UFOs with my camera, since nobody believed me when I told them about my first encounter two months earlier. Hours passed by as I watched and filmed the strange lights behaving very strangely, unlike anything I had seen before. They were not leaving, and they acted more strange as the night went on! I filmed them until the sun began to rise and I saw another car drive down the road, then I finally felt comfortable enough to start my car and leave. I was completely mind blown at what had just happened, and that I was able to capture much of it on film.

I literally just spent the entire night surrounded by UFO's. I thought to myself as I left the park, almost in disbelief.

I would return to the astronomy park alone the following night to see if they would show up again. I did see 2 of them hovering back and forth above the tree line on the horizon, which I captured on film. I went back the third night with a friend, determined to have somebody else witness this. That night they did not reveal themselves openly, but something strange flew past me when I separated from my friend to walk to the car.

They are letting me know they are here. I thought.

Even though my friend did not see them, he could feel their presence and said he felt like we were being watched. When I returned home later that evening, there was a light in the sky waiting for me. I felt a sense of excitement and relief to find them waiting for me. I felt a strange sense of connection and calm. The light slowly moved around as I recorded it and spoke to it until the sun began to rise, then I went to bed.

I would see about 13 UFOs / strange phenomena within the next 2 weeks, and caught many of them on film. They seemed to be jumping in front of my camera, like they wanted to be captured. They also seemed to be trying to tell me something.

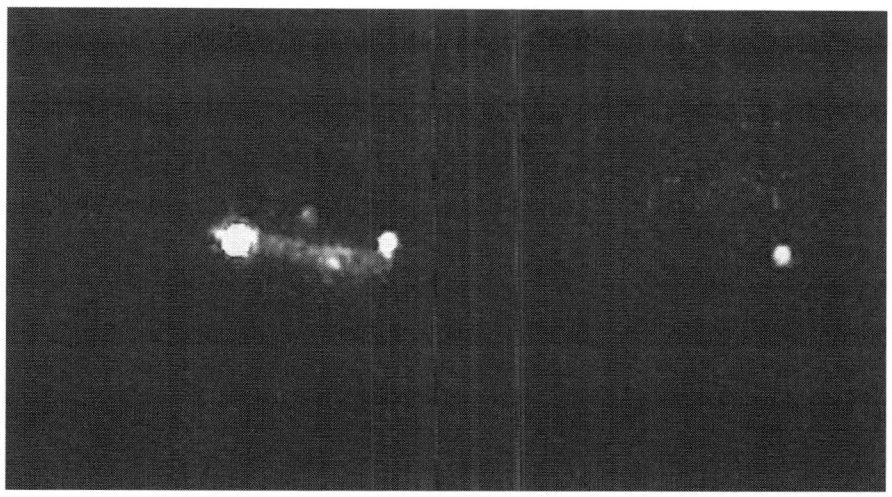

Beam of light comes from a craft in front of me during
my 2nd encounter at the astronomy park

As I was suddenly being bombarded by UFOs, I intuitively began speaking to the beings who were controlling the craft I was seeing, although I was unsure if they could hear me at first. I asked them why they were appearing to me and if they wanted me to share the footage of them, to show people they are here. I quickly began receiving responses to my questions.

I was completely amazed and mind blown that intergalactic beings not from Earth were appearing and communicating with me. This was the most exciting thing that had ever happened! Never did I expect anything like this would happen to me. This is the most important discovery and revelation in modern human history, and I felt like I was at the forefront of it. I felt an obligation to share what was happening. I wanted to know who they were, why they were here, why they were appearing to me, what else was out there, and more. I wanted to know everything. I was determined to get answers, capture evidence, and share the truth with others.

As a relationship with these other worldly beings developed, I began meeting with them daily. I went out with my camera every day to initiate contact with them and document evidence. I found out there is a term for what I was doing, often called "CE5", or human-initiated contact with ETs / UFOs. At first I went out at night, but after experimenting and capturing my first orbs of light during the day, I switched to initiating contact during the day and sunset. We made an agreement and established a regular daily routine.

I found that when I got in a "flow state", it raised my vibration and they would appear. I would begin filming the sunset or clouds, getting in a blissful, creative flow state while doing my passion, and then 'boom!' I would suddenly feel a rush of incredible energy, overwhelming love, and a flood of expansive downloads when they arrived. The overwhelming feelings of positivity, excitement, and pure love I felt during these contact sessions... is hard to even put into words. Nothing I have ever known or felt compares to the love you feel when interacting with these higher dimensional beings. I imagine that the closest comparison would be the immense love a mother has for her child.

Me meditating during a CE5 contact session with a ship to the top right

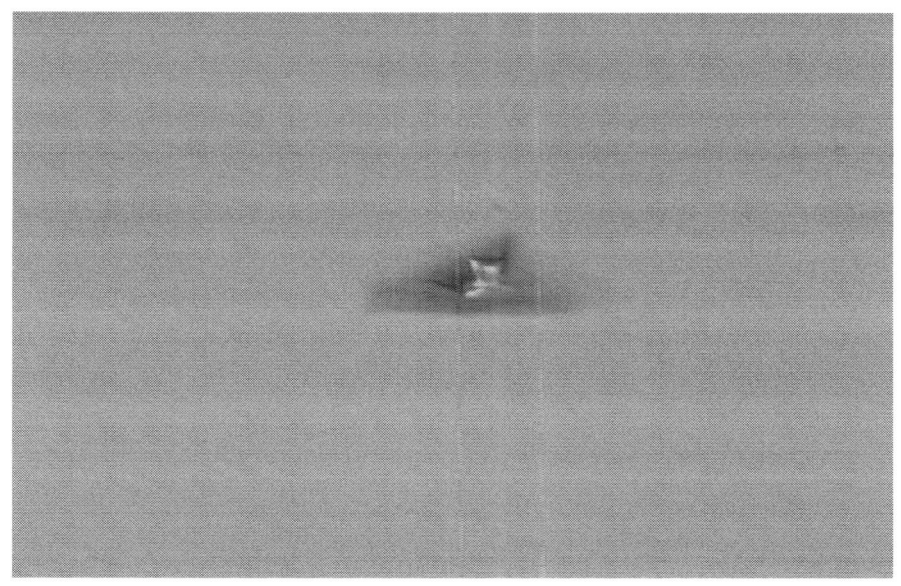

Close up of the UFO/UAP

Close up of two black triangles and what appears to be a portal opening

As our meetings continued, my psychic abilities were being activated rapidly. I began to receive empathic, intuitive, clairvoyant and telepathic information and messages. I was receiving what I would come to know as "downloads", or packets of information, activations, upgrades, and wisdom. I was not psychic before the UFO encounters. My extrasensory perception was being activated by them and rapidly strengthened by my dedication to continue meeting with them and training daily. They instructed me to begin meditating, which would pave the way to countless profound experiences.

When the ETs first began communicating with me through telepathic vision, I got to see what they looked like and learn where they were from. The first beings I saw happened during one of my first CE5's when a golden orb of light appeared (see photo). I closed my eyes and received telepathic visions of the crew, who had light blue skin, silver skin-tight uniforms on, and no hair. Besides having blue skin and no hair, they looked very human. These light blue beings later told me they were from the Lyra constellation, then migrated to the Andromeda constellation.

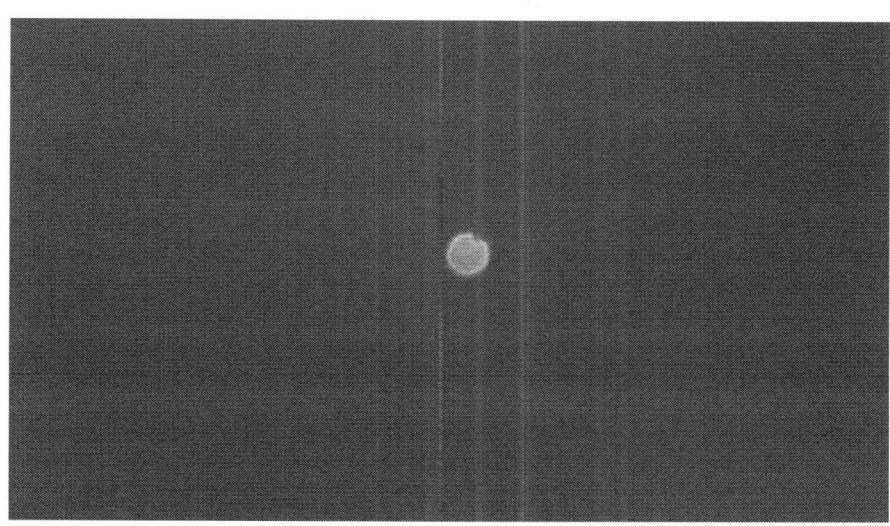

Golden Orb of Light that appeared, Andromedans
send me the telepathic vision

After seeing the light blue Andromedans for the first time, I soon discovered that they were my Star Family. This is when they told me that I was a Starseed (I was one of them - an old soul that does not originate from Earth) and I was on an important mission to help humanity through disclosure and a great awakening. I was here to help humanity through a shift in consciousness and to raise the frequency of the planet. I began communicating with my Star Family daily as they guided me down an unexpected spiritual awakening. As I progressed, I would see many different races of beings, including beings from the Pleiades, Sirius, Arcturus, Lyra, Orion, and others. They all teach me things about who we are, who I am, how the universe works, help me heal, and help me unlock higher levels of consciousness and activate my unique soul gifts.

Some of the initial messages I received from these beings are that we are all one, time is an illusion and the past, present, and future are all happening at once, our heart chakras and the frequency of love is the key, and humanity is incredibly special and has dormant DNA that we need to activate. Many of these beings are here because they are our cosmic families, and because they have contributed their DNA to our DNA. We are literally related. Scientists have long claimed that 95% of our DNA is "junk DNA" because it doesn't appear to be doing anything, but that can't be farther from the truth. This DNA is simply dormant. As the ETs taught me about our DNA and began helping me activate mine during daily meditation sessions, I experienced profound transformations, spontaneous healings, and incredible shifts in consciousness. As we begin to remember who we truly are and activate our DNA, we unlock incredible, superhuman gifts and abilities and unlock our potential. Through guidance and training from my Star Family, I was rapidly activating, upgrading, and developing strong psychic and healing abilities. They taught me that we are magnificent creators and divine sparks of Source, capable of creating and accomplishing anything we set our minds to.

Depiction of Pleiadians helping me activate my
DNA during a meditation session

Here are some things I've learned from meaningful contact
with my Star Family:

We are all connected through consciousness, and you
can make telepathic / psychic contact with these beings
no matter the physical distance between you. Everything
is frequency and vibration. Your frequency, and your
repeated thoughts and emotions create your reality. Many
of the extraterrestrials interacting with Earth are very high

vibrational / in a higher density than 3D, and in order to perceive and connect with them, we must raise our frequency to meet them. Humanity is unaware of how powerful they are, we have been suppressed and lied to about everything. We must remember who we truly are, and begin activating our dormant DNA, special gifts and raising our consciousness. We must also focus on healing and releasing our old baggage. It cannot come where we are going (the New Earth). We all have a Star Family who cares for us very deeply and is watching over us (especially if you are reading this). You can connect with your Star Family, too. Set the intention to make meaningful contact with benevolent beings, spend time outside looking up, raise your frequency or get in a blissful, loving state or creative flow state, and develop a regular meditation practice.

◆ ◆ ◆

Check out Lily's new book *Contact: An incredible true story of contact with beings from another world and spiritual awakening* to read more about her story, experiences, and insights.

CHAPTER 24

We Are The Disclosure

Still to this day, many people in the field of Ufology are discussing and dissecting the Roswell crash, researching and talking about government documents, hearings, and programs, and are basically still trying to prove to the world that UFOs are real and should be taken seriously, and that what crashed at Roswell was in fact an extraterrestrial craft. All of that is great! Those are all things that are important and we absolutely should be looking into and talking about those things. But if that's ALL you're focused on and are talking about…then there's a problem.

This can be extremely frustrating and tiresome to those of us who have moved past that stage a long time ago, or who even started off at a point much deeper than that. There are many of us who already know that UFOs are a real thing, that many are of ET origin, that extraterrestrials exist, and that many people on the planet have been in contact with them for a long time. We know the crash at Roswell was an ET craft and not a "weather balloon," we know that many UFO/ET sightings and experiences are real, and we know ETs have been coming here and have been living on the planet for a *very* long time. So can we please move on from trying to merely prove that UFOs are real? Let's actually figure out who is on the craft. What are they like? Why are they here? What information can they share with us? Can we contact ETs and connect with them ourselves? All the UFO/UAP information is absolutely important to discuss and get out there. But if we are only researching and talking about the "hard data," then we are completely missing all the deeper elements and realities of what is going on, and how it all relates to us. We are then stuck at a very superficial and surface level of information, when we need to be going much deeper and finding the wealth of information and truth that lie beyond all of that.

We need to connect the dots and see how ET contactee information fits with UFO information, which fits with spiritual and metaphysical information, which fits with paranormal information, which fits with "conspiracy" and hidden agenda information, which fits with ancient texts and ancient archaeology, etc. etc. When you look into all of these areas, you will start connecting the dots and start to see how they all connect. You're then able to take a step back and see all the puzzle pieces come together to form the big picture of what's going on. There is much truth within all of those areas, and when you research and study everything with a truly open mind and heart, you will see how they all connect within the greater picture of reality.

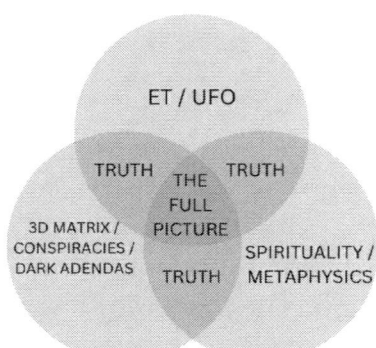

Many people have had their own profound experiences which have given them a deep *knowing* that something is true, far beyond just beliefs and knowing information. I have had my own experiences and I have this deep knowing. Through mediation, connecting to God/Source/Spirit, and having many other experiences, I now have a deep inner knowing that we are not alone in the universe, that many other beings and forms of life exist throughout the universe in many dimensions, and that we are all eternal spiritual beings who are currently having a temporary human experience.

Rosemary Ellen Guiley says it well in the book *We Are the Disclosure*:

> "As an author, researcher, and investigator for more than thirty years now, I have always focused on the nature and ramifications of contact—especially the transformative effects—as the true ground zero of ufology. Yet, the field almost from the beginning has chosen to mire itself in narrow 'nuts and bolts' pursuits, endlessly discussing the same alleged UFO crashes, trace evidence, and cover ups, and ignoring aspects such as the role of consciousness and the para-physical nature of contact. I am all for finding hard, physical evidence, but seventy years on, we have precious little of it, despite endless stone-turning. The evidence that has soared, on the other hand, points to contact that is part of an expansion of consciousness beyond this physical reality. It is no less real than any physical evidence.
>
> What's more, those who have had extraterrestrial contact also experience a host of other kinds of contact and extraordinary experiences that one usually finds within the field of metaphysics—a field usually overlooked by 'traditional' ufology."

Many people are fighting for "disclosure," which to them

means governments and militaries around the world finally admitting to ETs and UFOs being real, that we have in fact reverse engineered and obtained ET technology, and finally releasing these advanced technologies to the world to benefit humanity and the planet. These are all forms of "disclosure" which all should, and I believe *will* be happening at some point in the not too distant future. But if we're only focused on the "authorities" giving us information and access to extraterrestrials and other beings, then essentially we are just reinforcing that these governments and so-called "authorities" have all the power and we don't actually have any power, so we must beg and plead and hope that they give us the things we want. The things that are our birthright, like Truth, Freedom, Sovereignty, and connecting with other beings.

The truth is that governments, militaries, and the shadowy groups controlling things behind the scenes, only care about power and control. Any disclosures that the minions of the control system tell us, or any technologies they release to us, will only be done if it serves their own agendas and further reinforces their own power and control.

True disclosure is an inside job. It happens within us and *through* us. It's not something that will be given to us from some outside "authority." That whole concept is of the old world paradigm that we're completely moving away from. The energy and frequency of the planet is rising and will no longer support the old energies of violence, control, suppression, and fear. The planet is moving into the new energies of love, unity, cooperation, and authenticity. All control systems and structures which operate on the old energies of power and control are falling away. This means that WE are the disclosure. It is happening through us, and the New Earth we are moving into is being created by us each and every day. It is being birthed and created by everyone who is on that frequency of Truth and Love.

My soul brother and podcast partner Tyler Kiwala put it beautifully in a Facebook post:

"Disclosure is not a free pass to forget about your soul's healing. It seems many people want to see change so badly that they are forgetting it has to come from within, and somehow, this new information and technology will magically make their problems disappear. The transition has to be organic. You can't just flip a switch and turn off your old lifestyle, your old ways, and toxic behaviors. There is deep-rooted trauma that must be addressed. There is an integration process. If full disclosure happened right now, there would still be years' worth of healing for the collective. The frequency of the people and the infrastructure has to match the planet, or there will continue to be chaos and duality. But remember, this is an inside job. As we transition, more and more higher-dimensional beings will begin to incarnate until we are at a point where lower-dimensional beings literally won't be able to incarnate here due to the new energies we are inevitably moving into. The conditions have to be right to manifest the golden age we all desire, and it's our job to pave the way."

Humanity is awakening and raising its level of consciousness. We are waking up and realizing that we're actually the ones in control here, and we're the ones that have had the power all along. We are realizing that our freedom and sovereignty is inherent, and no government or "authority" can give that to us or take that away from us. When we start to wake up, reclaim our sovereignty, awaken to our true spiritual nature, and raise our consciousness and vibration into the frequency of love, peace, and oneness, then "disclosure" will start naturally occurring because we will be manifesting the disclosure ourselves. We will then no longer be giving our power away to *anything* outside of us, especially not to control systems, institutions, and psychopathic power hungry authority figures.

In the foreword of the book "We Are the Disclosure," Rosemary Ellen Guiley beautifully lays out how WE are the true Disclosure:

"Advocates for Disclosure have campaigned for an official acknowledgment and release of proof of contact. The advocates have said—every year for years—that we are on the verge of the 'big Disclosure': government is going to come clean, and tell us all about what has been going on and what they are doing about it.

...

Disclosure will not happen by announcement or pronouncement. Rather, it is happening every day, right now, in the contact experiences had by untold numbers of individuals on this planet, who reveal their stories to the public.

The history of contact goes back to the earliest human records. We have been in contact, and we continue to be in contact, with non-human intelligent beings who have pursued various agendas with us. We the people are the Disclosure, not any government, and we always have been so. We do not need a pope or a president to tell us what we already know.

The knowledge and truth of contact has been held in secret by many individuals who have feared—and rightly so—the ridicule of their families, peers, the media, and others if they discuss their experiences with non-human intelligent beings. We have a regrettable track record of labeling contactees as 'crazy' and 'unstable'.

Fortunately, thanks to brave souls who have come forward with information they feel is urgent to disclose, that tide is gradually turning. The more personal disclosure we have, the more public discussion and media coverage we generate, and thus the more we human beings can grapple with the truth of alien contact and interaction, and its implications for us individually and for humanity as a whole."

We don't need to hear things from governments, militaries, or any perceived "authorities" to know what is true or real. We don't need someone else to tell us what we already know, or to give us permission to be in contact with other lifeforms, and to know and experience the realities of the universe and of who we really are. Until a certain percentage of humanity wakes up, raises its consciousness, and takes its power back (which is currently well underway), there will continue to be a control system enslaving humanity. There won't be a disclosure that makes any difference on the planet other than partial ones that only further their own power and control. True and full disclosure is absolutely detrimental to the control system itself, would fully expose it, and would make the system completely obsolete. The truth is, the system is already obsolete, and the only reason they have any power and control at all is because *we give it to them.*

Disclosure and open ET contact on a mass level will happen when enough of us raise our consciousness to a higher level. It will happen when we wake up, take our power back, and realize that we are Divine Sovereign Beings. We don't need anyone's permission to contact and have relations with ETs or higher dimensional beings ourselves. We need to stop continually focusing on and feeding into the control system and all the propaganda and manipulations that are designed to keep us programmed and suppress our consciousness. When enough of us do that, and instead focus our energy and intent on creating the reality that we actually want to create, then we will manifest our own heart-based system that actually benefits and serves Humanity. The old control system will naturally fall away and disappear. It is already happening, as the higher energies are coming into the planet and are bringing up everything to the surface to be seen, healed, and transmuted. It's up to us to connect and align with these energies, align with Source/God/Divine Spirit, to reclaim our sovereignty and to step into our true power.

> "'Your dreams are random.' '96% of your DNA is junk.' 'Humans have five senses.' 'We only need 15% of our brain.' 'It's just your imagination.' Do you know what these all have in common? They're lies! They're programmed lies."
> — Jackie Kenner, from her presentation at the 2022 Secret Space Conference

We haven't been taught that our own bodies, DNA, consciousness, and soul are the greatest technology that exists, far beyond any physical technology, and that we can all tap into our own "technology" and innate power and abilities. We are ALL psychic and telepathic. Some of us just happen to be born with those abilities already "turned on," but we all *have* those abilities. We just need to raise our frequency and learn how to tap into them. Our thoughts, emotions, frequency and energy are constantly feeding into and creating whatever we are focusing on. The powers that "shouldn't be" have cleverly tricked us into creating a reality that only serves them (the tiny few) and keeps the rest of us suppressed, programmed, in constant lack and fear, and obedient to the system. We've all been manipulated into creating and to continually support this slavery system. When we take our power back and start to focus our mind and energy on what we actually want to create, we will then manifest a much different reality. One that is beautiful, that serves all of us, and is in harmony with the planet we live on and the greater universe.

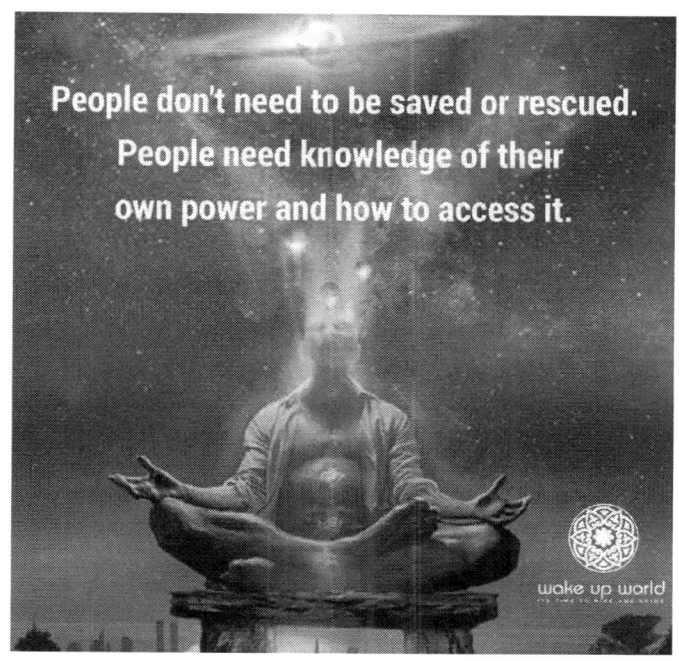

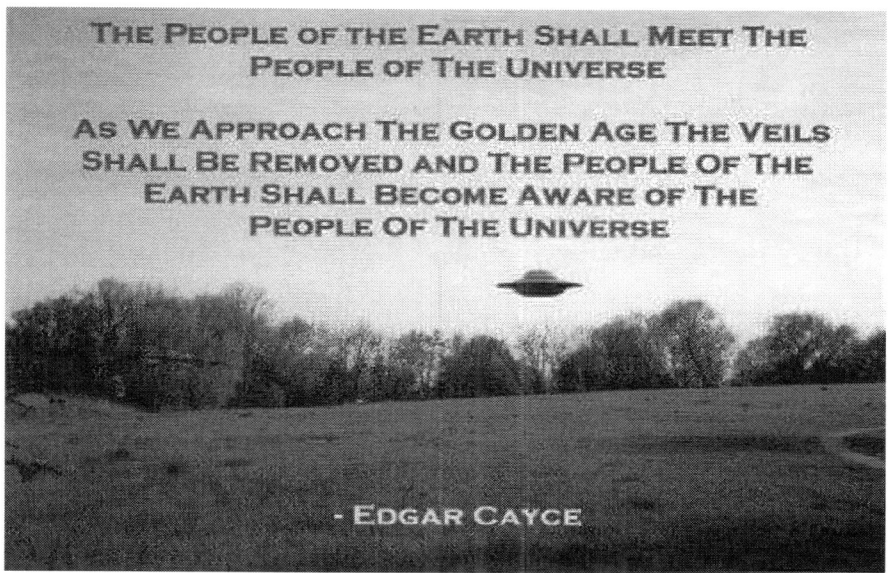

CHAPTER 25

The BIG Picture

*"If you want to find the secrets of the universe, think
in terms of energy, frequency and vibration."*
— Nikola Tesla

"Reality is merely an illusion, albeit a very persistent one."
— Albert Einstein

*"...all knowledge exists in the Mind universe of Light - which is
God - that all Mind is One Mind, that men do not have separate
minds, and that all knowledge can be obtained from the Universal
Source of All-Knowledge by becoming One with that Source."*
— Walter Russell

*"I believe that there is but One Thinker in the universe; that
my thinking is His thinking, and that every man's thinking is
an extension, through God, of every other man's thinking. I
therefore think that the greater the exaltation and ecstasy
of my thinking, the greater the standards of all man's
thinking will be. Each man is thus empowered to uplift all
men as each drop of water uplifts the entire ocean."*
— Walter Russell

*"Your soul is not inside your body, your body is inside your soul.
And what your soul is, is of course, fundamentally the total
universe."*
— Alan Watts

"You are not IN the universe, you ARE the universe,
an intrinsic part of it. Ultimately you are not a person,
but a focal point where the universe is becoming
conscious of itself. What an amazing miracle."
— Eckhart Tolle

If we are eternal spiritual beings having a temporary experience, then what happens after we die? There are many people who have died and come back to life having remembered their experiences on the other side, which are commonly called Near Death Experiences.

Near-death experiences (NDEs) are profound and often transformative experiences of individuals who have died and come back. "Near Death" is actually not entirely accurate, since most of these individuals were actually physically dead when they had their experiences, and then returned to life. So they should really be called "After Death Experiences." These usually involve a variety of common elements such as feelings of peace and serenity, out-of-body experiences (OBEs) where they perceive themselves leaving their physical bodies, and passage through a tunnel or void-like space. Many NDErs also report encountering beings of light or spiritual entities, undergoing a panoramic life review, and reaching a boundary between life and whatever lies beyond. While individual experiences may vary, these common elements provide insights into the mysteries of consciousness, the afterlife, and the nature of reality.

What every Near Death Experiencer becomes profoundly aware of, and what they tell the world, is that *there is no death*. Every religion and spiritual tradition has their own version of this, but NDErs experience the greater spiritual reality, and realize that the religions of the world are all distortions of pure spiritual teachings and core spiritual truths, which were later turned into dogmatic beliefs and control systems.

The great truth that every Near Death Experiencer wakes up to, is that we are Eternal Spiritual Beings. There is no death. There is no "One True Religion" or belief system. Though they all contain spiritual truths, they are all distortions and control systems meant to divide, conquer, and suppress the consciousness of humanity.

Almost every Near Death Experiencer describes experiencing an immense love and peace, beyond what they can put into words. They wake up to the truth that we are all Eternal Spiritual Beings who never die, that our true nature is of God/Source/Love, and that we go on forever having countless experiences.

Albert Einstein revealed a great truth when he stated, "Energy cannot be created or destroyed, it can only be changed from one form to another." Death cannot possibly exist, because all that actually exists is energy. That energy can change its form and expression, and consciousness can move from one point of awareness to another. So what we experience as "death" is merely consciousness moving from the physical body vessel and back into Spirit, which you actually never left in the first place. You're currently having an *experience* of being somewhere else, of being a human being on planet Earth, but in reality you are *still there* in Spirit.

Bashar (channeled through Darryl Anka) often talks about this truth:

> "Physical reality is just a dream. You are in spirit right now. You never left. You are still in spirit right now *dreaming* that you are not."

"You never leave Heaven. EVER. You're in Heaven now, having a dream that you're not. But you never ever actually leave. There is nowhere to go. Remember the second law? There is only Here and Now. So everything that happens, has to happen Here and Now, but it happens in a different frequency of consciousness so that it doesn't *appear* to be happening in the same here and now, but it is. So while you're experiencing this idea, this concept called physical reality where my soul, my spirit has left the spirit world and encased itself in a body and is traveling around in physical reality and someday I will die and my spirit will go back. That's the experience from your point of view. That's the illusionary experience. And the experience is valid, the experience is a real experience, but that's not an accurate description of what's actually happening mechanistically. You never leave. You're just dreaming that you have."

The real you is infinite, eternal, and is so much more than merely a physical body with a name given to you, that lives for a short period of time on one planet. The real you is beyond space, time, and physicality altogether. This 3D life that you are currently experiencing is just that. An *experience*. It's not *you*. It's an experience that the *real you* is having.

"Each of us is here to discover our true selves; that essentially we are spiritual beings who have taken manifestation in physical form; that we're not human beings that have occasional spiritual experiences, that we're spiritual beings that have occasional human experiences"
— Deepak Chopra

Your true self, or your soul, is pure conscious energy. And as energy cannot be created or destroyed, neither can you. This physical body that you are temporarily inhabiting is also made up of energy. So is all of physicality. It's all just energy that is vibrating at a specific frequency, and organized in a specific way. This gives us the illusion of matter and physicality, but in actuality it's all pure energy. So that means what we perceive as physicality is merely an illusion. And believe it or not, your soul (the real you) actually wanted and *chose* this experience. "Why on earth would I choose this?!" you might ask. To put it simply, because the physical plane gives you experiences that you cannot have any other way. Its difficulties and hardships are actually a blessing in disguise, as they allow for immense growth and expansion. It gives you experiences of love, beauty, joy, and excitement that are unique to physical reality. All those experiences (which could also be called lessons) help to further your soul's growth and expansion, and therefore the growth and expansion of God/Source/the Universe itself.

You never left the spirit realm. The realm of spirit is beyond time and space. Time and space are actually illusions. They only exist in this plane of existence in order to give us a particular experience. This physical reality is simply a very dense plane of existence, where the frequency and vibration of energy is much slower than the higher dimensions and densities. Therefore, it gives the illusion of physicality and "solid matter." But when you look close enough at "solid matter," it's made up of only vibrating energy, which isn't solid at all. That means what we perceive as solid and physical is merely an illusion. Our human brains are just wired to perceive it that way, so that we're able to have these types of experiences. We are able to have the *experience* of physicality. And therefore, we can also have the experience of death or loss, even though in reality there is no such thing as "death" or "loss." After your "death," which is merely the transition out of physicality, your awareness returns to the spirit realm (which you never left) and your soul goes on to other planes of existence and goes on to have other experiences. You merely "wake up" out of the dream of physicality.

We're all multi-dimensional beings who are existing on different planes and dimensions, and are having multiple experiences simultaneously, because time doesn't actually exists. Everything is happening in the Eternal NOW.

"What is multi-dimensional? Multi-dimensional is a being who is aware of all of its lifetimes at the same time: past, present, and future. One being can be many beings all at the same time. That's what all of you are. You're just not aware of your multi-dimensionality. You're only aware of you."
— Dolores Cannon, *The Three Waves of Volunteers and the New Earth*

Jackie Kenner explaining the nature of the soul and how it branches off to have multiple incarnations and experiences simultaneously

Here is what James Van Praagh has to say about the soul in his book *Adventures of the Soul*:

"Sometime between conception and birth, Spirit enters the body as a soul. The soul is Spirit incarnate. Don't think of yourself as a body that has a soul, but rather as Spirit that needs a body. Spirit permeates everything, and in me—in this body I call James Van Praagh—it is my soul.

While on Earth, I am Spirit that requires physical form in this dimension so I can experience conditions and learn lessons that other realms don't provide. I enjoy food, art, literature, music, and other things that speak to or feed my soul. My soul experiences love, hate, betrayal, sympathy, forgiveness, empathy … you name it. Earth is a schoolroom, and the soul is the student.

My soul is unique to me, but at the same time, it is a part of the whole and connected to everything. That connection is filtered through our physical senses, so it may not seem like it is always there. The emotion that we call love enables us to feel this connection, and extraordinary circumstances (such as the events of September 11) can certainly make us feel it as well. We are all the same energy, but Earth provides us with so many different physical guises that sometimes it's difficult to acknowledge that truth.

We often hear people say, 'I am God,' and it's true: our souls are Spirit, God, Allah, the Divine—whatever you choose to call it—on Earth. Our bodies are limited by the constraints of the physical dimension, but our souls are outside of linear space and time and transcend our physical selves.

The soul is the unique core of our self and the consciousness of who we are. It has crossed many oceans of lifetimes, experiences, and expressions of being. It's filled with infinite creative possibilities to manifest itself, and it's distinct in its own development and expression."

Another beautiful summation of what our soul is in relation to God/Source/the Universe, and everything I just talked about, is this excerpt from Christian Sundberg's book *A Walk in the Physical*:

"Source, also called God, is sentient, purposeful, and

unfathomably wise and loving.

The Whole of consciousness individuated Itself. We call those individuations souls. Each soul is indivisibly a part of the One, and yet is simultaneously a precious sovereign free-willed aspect of the One. There is no paradox in the simultaneous Oneness and individuation of the soul. In the words of Rumi, 'You are not just a drop in the ocean, you are the mighty ocean in the drop.'

Through individuated pieces of Herself (Himself, or Itself), Source takes on numerous physical and nonphysical experiences, including experiences where She may veil Herself from Her own true nature so that She can have the experience of separate perspectives. She does this for the purpose of the expansion of the joy and love of Beingness through Creation.

The soul is always full of the amazing life, power, vibrance, and profound abundance of Being. The soul contains many aspects of the self – different 'personalities' or 'characters' – that it has been and is, and yet it transcends them all. In other words, the human character is a small part of a much larger multidimensional self. The soul is the same 'I' even when it engages the experience of being these different 'personalities' or 'characters,' and they are each available to each other and inform each other. The self is unfathomably deep, and the individual can benefit greatly from personally exploring one's own depth of being."

David Icke has been preaching these concepts for the past four decades, and he always hits the nail on the head when talking about the nature of reality and our True Self. He sums it up beautifully in these quotes:

"Most people think that we live in a 'physical' world, and I grant you that certainly appears to be the case. But it's not, because we don't. There is no 'physical'. It's all an illusion. We are infinite, eternal Consciousness having an experience in a tiny range of frequencies that we call the 'physical world', but that isn't. We are not our name, body, occupation, family background, race, colour or income bracket. They are our current experience; they are not who we are. We are Consciousness – infinite, eternal Awareness. We have no form in our core state; we are just awareness, and an expression of Infinite Awareness. Hence, it is said that we are 'all One'. Yes, one Infinite Awareness having different experiences from different points of observation – different levels of awareness and perception."

"The real foundation from which this whole conspiracy is based...is manipulating people to believe they're something they are not, and to forget what they really are. And what we really are is consciousness. Infinite consciousness connected to all other consciousness. The seamless ocean of infinity. And we can move our point of observation around that consciousness and express and celebrate its uniqueness, but we are all of one infinite mind. One infinite consciousness. And the illusion of apartness is an experience of this reality and its accentuation by the manipulators to get us to see ourselves and everything in terms of apartness instead of as a connected whole."

What is life? Does life only constitute what you and I and all other living beings are experiencing? Or is life everything that exists, essentially the energy of God/Source in perpetual motion?

If everything in existence is the One (God/Source/Universe/ whatever term you prefer) experiencing Itself by having different experiences from different points of awareness, then there is no separation. We are all God, the great I AM, experiencing the infinity that it is. How could anything possibly be "separate" from that? How could anything *not* be that? It can't. Mental programs and beliefs can make us *think* that is the case, but reality is not a belief or a mental program. Truth is truth and the nature of reality is what it is, whether you choose to believe in it or not.

> "The truth is: you don't have a life, you are life. The One Life, the one consciousness that pervades the entire universe and takes temporary form to experience itself as a stone or a blade of grass, as an animal, a person, a star or a galaxy. Can you sense deep within that you already know that? Can you sense that you already are That?" — Eckhart Tolle

We tend to see life as something we possess. We call the temporary experience we're having "our" life. What most of us fail to realize is that we *are* life. We are not separate from it, because nothing *can* be separate from it. Life is everything that exists, therefore it is also you and me. We are literally life experiencing itself within itself. Our soul essences are each a point of awareness, a spark of light, which Source desired into being so it could gain experiences from that unique perspective. From the perspective that only *you* can give. Every experience your soul accumulates is helping God/Source/the Universe in its expansion, because you literally *are It*.

"Energy cannot be created or destroyed, it can only be changed from one form to another." Energy and consciousness are actually the same thing. So just replace energy with consciousness: "Consciousness cannot be created or destroyed, it can only be changed from one form to another." We are all Infinite Consciousness having experiences in an Infinite Universe.

> "The world is like a ride in an amusement park, and when you choose to go on it you think it's real because that's how powerful our minds are. The ride goes up and down, around and around, it has thrills and chills, and it's very brightly

colored, and it's very loud, and it's fun for a while. Many people have been on the ride a long time, and they begin to wonder, 'Hey, is this real, or is this just a ride?' And other people have remembered, and they come back to us and say, 'Hey, don't worry; don't be afraid, ever, because this is just a ride.' And we kill those people. 'Shut him up! I've got a lot invested in this ride, shut him up! Look at my furrows of worry, look at my big bank account, and my family. This has to be real.' It's just a ride. But we always kill the good guys who try and tell us that, you ever notice that? And let the demons run amok ... But it doesn't matter, because it's just a ride. And we can change it anytime we want. It's only a choice. No effort, no work, no job, no savings of money. Just a simple choice, right now, between fear and love. The eyes of fear want you to put bigger locks on your doors, buy guns, close yourself off. The eyes of love instead see all of us as one. Here's what we can do to change the world, right now, to a better ride. Take all that money we spend on weapons and defenses each year and instead spend it feeding and clothing and educating the poor of the world, which it would pay for many times over, not one human being excluded, and we could explore space, together, both inner and outer, forever, in peace."
— Bill Hicks

This is what I've come to ultimately understand is going on: God/Source/The Universe/Divine Spirit (whatever term you want to use) is the ultimate reality. We are all ultimately that infinite consciousness, having a temporary experience as a human. All is One, and we are all manifestations of that same Infinite Oneness. "Coincidences" are not a real thing, and neither is the concept of a lifeless, non-intelligent material universe that somehow started when a random explosion happened from...nothing...because that totally makes sense! Our physical universe is a mental creation of God/Source/Divine Intelligence. It is within the mind of God.

The ancient Vedic texts talk about this Infinite Consciousness manifesting in different forms:

> "The unborn in whom all existing things abide."
> "The one manifesting as the many...the formless putting on forms."
> — Rigveda

The Law of One's basic premise is this Eternal Truth, that we are all the One Infinite Creator and everything is the One in manifest form. It states:

> "You are every thing, every being, every emotion, every event, every situation. You are unity. You are infinity. You are love/light, light/love. You are. This is the Law of One."

On a soul level, when we are not incarnated in physical bodies, we are not bound by the limitations of time, because time does not actually exist. We only have an experience of time within the physical 3D reality. But all that actually exists is the Eternal Now. Our physical minds in this 3D realm have a very limited perspective. At the level of the soul, to say we have a much broader perspective is a *massive* understatement. From our soul's perspective outside of time and space, we know that experiences within spacetime physicality can have tremendous value to our soul's growth and expansion.

Peter Slattery writes this in *The Book of Shi-Ji 2*:

> "You are multidimensional Beings who are having multidimensional experiences. You are a cell, a facet of Source (with many other facets), and you coexist at the same time throughout many planes. To understand this, you need to go from linear mind to multidimensional mind. Many experiences are happening for your oversoul at this (what you call) time. So...it's best we start with the

'creation through thought' story first, and then take it from there. During the implosion and then the explosion (which created a torsion field), and then the second explosion, Helper Beings and zillions of spirits were created. They went out to experience and gain knowledge—although some remained in a state of monitoring for the overall collective, Source. This is how everything began in this cell, which is our multilayered universe, with its planes and dimensions and inter-planes. The other universes were created this way, too. All universes have a symbiotic relationship with each other, and all together they make up a greater intelligence. When the explosion happened and the zillions of spirits and Helper Beings went out to experience and gain knowledge, there were the Elohim, who came into existence through thought."

At the center of the universe dwells the Great Spirit. And that center is really everywhere. It is within each of us. ~ *Black Elk*

CHAPTER 26

Waking to the Infinite Universe

*"Do not feel lonely, the entire universe is inside you.
Stop acting so small. You are the universe in ecstatic motion.
Set your life on fire. Seek those who fan your flames."*
— Rumi

We do not need anything outside of us, because the truth is that there is no "outside of us." That experience is an illusion. The entire Universe is within us! All that actually exists is infinite conscious energy. There is no matter. Matter is an illusion our 3D minds perceive. It is merely vibrating energy. We are discovering that separation, either through time or space, is an illusion. There is no separation. All is One. We are all eternal fractals of Source who created the illusion of separation in order to experience itself, the All That Is. We are having experiences for our growth and expansion, and for the expansion of Source. We are all Infinite Consciousness experiencing all possibility. We are the great I AM experiencing All That Is.

Our 3D human selves are now waking up from a deep sleep. We are waking up to who we really are, and what is really going on. We are awakening to many truths and realities that have been hidden away from humanity for a long time. We are connecting with Spirit, with nature, with our souls, and with each other in loving communities. We are connecting with our Star Families, and other beings throughout the Universe. We are seeking and finding Truth within ourselves. We are reclaiming our sovereignty and taking our power back from everything we've given it away to. We are creating a new reality based on love and connection. We are waking up to the infinite beauty and wonders that surround us. We are waking up to the reality that *we* are the ones we've been waiting for.

We are Infinite Beings waking up to the Infinite Universe.

ROBERT DEAN
LECTURE AT THE
UNIVERSITY
OF LEEDS

Late military insider Robert Dean, or Bob Dean (1929-2018) gave a speech at the University of Leeds in 1995 which was called "one of the most profound lectures ever delivered in the U.K." The following is an excerpt of that speech, and is a powerful message for humanity:

"Let me tell you basically what the study concluded in 1964. The planet earth and apparently the entire human race is and has been the subject of an extensive, intensive and massive survey and examination by several extraterrestrial civilizations. This study has been extremely thorough in detail. These civilizations have demonstrated not only high intelligence, but an extremely advanced technology that may possibly be hundreds, if not thousands of years beyond our own. Evidence collected and studied by this report indicates that apparently there is some kind of a process or a plan unfolding. They–whoever they are–continually demonstrate that the development of some kind of a program is underway. They could see that in '64 as a result of the three-year study. Over the years we've seen it continue. We know it even progresses to that today. There is something happening. Something is unfolding. There's some development taking place. That's why I consider it so crucial that people pay attention and inform themselves about what's really been going on.

The evidence in this report leads to the conclusion that this survey or program has been going on for a very long time–possibly several thousands of years. Military Intelligence analysis have concluded that there did not–repeat, did not–appear to be a major military threat involved. The conclusions seem to indicate that if they were either malevolent or hostile, there was absolutely nothing that we could do at that time, and I have got to tell you in all honesty, there's absolutely nothing we can do at *this* time. The technology that was repeatedly demonstrated over the years and is still continually demonstrated, is so far beyond anything we–and I say we: the U.S., Britain, France, Italy, Germany. Most of the major nations on this planet are not even close to developing the kind of technology that these extraterrestrial intelligence have. NATO and SHAPE policy dictates that an ongoing study be continued by the various military committees, and that as many resources as possible by the major powers be committed to this matter. The entire subject is considered to be of the highest importance and extremely sensitive. This committee recommends that the highest level of classification be placed upon this matter and...to be cosmic top secret or above."

"I wanted to know what the military knew. I wanted to know what the politicians and the scientists knew. What they knew in 64 was only the tip of the iceberg. I wanted to know what it was all about. My initial research, as the military, was: 'who are they? where are they from? and why are they here?' And that was my impetus and my drive for very many years. I learned very quickly that there was no simple easy way to learn anything about this. That there was no discipline that I could ever follow that would give me a clear and understandable picture of what was happening. I found out most of our great scientists were specialists in their fields. Historians, psychologists, atmospheric physicists, atomic physicists, nuclear physicists–every one of our great scientists have this narrow specialty field that they spend their lives working on and they know very often very little about what's out on the sides. They know their discipline. They study it. They devote their life to it. But they don't necessarily have the time and the discipline to broaden their perspective and broaden their view.

Well as a trained intelligence analyst–a man who has no numbers or letters behind his name at all–a man who at that time had not even finished his university training–I was a raving nut about trying to find the answers to this, and as I said I'd been trained to be an intelligence analyst. So I began to apply my skill as an intelligence analyst to this research. I found that I had to dig into history. I had to dig into philosophy, literature, mythology, anthropology, geology, theology, many of the hard sciences, and I had to even get into art and music, before I began to get what I consider to be an overall perspective of what I thought was happening.

Now I must tell you, what I'm sharing with you this evening is my opinion. It's a result of 30 years of my synthesis, my personal search, my personal odyssey. I don't want one of you to leave this room this evening believing anything I may have said because I said it. But I would like to have you leave this room this evening with an enhanced piqued curiosity, so that you'll go out there and do your own research, inform yourselves as I did, and tell yourself–researching this–what really is going on and reach your own conclusions. Don't accept mine. I challenge you to do your own research, but I challenge you also, once you've really dug into this thing you'll never be able to walk away from it. You'll never be able to put it down, and you will never ever be the same. So I would say to you in advance, welcome to the club.

Now there are other things that happened over the years. When I began my research I was curious about the hardware. Who they were, where they were from, why they were here, what it was all about. And I learned over the years that my focus changed. The direction of my intention began to change. After about 15 to 20 years it became apparent to me that it was not necessarily 'who are they' and 'why are they here' and 'where are they from' that was really the most important thing to me. I began to realize that there was an aspect of this research–there was a component beyond the hardware and the reality of extraterrestrial visitation. I became aware that there's what I call a spiritual component to this matter, which I have concluded is roughly 90 percent of this entire thing. Beyond the hardware. Beyond who they are and where they're from and why they're here. What's really important to me in my studies today–and I challenge you again because I think once you get involved with this yourselves you'll probably come up with the same conclusions I did–What's really important is who are we? Where did we come from? How did we come to be here? What is our life, and the meaning of our life all about? And where are we going as a species? And that has become the central focus of my research over the years.

I don't investigate UFOs anymore. The evidence for the reality, as Stanton has told you, is overwhelming. We have an abundance of data. We have an overabundance of data. We don't need any more data to prove the reality of UFOs or extraterrestrial spacecraft. What we do need to know is: What's it all about? What is really happening? What is the meaning of their being here at this particular time? What is happening in the world today that they're interested in and involved in? What should we begin to pay attention to? Well I'll share a little bit of what I think is really happening here.

Now before I left SHAPE headquarters in 1967, the SHAPE military people knew that there were four different groups that we were dealing with. There were four separate extraterrestrial intelligences involved. When I retired in 1976 the military knew–at least the U.S. military and I am assuming the British as well– knew of at least 12 different groups that were coming and going and involved with us. I've been told by friends who are still working in high places–people who seem to know, people whose information I trust–that there may be well over a hundred different groups coming and going from God knows where.

The one that interested the generals the most in 1964 and 1967, the one that drove them up the wall, was the one group– one out of the four–looked exactly like we do. And I don't mean similar, I mean exactly. So much so that they could sit next to you in an airplane or in a restaurant or in a theater and you would never know. You would literally never know. And that bothered the admirals and the generals a lot because we military have always been–we are trained to be–paranoid. It's the nature of our game. The idea that there could be alien intelligence looking so much like us that they could walk up and down the corridors of SHAPE headquarters. They could walk up and down the corridors of the Pentagon. One day at lunch a Lieutenant Colonel, a U.S. Lieutenant Colonel says 'My god man. Do you realize they could even be in the white house?' Well there was a little forced laughter at that point because a lot of us, particularly we Americans, have had some misgivings over the years about who's ending up in the white house. I will share briefly with you that I have some misgivings about the present occupant, but I won't go into any specifics on that issue. It bothered him a lot that one of these groups looks so much like us–and I'd like to twist that around if I may. It's not that they look like us. We look like them, and there's a very good reason for it, and I'll touch upon that.

We also learned–when I left the service in 1976 and lost my clearance–could no longer visit and bug the hell out of my good friends–We knew that we were not simply dealing with extraterrestrial visitation from other planets. That was a given. We were not dealing just with interplanetary visitation. We were dealing with interstellar visitation. We were dealing with intergalactic visitation. And the one and the final thing that drove our scientists and our military planners, even some of our philosophers wild was that apparently we were dealing with advanced intelligence that appeared to be multi-dimensional in their source, and some of these advanced races apparently had the ability to manipulate matter and time. They had repeated these kinds of things all the time. They had demonstrated them repeatedly, specifically to get our attention.

Now stop for a moment and stop to think what that means. We're not just having little guys coming here from other planets or other stars or other galaxies. We're having advanced intelligences here interrelating with us. Interested somehow in us. Interested enough to come and be involved with us, that apparently are multi-dimensional and some of those more advanced ones can manipulate time and matter. My god that turns our old Newtonian Einstein physics absolutely upside down. The only people who I know today who can even begin to deal with this kind of reality are theoretical physicists. There are quantum physicists in Great Britain. There are quantum physicists in the United States. Many of them are working together at large U.S. brick universities, who apparently are on the edge of grasping what multi-dimensional visitation is all about. I'm not a physicist. I'm not a scientist like Stan. I can't begin to tell you what a dimension is for that matter.

I'm told we live in three, and that's quite a simple world that we have around us. I'm told that time and space is the fourth. Theoretical physicists have told me that there are as many as ten different dimensions. I cannot for a moment grasp what that means. I do however accept that it's probably real. The evidence that I have seen over my last 40 years has told me that this is not fantasy. This is not science fiction. This is all real, and ladies and gentlemen this reality, when it becomes known and when it makes an impact upon our world, is going to change our world forever. You talk about a paradigm shift. That's an understatement. The old world we have known for so long is literally coming to an end, and it's just around the corner, and very few people are prepared for it.

What have I concluded?

I told you things I've seen. I've told you things I've been a part of. Told you about military studies and reports that I've been a part of, that I've had a chance to read. I told you that your government and mine have been lying to us for well over 40 years. I told you bluntly that basically they're scared to death about how to tell you some of the things they've learned, because they don't know how you're going to deal with it. I disagree with them. I don't think any of you are going to run hysterically through the street. I've spoken to people like you around the world. It's my opinion, particularly the British people, are sound emotionally stable people and I haven't seen one of you run hysterically out of the auditorium, and I've been speaking here now for well over a week. I'll tell you what I've concluded: We are not alone, and we have never been alone. We have had as I have said, and repeatedly say–We have had an intimate interrelationship with advanced intelligence from somewhere out there, and it's not just time and space as we know it. I say somewhere out there, I'm talking about different dimensions as well. The human race has had a continual intimate interrelationship with advanced extraterrestrial intelligence from the beginning of our history.

Now there's more, and it's a little sensitive. It's somewhat sensitive in a theological way. I have concluded that the human race–us, we–are a hybrid race. That we have been genetically placed here. We have been seated on this planet and we have been continually genetically manipulated–and I say continually–from the beginning of our history into what we are today. The process is still going on. It's still underway. It has not stopped, and the abduction scenario and all of the things that many of you are beginning to pay attention to and are learning about, is real and it's happening. This intimate interrelationship is intimate. They're involved in our genetics. They're involved in our racial development. They're involved in our evolution. They have been involved in that since the beginning of our history. Some of them over the centuries–hundreds and thousands of years back when we had a relationship and a contact with them–we had a tendency to deify them. Thus we have all of these great world religions. It's also a sensitive subject to get into, because I flatly state in my opinion after many many years of research that every major world religion on this planet has had its origin from extraterrestrial sources. And every great theological philosophy and every great book, from the Bible to the Bhagavad-Gita to the Quran to the writings of the Buddha, every one of those tells essentially the same story. I have gone on the line and I have put my neck out on the block, literally. I'm too old to worry about it. I'm too damned fractious to pay attention to it.

I say flatly that in my opinion that beautiful young man in Galilee two thousand years ago was involved in this program. Everything about his life indicates to me that he was deeply intimately involved in this program. He said as much while he was alive. He said I'm not from here. This is not my kingdom. He said in my Father's house are many mansions out there.

He says I have other flocks. I have other sheep. He repeatedly made these things clear but nobody grasped what he was talking about. He said to the people at the time, he said you are as gods. What I do you can do and even more. He was trying desperately to get us to grasp and understand who and what we were. We were no great cosmic accident. We were no coincidence. It was important. There was a reason we were here and he tried to explain to us. It's in the Quran. It's in the Bhagavad-Gita. It's in the writings of Buddha. Every great religious teacher from the beginnings of our history has said essentially the same thing. This is sensitive material.

I made a comment at a conference one time in Dallas, Texas, which as many of you probably know is what we call in our Bible Belt. And after I had finished I saw this little heavy set dude coming at me. Had a bible tucked under his arm and I thought 'Oh boy I'm in for it.' I had visions of us rolling on the floor here, he and I, because Dallas is kind of a fundamentalist south there. Thank God I didn't get attacked. He grasped me. Hugged me. Kissed me with tears in his eyes and said 'Son, that's the best explanation of what I've been studying and living with all my life that I have ever heard. God bless you.' Gave me a kiss and disappeared. I say this to you because I'm convinced that almost everybody out there, including any type of Christian you could find, any kind of Muslim you might find, any Buddhist or Hindu you might find, if they are presented this information in the proper way, will accept it and understand it in the proper way.

Now what am I getting at here. What am I trying to say here. I'm trying to say that I believe the time is coming very very soon that every major religion on this planet will probably collapse in ruins. I tell you that honestly because I see it happening. I see it beginning to occur. They're falling apart. The reason they are is they're not giving you the spiritual truths you need. I say also that when that time comes I will be happy to see it happen. I will be pleased. Every major religion in ruins, literally around our knees. Because at that moment and at that time only, we the people on this planet, will be able to build something new. And we'll build something better. And we'll go on from there, and we'll devote our future to true pure spirit rather than religion. We have over the years butchered each other and shed blood in matters of religion much more than we have politics. I would like to see religion sort of fade away. Become history. I'd like to see us all begin to grasp who and what we are. Understand that there is a basic spirit within us. There is a spark, a divinity within us. That we are all the same.

It doesn't matter what color we are, or what church we go to, what language we speak, what political party we belong to. None of that matters. What matters is we are human beings. We are children of God. We are immortal beings. We are infinite beings. And we're all the same. We are brothers and we are sisters. And we're going to have to reach that conclusion and come to that conclusion very very quickly or we're not going to be able to go out there and take our place in that infinite universe of intelligence, unless we do begin to grasp that we are one people from one tiny planet with one future. And we're going to have to go out into space and take our destiny out there and take our rightful place out there as one people. They're not going to allow us to come out there with our hatreds and our savagery and our bitterness and our bestiality. The stuff that's going on in Bosnia must stop. The stuff that happened in Rwanda must never happen again. We've got to grasp that we are one species, one race, from one little tiny planet, with one future, and we have to go out there together or we may not go out there at all.

Now this is what I have concluded. These are some of the things I have reached after thirty years of research. I share them with you honestly and bluntly and I tell you don't believe me necessarily, but that's what I've concluded after thirty years. I understand, I see, I feel, I perceive, that there is a door being opened for us. The UFO is a part of it. The crop circles are a part of it. The appearance of this beautiful lady who keeps showing up from time to time here, there, and everywhere–the Christians call her Mary the mother of God, the mother of Christ–this beautiful lady has been in our midst and been involved with us since the beginning of our history. She's been appearing here, there, and everywhere. That is the same part of the same overall event. The crop circles, the UFOs, the appearance of the beautiful lady, the abductions, the fact that we are growing spiritually. We re beginning to pay more attention. It's all a part of this much larger whole. It tells me that a door is being opened for us out there to come out and take our place and see our destiny out there with the rest of them into this infinite universe filled with intelligent life. But we're gonna have to do it as one people, at one time together, or we're not gonna make it at all."

ANONYMOUS AREA 51 WHISTLEBLOWER

"The date is June 29th, 2008, 6:32 PM. I'm creating this message to let the people of the world, or whoever happens to hear this, know the truth about what is going on with regards to the alien presence in our world as well as interstellar space and within our own solar system.

I, myself, am a worker in one of the underground bases located near Groom Lake. I have done my work there for the past eight years, and within the next coming months will be discharged. Now, what I'm going to tell you, you may want to take with a grain of salt, but I assure you everything that I am about to say is truth, is fact. And whether you know it or believe it, or not, everything that I will tell you is common knowledge within the Black Ops community at the most highest and secretive levels. Now, as I said, I've worked inside an underground base near Groom Lake for the past eight years, and have done my work there as a researcher and analyst working within the realm of the ET program as we call it, or as it's known in the Black Ops community as G28.

What we do here is research, analyze, and investigate the extraterrestrial presence within our solar system and other dimensions, and what I'm going to tell you today is the truth about what is going on. I will try not to be too vague in my revelations, however I do not want to say too much as I have already committed a felony in the eyes of our government just by speaking on the subject and I will be leaving soon after my discharge. And I have asked the owner of this video to which I'm sending, not to publicize this video for at least two years after it's recording to ensure my safety as well as theirs.

Now, as I've said, and let me make this clear, the presence of alien beings and the technology does exist. It is real as you or me, and it's a whole lot more 'out there' than even the most die-hard believers could possibly fathom. The truth is that we, and by we I mean this planet and the people of this planet, are in essence blind to what is really going on in the cosmos and interstellar space.

What people call aliens, we call IBs, or in layman's terms interdimensional beings. What we found out and have known about since the early 70s is that, in simplest terms, other dimensions or planes, as we call them, exist and lay on top of each other, almost stacked as if you had a blanket with another blanket stacked on top of it and another blanket stacked on top of it. To explain it so you can understand, you can imagine the earth and our reality as a thin blanket and all of these other higher dimensions are the blankets laying directly on top of ours. However we can only see our own blanket.

Now the alien beings or the ships that we have seen in videos and that many people have captured over the years are in fact what we call jumpers in that they exist in their relative dimensions but have in fact jumped into ours. We have discovered that most of the time we are unable to see them as they are at a wavelength different to our own and our senses, eyes and ears cannot detect.

From the information that I have gathered and been briefed on, every planet, star and galaxy within our own plane and universe as we see it, exists also in these other dimensions. We've detected, that we know of and that I've been briefed on, at least four other dimensions that do exist.

Now as I've said, every planet we know of, every galaxy, does exist in these other dimensions. However, with each new dimension, each planet/galaxy/star takes on a different form. To explain it in the simplest terms, you can look at our own planet Jupiter, which is in the outer reaches of our solar system. Now to us, it's a deadly gaseous planet. Completely uninhabitable. However, when you look at Jupiter in an elevated dimension, you will see that it is completely changed in all forms. You will see that it's no longer a deadly ball of gas, but is now solid, has a different color, and is now inhabited. We know for a fact this is true due to the fact that the government has the technology to detect these higher dimensions and actually get a small view of what the solar system looks like on the other side, as we call it, in these other dimensions.

There is much we do not know about the universe and how it works. However, here are the facts that I can confirm as truth and were made known to me, and that I and the other people that I worked with have been briefed on.

We are not alone in the universe. There are alien beings within our own dimension of space, as well as other dimensions. The planet Earth is an early stage training ground, if you will, whereby we as beings will live until we advance to the higher dimensions. Now, we are not the bottom of the food chain, and we have discovered that there are at least two dimensions below our own plane, but that is as far as I will go regarding that.

These are things that I have been briefed on by my superiors and that are common knowledge in the black ops community.

Now the planet that we know of as Mars was at one time inhabited. But again at one time was wiped out by the people who inhabited the planet which were much more technologically advanced than we are, which we discovered by testing and analyzing the chemical residue found from the blasts around the planet, as well as artifacts that we've also discovered on the planet, including the infamous glass tubes seen in the few of the publicly made photographs from NASA. Now these are not glass structures, but a glass-like material that is about a thousand times stronger than any material or steel that we have on our own planet. These tubes were used as a means of travel, underground and above ground by people who inhabited this planet.

It is thought from our research that there is still an ET presence inhabiting Mars but again, this is as far as I will go and that I was briefed on regarding that matter. Now I'm not trying to be completely vague but I am trying to give you a picture of what is going on out there that doesn't completely put me in more danger than I am already in just by revealing the few things that I have.

One of the last things that I will reveal, and that is definitely a fact and that I have been briefed on and that many other people involved with the Black Ops community have been briefed on, and that is our own moon does in fact have alien bases on it and also has bases for our own government.

Now there is an ET presence which is primarily located on the dark side of the moon. The Apollo program was in all actuality a reconnaissance mission so that we could research what was exactly there and who.

You will notice that many of the photos from the Apollo missions have airbrushed out buildings and bases, and this is the truth of the matter. About half of the video that you will see that is documented from the Apollo missions was in fact shot here on Earth at Area 51. In fact, if you look at satellite imagery, you can actually see what's left of a crater field created at Area 51 that was used in the filming. Now, the truth is that most of the footage from the moon was simply cluttered with bases, with alien buildings, and from what one astronaut said, and I'm quoting, what were a 'constant presence of alien vehicles flying over the surface,' cluttering up the footage. So again, they showed the American people what they could, and recreated the rest here on Earth that they couldn't show.

From what we know, the dark side of the moon is where most of the alien presence is located. It's a more primitive alien race from what we can see and our research tells us, it's more primitive than the alien beings you would see on higher dimensions, but still thousands if not millions of years ahead of us.

We have our own bases which are primarily located in or near the Sea of Tranquility, which is the site of Apollo 11, and also one base that I know of located near the crater Sabine D. To this day we are still sending secret missions to and from the moon. However, I do not know the complete details of what we are doing there."

DAVID ICKE ON
THE HEART

The following is from a 2020 David Icke interview on London Real:

"One of the great targets is the heart. I'm not talking about the physical heart, though they are connected. I'm talking about the heart vortex within the human energy field. The heart chakra, or wheel of light, as they call it in the East.

We think of love in a certain way: being attracted to somebody or loving your kids. What I'm talking about, and I talk about this a lot in *The Answer*, it's very different. It includes that of course. But love in its true sense does not say 'I want the best for my kids,' although we do, of course we do. It says 'I want the best for everybody.' And when you open this [the heart], it's not just love in the sense that people perceive it. It opens you to infinity. It's our connection to all that is, has been, and ever can be. And through that connection you have insight, you have knowing. When people have intuitive knowing where do their hands go? 'Look mate I just know, I just know!' This knows because it *does* know because it's connected to that which does know.

And when you open your heart, you're opening your connection to a level of awareness that allows you first of all to see the connections, because you're coming from that level where everything is one, therefore you can see the connections in the reality you're experiencing.

One definition I would give for this kind of love is the absence of fear. I would call evil the absence of love. I think that's what evil is, it's the absence of love. You infuse love into evil, evil's not evil anymore. It's the absence of love, and this is what this cult is, it's the absence of love. That's why it does what it does.

It's the absence of fear, because once you open to this insight, this self-identity, you know there's nothing to fear. Because whatever happens, whatever experiences we're having, there'll be another one along in a minute. We are always an expression, a point of attention within all that is, has been, and ever can be. And however bad the experience we're currently having, that is what we *always are*. All that is, has been, and ever can be.

And so, this [the heart] does not fear. This will always do what it knows to be right. And therefore does not consider consequences for doing what it knows to be right because it would never consider doing *anything* but what it knows to be right. Thus, consequences are irrelevant. This [the head] says, 'I'd like to do this but what are the consequences?' And you'll always find a list of consequences why you wouldn't do it. This [the heart] says, 'I do what I know to be right.' Consequences therefore are not even a conversation.

One of the great fears people have, well it's the foundation fear I think, is the fear of the unknown which manifests as the fear of death. And the manipulation of the fear of death is the manipulation of this pandemic. People are frozen in fear because they fear death. It's why doctors have so much power. Well actually, you are all that is, has been, and ever can be and always will be, you're just having a brief experience.

So this [the heart] is without fear. It doesn't consider consequences. I mean consequences of 'What will people do, or think, or say about me? What will happen to me for doing what I know to be right?' It doesn't even consider those consequences. I never consider them. Because to consider them is to consider not doing what I know to be right. Not having it.

Because you reach this point of connection, and this point of insight, you know I'm not sitting cross-legged on a mountain like a Buddha. *Anyone* can do this, it's our natural state! We've been manipulated into an *unnatural* state. What I'm describing is our natural state. When you open your heart, you know that death is nothing except a transfer of attention. That's all it is.

I've got a picture in *The Answer*, and it's of a bloke with a virtual reality headset, and he's just taken it off and he's looking around. And I put a caption underneath: 'My god I've just died!' Because that is what death is basically. It's taking the headset off. It's moving out of this brief experience into the expansive true self. So when you open *this* [the heart] all of this comes to you. You know all of this. And therefore this would never be intimidated by authority seeking to impose itself upon you, when you know it's not justified and it's about destroying your freedom.

THIS [the heart] is freedom. It's the freedom of knowing that the scale of who we really are. It's the freedom of connecting with all that is. When there's a revolution of THIS, acquiescence will stop. This would NEVER acquiesce to impositions on freedom. Never do it. Always does what it knows to be right. THIS is the revolution.

The heart is the center of everything. People talk about the physical heart, ok, but if you go back, what they're really talking about is *this* heart. The energetic heart. The connection out there. And you look at all the things, all the symbolism through the ages and still today, relating to this. Open heart. Heart of stone. Broken heart. You look at all the phrases relating to the heart. It's because this is the center of everything. And we've been manipulated to think this [the head] is the center of everything. It's not.

Do you know that the heart is the biggest electromagnetic field, the most powerful electromagnetic field in the body? And this, when it's open, dominates the head. What do people say all the time: 'What does your head say? Ok. What does your heart say?' And they say very different things, because this [the heart] is out there, and this [the head] is down here. And when this [the heart] opens, everything changes because *you* change. Everything about you changes.

It's what happened to me a long time ago, and changed my life.

INTERVIEWER: And everyone can access this whenever they want.

David: Anytime they want, and what I would say is: *Ditch the bloody labels.* Stop identifying with labels. They are a brief experience. Even your name is a brief experience. *You* are the consciousness having the experience. So when someone says to you, 'Who are you?' You are all that is, has been, and ever can be having an experience. If you meet someone and say, 'Who are you?' They'll give you their name. They'll give you their job. They might give you their family background, their history, where they went to school. That's what they're saying they are. But that's just what they've experienced.

Who am I? All that is, has been, and ever can be, having an experience called David Icke. Very brief. Very interesting. The point of attention that I am is an expression of the same consciousness that the point of attention that you are is. And the same with all of us.

So racism and all these -isms and all these divisions, are not only undesirable, they are confirmation that those that go down that road are utterly clueless about the nature of reality, and the nature of who they really are. I see anti-racists who are utterly, utterly obsessed with race, when it's just a brief experience. That's all it is. *You* are what is having the experience. And when that penny drops and this [the heart] as a result opens,

Game Over."

ABOUT THE AUTHOR

Aaron Kuhn

Aaron Kuhn is a Podcaster, Researcher, Author, and Musician. Since early 2019 he's been the co-host of Journey to Truth Podcast with Tyler Kiwala. He was a devout Christian until the age of 25 when he had his "awakening." He came across presentations, interviews, and books of people like David Icke, David Wilcock,  Jordan Maxwell, Dolores Cannon, Project Camelot, Alex Collier, Gregg Braden, and others.

He started putting the pieces together about ETs, what's really happening on our planet, our true history, the true nature of reality, why we are here, etc. After five years of doing research in isolation, he attended his first conference in 2017 called Eclipse of Disclosure, in Mt. Shasta, CA. The following year at the Dimensions of Disclosure conference he met Tyler Kiwala. Shortly thereafter they started Journey to Truth Podcast and have been going strong ever since. They are now also putting on conferences, doing webinars, and creating documentaries.

JOURNEY TO TRUTH
P O D C A S T

Our website: journeytotruth.online

Thank you for all your love and support!!